Hey TRUE BLUE

JOHN WILLIAMSON

Hey
TRUE BLUE

MICHAEL JOSEPH
an imprint of
PENGUIN BOOKS

MICHAEL JOSEPH

Published by the Penguin Group
Penguin Group (Australia)
707 Collins Street, Melbourne, Victoria 3008, Australia
(a division of Penguin Australia Pty Ltd)
Penguin Group (USA) Inc.
375 Hudson Street, New York, New York 10014, USA
Penguin Group (Canada)
90 Eglinton Avenue East, Suite 700, Toronto, Canada ON M4P 2Y3
(a division of Penguin Canada Books Inc.)
Penguin Books Ltd
80 Strand, London WC2R 0RL England
Penguin Ireland
25 St Stephen's Green, Dublin 2, Ireland
(a division of Penguin Books Ltd)
Penguin Books India Pvt Ltd
11 Community Centre, Panchsheel Park, New Delhi – 110 017, India
Penguin Group (NZ)
67 Apollo Drive, Rosedale, Auckland 0632, New Zealand
(a division of Penguin New Zealand Pty Ltd)
Penguin Books (South Africa) (Pty) Ltd
Rosebank Office Park, Block D, 181 Jan Smuts Avenue, Parktown North, Johannesburg, 2196, South Africa
Penguin (Beijing) Ltd
7F, Tower B, Jiaming Center, 27 East Third Ring Road North, Chaoyang District, Beijing 100020, China

Penguin Books Ltd, Registered Offices: 80 Strand, London WC2R 0RL, England

First published by Penguin Group (Australia), 2014

1 3 5 7 9 10 8 6 4 2

Text copyright © John Williamson © 2014
The moral right of the author has been asserted

Design by Alex Ross © Penguin Group (Australia)
Text design by Pauline Haas © Penguin Group (Australia)
Front jacket, case and endpaper photographs by Paul Harris, Seesaw Photography
Photographs in the book are from the author's private collection unless otherwise stated
Typeset in Sabon by Pauline Haas
Printed and bound in Australia by Griffin Press, an accredited ISO AS/NZS 14001
Environmental Management Systems printer.

National Library of Australia
Cataloguing-in-Publication data:

Williamson, John, 1945– author.
Hey true blue / John Williamson.
9781921901744 (hardback)
Williamson, John, 1945-
Country musicians–Australia–Biography.
Composers–Australia–Biography.

781.642092

penguin.com.au

For my dear parents, Keith and Shirley,
who encouraged my musical journey
and surrounded me with security and love

CONTENTS

And they sang and they watched and waited ... 1

Chapter 1
Oh God it's so small, but it was my world 5

Chapter 2
And I don't mind at all if you call me a Mallee Boy 17

Chapter 3
He still toes the dirt and predicts the rain 25

Chapter 4
You taught them all you know 35

Chapter 5
That unselfish, unsung hero of the land 41

Chapter 6
To walk in my old man's shoes 49

Chapter 7
It's just plain dirt but it's the world to me 57

Chapter 8
There you were beneath the stars 69

Chapter 9
Boy leaves home to make a crust 73

Chapter 10
Easier ways to make a quid 81

Chapter 11
Now look out for the funny drunk, a regular heart and soul 89

Chapter 12
But you are young, and stuck out on the dryland 97

Chapter 13
So I'm tired of 'Kangaroo', he won't catch 'Old Man Emu' 103

Chapter 14
Headin' for the Alice with a dinkum show and crew 119

Chapter 15
True Blue 125

Chapter 16
Why don't you take your best mate and sail the Nullarbor 133

Chapter 17
If you're livin' in a Lawsy town 141

Chapter 18
It's in my blood gonna make a stand 147

Chapter 19
Maybe it's not too late 155

Chapter 20
Put your men through the toughest test 161

Chapter 21
Where dreamers and good old drifters go 175

Chapter 22
We must have a flag of our own 185

Chapter 23
The kookaburra tries to laugh as the tin-pot trailer falls in half 191

Chapter 24
Like a boomerang, we shall return, with another story and song 197

Chapter 25
It's raining on the Rock, what an almighty sight to see 207

Chapter 26
And I am proud to know you, the Keeper of the Stones 213

Chapter 27
See y'later Birdsville, you're far too flash for me 221

Chapter 28
To show their pride, pay respect and 'Don' the Baggy Green **229**

Chapter 29
Tomorrow there'll be time to cry **241**

Chapter 30
Yeah, c'mon wattle soldiers, wildlife warriors get angry **247**

Chapter 31
Ah that's what it's like to be a country balladeer **253**

Chapter 32
Lay a little frangipani gentle on the water **265**

Chapter 33
Oh it's December in Australia **271**

Chapter 34
As the dusty roads unwind **287**

Chapter 35
Land him on the beaches, eight thousand never came back **293**

Chapter 36
I'm sorry but I don't understand **303**

Chapter 37
And you ask is he happy **317**

Chapter 38
Give it to me straight, face to face **323**

Chapter 39
I led you up the Hillbilly Road **327**

Chapter 40
Being what you really wanna be **343**

Discography **351**
Notes **371**
Acknowledgements **373**

AND THEY SANG AND THEY
WATCHED AND WAITED ...

Wallabies coach Rod Macqueen says, 'John, you've gotta sing "Waltzing Matilda" straight after the All Black's haka. That'll stir 'em up. That's what the Wallabies need.'

I agree, but will I get away with it? I'm treading on rugby sacred ground here. All hell could break loose. Some big Maori will kill me. The haka's over. Go! Go! Go! The television camera is pointing in my direction. It's just the microphone and me. Dark green shirt and gold scarf. No guitar. I need a spare hand to conduct the crowd ... if they sing ...

Well, they sang alright – 70 000 Aussies in full tonsil. They really belted out the song like never before, especially when I stopped singing for a moment on purpose. That always works. That's when the crowd sings louder because they don't have to listen to me. Through my in-ear headphones the crowd sounded faint but I could feel and see what was happening. Great comments afterwards confirmed what I felt, but the greatest compliment of all came from Wallaby front-rower Phil Kearns after the game. 'Mate, I felt about a metre taller as the crowd sang "Waltzing Matilda". You know, traditionally, the All Blacks are on the front foot after their haka, but tonight you turned the tables.'

John Eales raised the Bledisloe Cup high that night in 1998. And the Wallabies went on to win the World Cup the following year at Cardiff Arms Park in Wales.

♪

To me, 'Waltzing Matilda' is our larrikin anthem. It describes things that are deep down in our Aussie psyche and will never die: affinity with the underdog, love of the bush and the campfire. I've always loved the song and have had some amazing experiences when I've been asked to sing it publicly.

My forty-four years in music have been quite a journey. But my life has not really been about music, more a continuing love of the Australian character and especially the bush. Songwriting became my way of expressing how I feel. Nature has been my enduring inspiration, the songs have flowed from that and I've been blessed that some of them have become well-known celebrations of our great land and its people.

This country is what makes me tick.

Waltzing Matilda

There once was a jolly swagman camped by a billabong
Under the shade of a coolibah tree
And he sang as he watched and waited till his billy boiled
You'll come a Waltzing Matilda with me

Down came a jumbuck to drink at the billabong
Up got the swaggie and grabbed him with glee
And he sang as he stowed that jumbuck in his tuckerbag
You'll come a Waltzing Matilda with me

Waltzing Matilda, Waltzing Matilda
You'll come a Waltzing Matilda with me
And he sang as he stowed that jumbuck in his tuckerbag
You'll come a Waltzing Matilda with me

Down came the squatter mounted on his thoroughbred
Up came the troopers One Two Three
Who's that jolly jumbuck you've got in your tuckerbag
You'll come a Waltzing Matilda with me

Up got the swaggie and jumped into the billabong
You'll never catch me alive said he
And his ghost may be heard as you pass by that billabong
You'll come a Waltzing Matilda with me

(Original words by A B 'Banjo' Paterson.
This version arranged by John Williamson.)

Oh God it's so small, but it was my world
Never enough daylight to play
In a town where imagination ran wild
Why did we all move away

Chapter 1

OH GOD IT'S SO SMALL, BUT IT WAS MY WORLD

I am proud to be born a wheat farmer's son.

I came into the world on the first of November 1945 in Kerang, about 280 kilometres north-west of Melbourne in Victoria. I popped out in Kerang District Hospital, stayed for two days and returned home, 26 gravelly miles down the road. So I have to put Kerang on my passport, which irritates me because before that, my mum carried me around in her stomach for nine months in a great little Mallee town called Quambatook.

My heart still warms at the sound of the name Quambatook: 'resting place beside a river'. That's what I'd like on my passport. I don't know what Aboriginal language it comes from but the name is perfect. The locals affectionately call it 'Quamby'. There used to be a Ninnynook and a Chinkapook nearby.

My mother, Shirley Ellen Manuel, and my father, Keith Williamson, were an obvious match. They both grew up on the land and in the same district in the Mallee. But even though their farmhouses were only 64 kilometres apart, the farms were completely different. Dad lived on Cannie Ridge: pure sandy loam, wheat country in the Mallee scrub. Mum came from the eastern side of the forest on an irrigation farm; her dad bred fat lambs on the grey soil around Kerang. On Mum's side of the forest there are no mallee trees. West of the swamp, the mallee trees exist all the way to Western Australia. Heading towards Kerang from Quambatook you come to the western edge of the Wandella Forest of swamp box trees; this marks the boundary of the Mallee scrub. It always fascinates me how the Mallee red soil stops on a fence line about ten kilometres out of Kerang.

Mum was like new stock in the Mallee district. She loved singing and so did Dad. Dad's brother played the violin and Mum's brother played the ukulele. In fact, my first ukulele belonged to my Uncle Rolly.

Like most Mallee district towns, Quambatook was completely dominated by the tall concrete silos built during the First World War. The little town really only exists because of farming. Dad and his brother, Arthur, jointly owned blocks of land north and south of Quamby. The blocks north were roughly 16 kilometres away and totalled about 3000 acres. They were called Cannie Ridge (where Dad grew up with Arthur and two sisters), Templeton's and Mahar's Hill. The other blocks were named after their original owners. We also had Knight's Lake and land around the cemetery south of the town. So it made sense for both Williamson families to live in Quamby. We were constantly driving tractors and machinery back and forth through the town to work the different paddocks. Uncle Arthur had a workshop and shed and so did Dad. Uncle Arthur managed the sheep and Dad managed the wheat farming.

♫

Being the first born, I pretty much had things my own way for a few years. My brother Willy turned up three years after I was born. We shared a bedroom. Robin arrived next and eventually shared my single bed, which meant I would often lie in his warm piss. Then Peter arrived and he shared Will's bed. Jeff came along much later.

Will, Pete and I were born on 29 and 30 October and 1 November respectively, just under nine months after Dad's birthday. That's a fact us boys have chuckled about over the years.

We were no better or worse off than most kids in Quamby. I didn't complain about sharing a room as I didn't know or expect any better at the time. I often wondered why Mum kept a double room at the front of the house for guests. It was hardly ever used. If a mate from a farm came to stay, he had a better bed to sleep in than I did.

I'll never forget some things from the early days in Quamby.

One terrible morning Mum tripped over baby Will, who was crawling on the floor. She spilt a fresh pot of tea all over my arm and back. I was about four years old. The neighbours came running to Mum's assistance but despite all the attention no one seemed to know what to do. Back in those days, people didn't know that the best thing would have been to put me under a cold shower. Dad pulled off my singlet, skin and all, and wrapped me in a blanket. The nearest hospital was in Kerang. It was very traumatic, turning over and over on the bench seat of the old army Chev ute, shivering, as we sped along the gravel road. I kept saying to Mum, 'Why did you do it?' I still count my lucky stars the hot water didn't land on my face. It probably would have looked like my right upper arm, which bears a large patch of scar tissue. Even today, when I get hot or too tired I can't help but fidget my shoulders. I'm sure my body remembers that day.

I also remember poor young Willy's shocking asthma. He was allergic to cows' milk and wheat dust – hardly a good start for a wheat farmer's son. He could barely breathe when the asthma came on. I would lie awake some nights hoping he wouldn't suffocate. Dad bought a couple of goats so Willy could have goats' milk. Will had Mum's positive outlook but the asthma gave him a bad start; he was always very skinny and quite weak as a kid. Hard to imagine nowadays, as he grew to about five foot ten and his hands are much wider than mine.

I was five years old when Robin arrived and really didn't need another brother to land on our family doorstep and disturb the peace. By the time he was four, I'd decided that that was the worst age for a boy. Robin had no respect for the rules. He delighted in unrolling the tyres off my micro-model car collection, which obviously upset me no end. Those toys were special to me. I'd save halfpennies and pennies to raise two shillings to buy them. Everyone said Robin was like Pa, my dad's father.

I was into the movie *The Dam Busters* and loved to make a dam in my sandpit and blow the banks to the shithouse with a bunger. One day, my cousins Doug and Gerald and

I were building a dam. We just about had it finished when Rob turned up. 'Piss off!' I said and we pushed him aside. I knew he wanted to bugger it up and destroy the dam bank. Next minute he'd found a metal hearth shovel and donged me on the head, splitting my head open. There was blood everywhere. I was bawling my eyes out and Pa said, 'Serves y'right for not letting him play with yer.' I think old Lew, my grandfather, saw something of himself in Robin.

I have never thought about having a favourite brother. Willy and I weren't overly close as kids; we both had plenty of mates our own age. I suspect siblings are closer when they're isolated on a farm, rather than living in town as we did. Robin was a stubborn little bugger. However, Peter, the next in line, couldn't do anything wrong by me. Maybe it was because we are so much alike. When we catch up these days, his wife, Annie, always tells him, 'That's how you'll look in ten years!' I hate that. I feel as young as he looks.

The novelty of having brothers had completely worn off by the time Jeff was born. I was fourteen. I love him as much as the others, but we all wanted a girl in the family.

♪

It suited Mum to live in town rather than on the farm; it was much more convenient. We could walk to school and the shops. A local dairy farmer delivered the milk, and Tom Hogan, our next-door neighbour in Kerang Road, came around once a week with pencil and pad and took our grocery order. He could recite every product in his store. Vegemite (no thanks), Weeties (yes please), Vita-Weat (yes, two packets) and so on. He delivered the groceries in his 1948 sandy-coloured FX Holden ute.

As you can imagine, life in Quambatook was idyllic for a country boy. I had the fun of being from the land as well as having mates my own age in town, which brought me many adventures. Our house was a stone's throw away from the Avoca River, a peaceful little stream full of plate-sized redfin and yabbies that was perfect for fishing. Not like the Murray River, which is deep and full of dangerous whirlpools. My mates and I found the fish easy to lure using copper spinners with red tails. A bit of steel wool and Brasso kept them shiny. It spoilt me from fishing with worms forever. Close to home there were so many things a boy could enjoy – finding mushrooms for the table, shooting and digging out rabbits and foxes, swimming in the river. A game of hide-and-seek took in the whole town with a game called 'black trackers'. One kid would go ahead with a lump of limestone and draw arrows on the footpath in the direction he was headed. But you could lead the hunters astray by pointing them to a dead end and backtracking.

The biggest adventure in Quamby, and the most daring, was to climb the 120-foot high silo. This was entirely a no-no but, of course, that was half the reason for doing it. Only one person was officially allowed to climb the wheat silo and that was the man working for the Wheat Board. On the rare occasions this man mistakenly left the door open, our neighbours the Pepperell kids and I took advantage of it. We had it all planned; we'd always have a bag of paper aeroplanes ready to throw off the top. There were about six skinny little ladders with a platform at the end of each one. No safety cages. Everything was covered with a centimetre of fine wheat dust. Willy wanted to come too, but at least I was responsible enough to make him stay on the ground. Being an asthmatic, the wheat dust would have nearly killed him.

Well, for a kid who was brought up on flat ground, the view from the silo was breathtaking. I could see everyone's backyard at once. What a small town! I could also see the wheat silo up the railway line at Cannie, 14 kilometres away. The aeroplanes worked well too. The Pepperell boys were always a bit more daring than me. They crawled right to the edge (remember, there were no safety rails) and stuck their heads over and spat on whingeing little Willy on the ground. My main worry was that Dad would see me from home. He might as well have seen me, because the next time Willy and I had a fight, Willy cried and told Dad and Mum, 'Yeah, well, John climbed the wheat silo yesterday.' We both got six of the best of Dad's big hand on our bums – me for climbing the wheat silo, and Willy for telling on his big brother.

At Christmas time, the organ from the Catholic church was loaded onto the back of a truck and Miss Graham, the organist, pumped out Christmas carols. Mum and Dad and anyone else who could sing piled onto the truck and sang carols all around town. We'd stop in front of any house where the people came out. But Christmas in the Mallee as a kid was really all about Lake Meran, near Kerang. My uncle had a speedboat for waterskiing, something I never really enjoyed. It always seemed like hard work. It was the farmers' traditional games, such as stook-tossing (where a stook of hay is thrown over a high rope with a pitchfork) that I remember. This, and the egg-and-spoon and sack races gave the lake a great atmosphere.

Lake Meran was about half an hour away and Kangaroo Lake not much further. The summer holidays meant many weekends having picnics on the banks of these lakes. Kangaroo Lake, between Kerang and Swan Hill, was probably our family's favourite; it seemed to be much bigger and more peaceful. In the twenties or thirties someone planted weeping willows on the edge of the lake. While many people now deem them as a pest along our rivers, they were perfect for shade and summer picnics. We just loved being together under the willows.

Today it's hard to believe that even during harvest time we would have Sunday off. They don't close the silos on Sundays now; the weather has become too unpredictable. Rain in the wheat can cost you many thousands of dollars with loss of protein through bleaching.

There were other lakes in the district that were left alone for the birds. Except on duck opening day. Being such a bird lover now, it's weird that I had a day duck shooting with my Williams cousins (yes, my mother's sister married a Williams, so it's confusing). My dad wasn't into duck shooting but my uncle Ralph Williams was. I have to confess that I didn't hit one duck but my cousins bagged plenty. The ducks were divided up and eaten and were absolutely delicious. Duck opening day was unbelievable. It was called 'duck opening day' because duck shooting in Victoria was allowed for a short period only. I don't believe it was to save the ducks for conservation reasons but to make sure they weren't shot out for the next duck season. I guess this all seemed reasonable in the early days when the sky was almost blacked out by birdlife in these areas. But that didn't mean you just pointed the gun, shot into the air and hit one. It still required skill to follow an individual duck that was flying at high speed and to bring it down. The really keen shooters had bird dogs, such as Irish setters and retrievers, to swim out and grab the duck. This often caused arguments over whose duck it was. Bloody hell! How could you tell?

When a flock came through at sun-up, the guns went off all around the lake. The shooters were about 20 metres apart. Pellets dropped all around you. What annoyed me that day was that the guns went off when swans and shags flew by. My uncle was annoyed too. 'Those bloody city slickers would shoot anything,' he said. It wasn't as though you could eat those birds. Years later, it would give me a couple of lines for my song 'Mallee Boy'.

So I had the best of both worlds, I reckon. On the weekends I could spend time with my mates, or just be with my dad as he went about doing all the things he had to do on the blocks of land outside town. For us boys – my brothers and my cousins – it was quite normal to ride with the dogs in the back of the old army ute, or stand next to Dad as he went round and round the paddock with the plough, or sit on top of the load of wheat all the way to the wheat silo at harvest time. I can still see the mallee trees flickering through the sun in my eyes as I lay in the back of Dad's old Chevy ute down a mallee lane, or standing with the kelpies enjoying the wind in our faces, thumping the cabin when we spotted a fox. There was always a .22 rifle in the cabin. The only time I fell out of a ute was when it was stationery.

Harvest time was very special. In the early days we would ride on top of the bags of wheat or wool bales in the back of the old Maple Leaf truck. Then came the time we could sit on the bulk wheat. With our legs well and truly planted in the grain, it couldn't have been safer heading to the silo on the truck. Nowadays that would be frowned upon and illegal. So I feel lucky to have been a kid before all the safety issues were introduced. We taught ourselves to be careful through experience. Such was my world in Quambatook and I am forever grateful for it.

Dear Little Quambatook

My little town hasn't disappeared yet
Quambatook take a look, I'll never forget
Warm in the shade of a peppercorn tree
Dear little Quambatook, hometown to me

It's as flat as a tack in the old Mallee bush
Billy-carts were useless, you needed a push
But we had a river; you could ride on a drum
Dive off the bridge get a leech on y'bum

Oh God it's so small, but it was my world
Never enough daylight to play
In a town where imagination ran wild
Why did we all move away

And I still love the smell of that sandy soil
Some say it's dusty, some say it's gold
Cause it grows the sweetest fat lambs the markets ever sold
And I don't mind at all if you call me a Mallee Boy
No I don't mind at all if you call me a Mallee Boy.

Where you can lose an ear on duck opening day,
Where slickers bring their shotguns from miles away,
And shoot the life out of shags and swans that fly their way.
Where a bloke grows as stocky as a Mallee bull,
Where they come from miles around to see the tractor pull,
When the paddocks are clean and seed silos are full,
And I don't mind at all if you call me a Mallee Boy.

(from 'Mallee Boy' © 1986 Emusic Pty Ltd)

Chapter 2

AND I DON'T MIND AT ALL IF
YOU CALL ME A MALLEE BOY

In the 1950s, the district population for Quambatook was about one thousand people. It reduced slowly once they sealed the roads to both Kerang and Swan Hill. But when I was a kid it was quite self-contained with a bank, a chemist, three cafes, two pubs, two garages, a bakery, stock and station agent, grocery store and the Quambatook general store. It had a menswear and a ladies fashion shop, and right up to at least 1964, young lads could pick up their numbered jersey for the footy team at the menswear store. What a beautiful memory.

Sport played an enormous role in giving my little town a feeling of togetherness. It still boasts six or seven grass tennis courts – quite a number for a town of that size. For five shillings I was a junior member and played often. However, if a senior member wanted the court, you had to move. I was always indignant about this rule and could see no reason why an adult was more important. I would have paid an adult membership fee if it made a difference. I guess it was always part of my nature to question things. Some of the adults probably thought I was an arrogant little bastard.

In my day, there was even a golf course, which was mainly on a claypan with gravel greens. There was a gun club: a small-bore club. I didn't mind the small-bore and have a silver serviette ring that was a prize from a gun-club competition.

But the main game in town was Aussie Rules. We simply called it footy. We were completely unaware of any other code and until I went to boarding school I'd never heard of rugby. To a small boy like me, who enjoyed competitive team sport, footy was wonderful. In winter every evening, till it got too dark, I could always find a mate to kick the football with, someone who would stand at the other end of a little paddock. The best fun was when you could muster a group for each end. This is where we learned to compete in the air for the ball. In my later years at school in Quamby I enjoyed playing half-back flank. I found defending fairly easy. If I stood ten paces in front of my opponent instead of niggling him, side by side, I would generally win the ball. You see, in the country, the kicks fell short of the mark.

It's curious that Quamby has gone through several changes in team colours. When my grandfather played, they wore Richmond colours: black with the yellow diagonal stripe. When Quambatook joined the Mid-Murray League, my father wore South Melbourne (now Sydney Swans) colours: white with the red V. Now they wear the St Kilda colours because they changed leagues again.

As a kid, the numbers on the local senior team's footy jerseys were legendary. We all knew who wore what number. So it was a huge thrill to be finally given number six down at the local menswear – a red six to sew onto my red-and-white jersey. Many good players had worn the same number six over the years.

I wasn't what you would call a natural footballer but I never gave up and managed to win a few best-and-fairest Pelaco shirts. Then it all came to a sudden halt. I had finally found my best position on the field then we moved north to Moree where there was no Aussie Rules. So I joined the local rugby team because all the farm boys played rugby. But that's another story.

♫

Quambatook Group School had a seventh year tacked onto the normal primary school. They were very happy days for me. I always found the lessons easy and was always third or fourth in class exams.

Maybe because I didn't have a sister I enjoyed being with girls at school. By the time I was six I had a girlfriend named Judy McCann. She came to school by bus from a farm north of the town. In those days, love to me was just sitting next to her. I thought about her all the time. We both understood that we were boyfriend and girlfriend but were always extremely shy about it. I drew a portrait of her in pastels and on parents' day at school both mothers were delighted with it. They saw no harm in our friendship and, after all, we were both Protestants. That mattered in those days.

I prided myself in having the best-looking girls (and most intelligent) as partners in folk dancing. The dance involved a boy with a girl on each arm. I was always first in line. Perhaps the teacher realised I had a natural rhythm for dancing and would encourage the other boys. I became the drummer boy for assembly as well.

You'd think I would have owned a horse when I was a kid. Perhaps if we'd actually lived on the farm instead of in town, I might have. The butcher's son used to ride a beautiful big black mare around the town, bareback. This inspired me to ask my parents for a horse but my request was very quickly rejected. 'What do you want a horse for? We don't need a horse,' was the reply. It was true. In the wheat-farming district, horses were long gone. As a kid, Mum had to ride to school every day and when Dad was in his teens he had to feed, water and hook up a horse team for ploughing. I think his dad was the first to buy a tractor in the district; Dad saw the transition from horses to tractors that started his love of motor machines and mechanics. So I understood that they had no time for horses anymore. They were unnecessary, a waste of time, a nuisance and a headache.

My young girlfriend, Judy, brought her pony in from the farm to give the town kids a ride at our school fete one year. Of course I had to have a go. But as I'd had no experience at all (thanks, Mum) I just slid off its bare back almost immediately. No one told me you had to hold on with your knees. What an embarrassing moment that was, and not one I got over easily. I'll never forget Judy having a chuckle.

That same day there was a contest for the most unusual pet as part of the fete. Well, I thought I'd win hands down. During a flood in the district, a little blue baby fox had been stranded. He was about 15 centimetres long. When they're babies they are a deep smoky blue colour. I could carry the fox to school when it was young, despite all the dogs around.

It was nervous but quite comfortable in my arms. I got second prize in the unusual pet competition, losing to a kangaroo. What was so unusual about a kangaroo? Bloody idiots! I kept that fox until it was fully grown but it never got used to being kept on a chain in the shed while I was at school, in the way a sheepdog does. I don't know how it didn't break its neck running full-pelt all day, until the chain snapped him back. Eventually the chain broke and he cleaned up most of the neighbours' chooks. Uncle Arthur was commissioned to shoot the poor thing the next day. Dad couldn't do it. Nowadays I have no time for foxes.

♬

My cousins Doug and Gerald were roughly my age and lived across the paddock. Our dads were partners so we spent a lot of time together on the land. My neighbour Lawrence Pepperell was great at making things (his dad was our woodwork teacher) and we loved watching *The Goon Show* together. They came from the Dandenong Ranges near Melbourne and brought a refreshing new way of seeing things.

I also had a couple of mates who enjoyed collecting birds' eggs. The rule was to take only one from the nest. Of course, sparrows, starlings and even native crows were treated with contempt. They were always attacking our orchard and vegies, and they're an introduced species. Lawrence and I had a birds' egg collection together that my mate Normy Free would inherit from me when we left Quamby. Neither of these boys had the gift of self-preservation and would climb further out on a tree limb than I would. Consequently, Normy broke his arm at least once. The normal way to climb down a tree with a bird's egg was to put it in your mouth. Lawrence and I found that by piling up a big heap of barley grass you could drop the egg onto it with great success. Much better than breaking an egg in your mouth! So I was generally the expert egg catcher.

Mr Pepperell encouraged me to join the Gould League of Bird Lovers. I loved to draw birds and sent quite a few pictures to the Gould League. They would send back a certificate of merit. It was a fantastic way to make kids aware of the beauty around them. But you know, I think I am the only one in my class who carried on with it.

I often played a game with Lawrence and his brother, Geoff, catching mice and filling up kerosene tins with them. This was easy. Mice in wheat country are part of life. Rarely would you lift up a sheet of tin or a wheat bag without revealing a nest of mice. Dogs, kids, dads: all were mice killers. The huge temporary storage for bagged oats in Quamby was held up with long railway sleepers and corrugated iron. Each ripple against the iron usually had a mouse hiding there. Poke a stick through it and the mouse would land in the tin. With a writhing tin-full we could take them out into the middle of a claypan then let them go, one at a time. The first kid to stomp on the mouse got a point. This is a skill that I haven't lost. A mouse will never make it across a room with me around. Trouble is, I'm not fond of cleaning up the squashed dead body. The chook yard attracted mice so I set up an old greasy beer bottle with butter on the end, over a bucket of water, and drowned hundreds of the things.

Mum always had cats, which also served to keep snakes away. A snake bit Mum's sister when she was a kid and she's still traumatised by the incident. Her dad cut the bites with a razor blade and sucked the poison away. I can imagine the horror in my mum's young eyes back then. I was brought up to kill any snake I saw, too ... usually with a shovel.

Looking after the chook yard was my job, along with cutting the pine kindling for Mum's wood store. I had bantams too. I absolutely loved their chicks. I miss not having a chook yard. Setting up their nests in four-gallon drums was always such a wonderful experience. And their first egg was a triumph!

In my teens in Quamby I tried to be enterprising. I killed snails for my mum (a few bob a bucketful). I also delivered the *Quambatook Times* for fifteen shillings. This included melting down the lead from the printing machine and folding the papers. I can still feel the awful burning sensation of rubbing my fist along the fold.

Before the introduction of myxomatosis and now calicivirus, rabbits were a part of farming life. I wonder if the saying 'skin a bunny' is still used in the bush? My mum used to say it to us when she pulled off our singlets before bath time. Selling rabbit skins was another money-making idea but I chose to do it during a rabbit plague and was offered only a halfpenny a skin. And I think that was only after Dad had a quiet word to the dealer for a favour to encourage my enterprise.

My attitude towards native animals has changed completely since those days. Recently I have carried whip snakes out of my shed on a long stick and thrown them back into the forest. Unfortunately they come back because the native mice are delicious.

And it goes without saying, my old man
Was born of the soil, no particular plan
Just bent on doing the right thing
He still toes the dirt and predicts the rain
And I'm sure if he had his life again
He'd be on a tractor singin' a song

(from 'It Goes Without Saying' © 2003 Emusic Pty Ltd)

Chapter 3

HE STILL TOES THE DIRT
AND PREDICTS THE RAIN

It seems to me that Mum and Dad lived through the best times for wheat farming. The commodity prices were pretty good and if you had a bumper crop the reward was there. We sold up in 1965 and I don't remember a real drought in the Mallee. Sure, some years we might have only broken even, but I don't recall Dad ever complaining about a loss. The average crop yielded about seven or eight bags per acre over the years. The cost to sow the wheat was probably five bags per acre. So we weren't rolling in money but we had all we really needed as a family.

Dad loved his cars and always managed to own a reasonable one. Our first family car was a second-hand Chevy ute sold off by the army. It was very solid and the steering wheel was big enough for me, as a little kid, to sit in and swing from side to side. We kept that ute well into the sixties. It was capable of carrying four-gallon drums full of fuel, which was ideal for paddock work. I wish I had it now, I would cherish it at my place at Springbrook.

One of my favourite pictures of Dad shows him with the old ute. I reckon the photo was taken in the mid-1950s, by which time the ute had become the farm car. It was the first vehicle I drove, at the age of nine. That's one big advantage of being a farmer's son – there were plenty of paddocks where I could learn to drive a car. In the picture, Dad is proudly standing alongside a dead wedge-tailed eagle. In those days it was seen as a trophy; farmers would shoot and string out a wedgie on a fence to show off its wingspan. Back then, they believed the wedgies killed lambs but this has since been proven to be a myth. Now, the wedge-tailed eagle is one of my favourite birds. With all the roadkill, I see them everywhere in pairs. I think they have bred up very well.

Our second car was a Morris Six. It looked like a large Morris Minor. My strongest memory of that car goes back to one rainy day in winter in Quambatook when I was walking home from school. About halfway home, I saw the maroon Morris Six slowing down on the road. *Beauty! Thanks, Dad.* I quickly climbed in to find myself surrounded by Ned Doyle's family who were most amused. They had exactly the same car! That kind of embarrassment isn't easily forgotten.

Our third car was a Ford Customline. We were starting to realise that Dad liked a car with balls. When we were old enough to go camping, Dad would tow a little caravan that was really just a double bed on wheels. The boot opened up to reveal an outdoor kitchen and there were cupboards above the bedhead inside. Dad had roof-racks on the caravan and on the car. He'd park the car alongside the caravan and lay a large tentpole between the two. Then he'd simply pull a canvas over the lot and we had a tent. Mum used to stuff something onto the floor of the Ford to extend the back seat into a makeshift bed where Willy and I slept. They were great days. The smell of kerosene always reminds me of our little camping stove.

Our cousins in Quamby always went to seaside Dromana with their caravan in tow but we went to many different places on our traditional two weeks' holiday after Christmas: Lakes Entrance, Torquay, Lorne, Victor Harbour and Sydney. Mum has always been the restless type and I think we all benefited from that. So we ventured as far north as the Sunshine Coast in Queensland. Lakes Entrance in Victoria was the best place to go. I thank Mum for opening my eyes to wider Australia.

When it came to listening to Dad explain mechanical details, my eyes would glaze over and I'd become quite deaf, but nod my head anyway. (I did inherit Dad's leadfoot though!) In fact, the only way you could get Dad to talk was to talk cars. He reckoned the Ford Galaxy was his all-time favourite: lots of headroom and space for Mum's picnic hamper and flask, and it went like the clappers with a huge V8 engine. It was a car that completely ignored cattle grids.

♫

As far as I knew when I was a kid, neither of the Williamson families went into either of the two pubs in town. We were Protestants, and it seemed to be something the Catholics did. The strong malt smell that engulfed me as I walked past the Railway Hotel struck me as evil, especially as there always seemed to be someone sitting outside, coughing and spitting on the footpath. It actually frightened me, even though we laughed at Mick Hickey, one of the locals, struggling to get over the very slight rise in the road, with a half-empty beer bottle in his hand and a couple under his arm.

The first time I discovered that Dad drank was when the publican's son, Wayne Barnes, told me at the end of harvest one year. Apparently Dad came into the hotel and downed a few beers really quickly. It turned out that he always shouted the men a beer after harvest. And I bet all the regulars raised their eyebrows to see Dad there. I think Mum and Dad were relieved to move to north-west New South Wales where, by 1965, there were no wowsers left. It's almost as though pubs brought the Proddos and Micks together at last.

Dad was a god-fearing man. He died in March 2014 at 93 and he seemed very comfortable that his god had a place for him in heaven. And if there *is* such a place, I think he's up there in his favourite dream car, zooming through the clouds. I've never been convinced that there is a personal god, but I never discussed this with Dad for fear he would call me a fool. But Dad also feared his earthly father, Lew. I had very few beltings as a kid from Dad, but after one episode (which I probably deserved), he felt bad and told me he never wanted me to be afraid of him, as he was of his own father. I think there is something in that story that kept him a quiet man all his life. But he played a loud banjo! Happy cruising, Dad.

I remember distinctly the last time Dad tried to belt me; I took off out the back gate and ran down the lane. He couldn't catch me. We ended up laughing our heads off. He never bothered me again. That was at Kerang Road, so I was probably about eight or nine.

Wheat-harvest time was a great opportunity for me to bond with Dad. I can just remember when there was no bulk wheat carted. The wheat was all put into bags that had to be tipped individually into the pit at the silos. When I was old enough to lift a 180-pound bag full of wheat off the ground, I could help with bag sewing. The seed was graded first through a grader that came to the district every year. It was a wonderful contraption that separated cracked seed from wild oats and poppy seeds from the sample. It was then put back into bags to be sewn and carted to the barn. We stored seed for the next year in bags.

I became quite skilled at bag sewing and took great pride in being able to sew quickly and neatly, first making an ear on the left then stitching neatly on an angle to the right side and finishing off with another ear. The ears became handles for maneuvering the bags around the barn or truck. You needed to lift the heavy bag off the ground and dump it a few times to make sure it was tightly packed before sewing it up. The main reason for this was because a tight bag was easier to carry on your back when stacking or carrying from truck to the seeder (or the combine, as we called it). It wasn't until I left school that I had to actually carry these 180-pound bags across my shoulders. It's a wonder my knees have held out from that experience. That's when I really knew how important a tightly packed bag was; a sloppy bag was like carrying a dead animal. It wasn't easy balancing those bags on your back across the fallow ground, while stepping carefully over the harrows that could easily trip you on your way to the seeder.

By the time I was a teenager, I had developed quite big thighs. When I first arrived at Scotch College as a boarder

in 1960, the other kids remarked on my big thighs. This was
from bag sewing. Your knees played a big role in lifting the
bags a little off the ground when dumping, so your thighs
became quite developed.

This was all before we changed to bulk storage with seed
wheat. Since I've left the land it has all gone bulk, and now
wheat bags (or potato sacks) are becoming quite rare in
wheat country.

A lot of things are said during long days in the hot January
sun, sewing bags in the middle of a paddock. I learned a great
deal from Dad and Jim Hanson (his right-hand man) in those
days. I remember Dad telling me that his father could lift a bag
of wheat with his teeth! He would bite one ear, put his hands
on the bags each side and lift it off the ground. It sounds like
Pa Lew would have been a good front-rower! Apparently he
was quite fierce on the Aussie football ground. There was a
story that one day on the footy field Lew had trouble with the
toenail on his big toe. He yelled out for a pair of pliers, ripped
the toenail out and carried on playing. Mum still says he was
an old show-off. They didn't get on at all.

I think I must have been a good kid in Dad's eyes, even
though I found motor mechanics boring. I was keen to learn
what I could on the land. Was it tough living on the land?
Not that I was aware of at the time. The work was hard and
long but that's the way farming families are brought up.
It wasn't until I got away from it that I realised how hard we
worked. The smell of freshly turned sandy loam, the beauty in
a straight furrow, the hours being your own boss, the pride in
the achievement when you see wheat pouring into the truck –
I was always happy just being out in the bush. That has never

left me. But I couldn't go back to the heat of summers out there now. I have become soft.

♫

Dad was very musical and played rhythm banjo at every dance in town. The town hall was at the end of our street, so from our house I could often hear the bass drum beating out the foxtrot. Ted Andrews, another farmer, played drums in Dad's band in Quambatook and Uncle Arthur played fiddle. Well, it wasn't really a band, just whoever was available to play at a dance. Dances were put on for any excuse, a 21st birthday party, a fundraiser, an engagement party; they were the original weddings-parties-anything band. They never got paid; it was all just for fun. Dad's banjo strumming was confident and strong and perfect to get people jitterbugging and foxtrotting. I love to tell the story of how Ted Andrews played drums like he was still sitting on the old tractor, bouncing up and down. Dad taught me to play ukulele, so when I was about ten years old I could easily give him a break on the banjo so he could have a dance himself.

Dad was also quite an accomplished tenor. While I didn't inherit his tenor voice, I did inherit his sense of rhythm. Maybe even as a baby I had rhythm drummed into me. It's my rhythm, even today, that holds my music together.

Towards the end of his life I think Dad reflected more and more on how he had missed his calling as a tenor. I sensed a touch of sadness and regret that he didn't break out professionally and take his singing talent further. I'm glad he didn't. At one stage Dad joined the ABCD Quartet from

Kerang and their most requested song was 'Three Bells'. His voice would have been classed as an Irish or Scottish style tenor. He loved to sing 'Pedro the Fisherman'. Being that kind of tenor would have sent him broke, I reckon, by about the seventies. He would have spent the end of his working life singing at clubs on Sunday mornings for the elderly. As it was, Mum and Dad sang for the elderly at the retirement village in Moree until 2010 when they became residents there themselves.

Most of all, my father was a man of the soil. In Quambatook he volunteered to be the grower of new wheat seed trials. The CSIRO had field days on Dad's land to discuss the benefits of new varieties. He set a great example for five sons on the land. He was supremely honest and hard working, with arms and hands that belonged to the land, and that's where he remained until he was eighty. Dad had all that was required to be a successful farmer and he was very strong physically. I was always proud of his achievements but I don't think he realised what a legend he was as a wheat farmer.

It Goes Without Saying (Dad's Song)

It goes without saying myself and m'dad
How we love each other and always glad
Just to be together goin' up the road
And I speak for m'brothers, I'm sure of that
I love the smell of his dusty hat
With the diesel and sweat and the smell of dogs

And the cracked old hands from all that work
The bandy legs and the rolled-up shirt
The snort and the spit on fallowed ground

And it goes without saying, he's proud of us
He didn't spell it out, or make much fuss
Just whistled along and showed us the ropes
And I speak for m'brothers, that's for sure
If we asked for it he gave what for
Not a hard man, just as good as they get

And it goes without saying, my old man
Was born of the soil, no particular plan
Just bent on doing the right thing
He still toes the dirt and predicts the rain
And I'm sure if he had his life again
He'd be on a tractor singin' a song

It's gonna be hard, when he's not around

Now it's considered normal
To pass your acres down
But if you've got more children
Well you try to buy more ground
So you borrow heaps of money
Just to give your kids a go
After all that's said and done
You taught them all you know

(from 'The Farming Game' © 1994 Emusic Pty Ltd)

Chapter 4

YOU TAUGHT THEM ALL YOU KNOW

I had a charmed childhood waking up to the sound of a fine soprano voice coming from the kitchen. Mum was always rehearsing something. In fact Mum and Dad both had voice training in Kerang by Mrs Brooker, who I think was conservatorium trained. They really did sing beautifully, and those who remember them in the Mallee, and later in the Moree district, will testify to that. Mum would never sing without Dad, though; she lacked confidence to be a solo artist. Ever since I sang 'Oh what a beautiful morning' in my mother's rose garden in Quambatook – the year that the musical *Oklahoma!* became a hit in Australia – I've been conscious of my love of music.

Mum and Dad thought it would be ideal if I learned the piano, as they probably wished they'd done. I'm sure they saw me as a potential built-in piano accompanist for them. Miss McCulloch, a piano teacher from Kerang, would come to Quambatook once a week and give lessons. I did as I was told and endured the most boring hours of my childhood. Miss McCulloch was a dear old girl but she did nothing to change my hatred of being stuck at the piano. As a kid, I had no ambition to be a pianist and found the endless repetition of scales both tortuous and pointless. My mates were outside in the paddock kicking the footy and I was in the front room of the house practising the A minor scale. By the age of seven I had learned to play a couple of pieces by heart, including a trio piece called 'The Gallop'. At local concerts, including the Kerang Talent Quest, I played this trio piece with my cousins, Doug and Gerald. Everyone thought the trio was wonderful but I still hated it. I also sang 'Tell Me a Story' with Doug.

I used to have my piano lessons in the local weatherboard town hall (the Mechanics Institute). One night I left my music on the piano and that same night the hall burned down, piano and all. I must admit thinking, *You beauty!* (It wasn't me who started the fire, if that's what you're thinking.) Ironically, thirty years later an ex-teacher of mine came to one of my concerts in Bendigo. She told me that Miss McCulloch had passed away and that she used to tell people often that I was her favourite student because I had a soft touch. Apparently I was 'her John'. Bugger me! She must have had some crook students.

I tried to please my parents by keeping the piano going when I went to boarding school, but I was not, and never will be, any good at reading music. I found it very taxing. It didn't come naturally to me at all. I just thumped bass notes with my left hand and played chords with my right, which worked well enough if there was another person playing the melody at the high end. I guess familiarity with a keyboard has helped me as a writer to understand sharps and flats and intervals and so on. So now I can write a music chart but it is laborious and generally unnecessary.

Bugger the piano. I've always had a piano in my house but it never beckons me. You can't play it around the campfire. I like that Larsen cartoon of the good old cowpokes in their chaps and tall hats sitting around the fire. One of them says to another 'Pull that piano out of y'back pocket Jed and play us a tune.'

So with Mum's enthusiasm and Dad's banjo playing and his voice, it's no wonder one of us boys would lead a musical life. Mum didn't mind writing the odd poem either, so I guess that's where my writing talents come from.

♫

It was Mum's idea to send me to Scotch College in Melbourne in 1960. The local Mann family sent their boys there. If it was good enough for the Manns, it was good enough for her boys. Going to Scotch College for four years was one of the best things that happened to me. Not only did it open my eyes to how other people lived, especially in the city, but also to a range of music styles.

The music scene in Melbourne in the early sixties was a mixture of traditional jazz and folk singing, at least in the upper middle class suburbs around Scotch College. Coffee lounges were all the rage. They had either jazz bands or folk singers. It was very trendy to be a member of a jazz club. Little dance halls all over Melbourne were in full swing. Out of this era was born Judith Durham and the Seekers.

I was a boarder at Scotch so I was only able to go to these places on a weekend if I had a suburban Scotch College mate to stay with. Even before I had the freedom of being a boarding house prefect, my mate Zeke and I used to sneak out at night and, in the junior school playground, change our red school ties for skinny black ones. We'd go to the bohemian-style jazz clubs and coffee lounges until three in the morning. We were never caught.

It was here that I heard Martyn Wyndham-Read sing 'Waltzing Matilda' like it was the last song he would ever sing. I can't explain it, but there was a power there that I'd never heard before. I'd already been to a Pete Seeger concert at Melbourne Town Hall and been blown away by the rustic texture of his banjo playing and the clear message songs he sang. He opened my ears to real folk music. And I'd fallen in love with the pure sexy voice of Joan Baez. Her voice just melted my soul. She played a fingerpicking style on a nylon string guitar. I had to have a guitar like hers and that's when I started the double-thumbing style that I use. (My song 'Wonthaggi' is a good example of this.) Of course, Bob Dylan came out of all that, too. Pete Seeger made a couple of Dylan's songs famous. Bob Dylan hooked up with Joan Baez and eventually became more famous than any of them. My fans have often related my harmonica playing (while playing the guitar) to Bob Dylan's, but I guarantee I was playing harmonica before he was. I started in 1950, when I was five. But despite these influences, for me, the Aussie seed had been sown.

I formed a group at Arthur Robinson, our school boarding house, and called it The John D Four. There were three Johns and one David. Our only claim to fame was to sing at the annual Boarders' Hop and the school dance. Everything we did was a direct copy of The Kingston Trio. We had a lot of fun working out harmonies. I played the only guitar, my

Maton nylon string, and John Thompson played a bongo drum. It wasn't really until I left school and started studying the little American folk songbooks (I think they were called 'Folkways') that I really became interested in performing solo.

I also joined the Scotch College choir that joined up with St Catherine's and MLC, two of the nearby girls' schools, to perform Handel's *Messiah*. I was a second tenor. It was a good way to meet girls.

She's my mother, she's my aunty, she's many that I've known
The backbone of the bush, where country kids have grown
She's raised and she's nurtured those children of her own
While her man does his battles on the land
And he comes in from the shearing, still aching in the back
The kids are finally tucked away, her days are never slack
But she makes it look so easy, as she cooks him up a storm
That unselfish, unsung hero of the land

(from 'Woman on the Land' © 1997 Emusic Pty Ltd)

Chapter 5

THAT UNSELFISH, UNSUNG
HERO OF THE LAND

From my position as the oldest of five boys, I can say I'm sure
Mum and Dad would have loved dearly to have a daughter.
With four sons, there were more than enough boys to take
over the land.

My youngest brother was always a different boy to the
rest of us. One Christmas holiday we went to Mildura to
take advantage of their new Olympic swimming pool and
Jeff surprised us all. There was a moment at the pool when
we couldn't see him. What a worry that was! Next thing
there was a triumphant 'Up here!' and there he was, three
years old, up on the high diving platform. He seemed to have
no fear.

Another day I was in our backyard when I spotted him on
top of the chook yard roof. He yelled out, 'Wait there!' He
disappeared to the other end of the shed then came hurtling
towards me with a running jump. It was my responsibility to
catch him. *Shit, Jeff, you could've warned me!* I thought.

I've always felt sorry for Mum that she didn't have a girl,
although it's hard to know if she would have got on with a

daughter. I reckon Mum would have been quite competitive and dominating so a girl would have had to stand up to her.

To us boys, though, Mum was always very affectionate and quite soft in her approach. The only time she lashed out at me was when she grabbed a light wooden coathanger and feebly tried to hit me with it. It was almost laughable. I found it very easy to cry anytime I didn't feel like going to school and she would let me stay at home (not that I didn't enjoy school).

One of Mum's great qualities is that she doesn't speak badly of others and she definitely has never had a prejudiced or racist thought. She would invite kids from all around town to play in our yard. She was also very encouraging of our creativity. The Quambatook Presbyterian Church had an annual fete so I was always pushed to make something crafty to enter in a competition. She told me, when I was very young, that if I built a little house made of moss for fairies, they would reward me with a penny. So I broke off the moss from around the gutter and built a wee little hut. Sure enough, the next day I found a penny. This was very cool; I didn't have to lose a tooth to please the fairies. I'm forever grateful to my mother for the fairies in the garden. I'm sure it stimulated a young boy's mind and was my introduction to creative thinking.

Mum loved to create magic and wonder in our young lives. On Christmas morning we didn't just find our presents under a tree. No, Santa Claus left notes for us to follow a string all around the house, through the laundry, around the verandah and *Wow!* a new Malvern star pushbike gleaming metallic blue in the garage! I was sworn to secrecy not to blow Santa's cover with my younger brothers. I always played along. And today I'm cross with parents who destroy that magic for their kids in the name of honesty. How can they spoil such wonderful imagination? And I wish I could ban all those fake Santa Clauses that have grown to plague proportions in shopping centres. Shame on you retailers behind this! A child probably wakes up to the myth in no time these days.

Putting on birthday parties was another of Mum's fortes. Just about every kid in town was invited. All down a long trestle table on the lawn, plates were piled high with bread and butter smothered in hundreds and thousands. Then there would be a treasure hunt. Little notes were hidden all around the yard explaining where the next note was to be found. She was always bringing magic into our lives.

♫

It was the town life of Quambatook that Mum enjoyed most of all. She was a born organiser and involved herself in many things including the Country Women's Association (CWA) and the church. She was also a bit of an amateur architect and designed the baby health clinic for the town. After the old weatherboard town hall burnt down, Mum became very involved in designing the new one that is still there today.

Mum has always had the knack of encouraging locals to perform and the energy to make things happen. Anytime the town needed to raise money she would gather the local talent, which always seemed to be in abundance, to put on a concert. I'm sure part of the reason for concerts was that she loved to sing and when else does a farmer's wife get the opportunity to perform? Often a special guest from another town nearby was invited. I remember one year she had the entire Quambatook football team dress up in grass skirts with half-coconut bras on elastic. These concerts were always a huge success because there's nothing more entertaining than the locals making fools of themselves. Mum knew there was a performer inside most people once you got them started.

It still blows me away that a town the size of Quambatook, with a population of maybe one thousand, including farmers, would attempt to put on several Gilbert and Sullivan musicals, but they did. Mum was always a driving force behind that. I remember seeing *The Mikado* and *The Pirates of Penzance*. Dad would take a leading role, Mum would be in the chorus. They were often guest singers in other towns too. They performed Jeanette MacDonald and Nelson Eddy songs as well as any professionals.

Aunty Hazel told me I was the golden boy in Mum's eyes and I didn't do too much wrong to destroy that perception. I wasn't a goody-two-shoes but I enjoyed being a good boy, I suppose. I was happy to feed the chooks, cut the kindling for Mum's fuel stove, and pick up half a loaf of brown bread from the local bakery on the way home from school. (I was sweet on the lady who served there. She showed me how to break string with my fingers.) We were five minutes' walk from the shops in Quamby, and the shops were halfway to school. I might have whinged a bit about it at the time but I do remember quite enjoying being Mum's errand boy. I always bought her a cup and saucer or something similar for Christmas.

It was only as I grew older that I thought she seemed to be too demanding of Dad. That got to me and I fought against her. It used to bother me that Dad didn't stand up to her, so I tried to do it for him. A true matriarch, she always got her own way with Dad but he didn't seem to mind, as long as he had a good tractor and a good motor car. I've often said that Mum was one of the early women's libbers.

During hard times on the land Mum always kept our chins up. 'Don't worry, the rain's coming. Look, the half moon is upside-down. That means rain will fall out,' she would say. Mum will turn 91 in 2014 and, while her short-term memory is going, on the phone she still sounds twenty years younger. Apart from being very forgetful, she is as full of life as ever. And despite being a woman who designed two large houses to live in, she was as happy as Larry with Dad in one room in a retirement home in Moree. 'I am so happy here,' she'd say. 'They gave us the best room.'

I'm very much like my mother in many ways. I will never rest on my laurels. I have enough projects to keep me going until I die. 'Same old, same old' leaves me a bit bored. It gives me great confidence that, all being well, I will kick on with the same energy until my bones just get too old.

♪

In our old weatherboard house in Kerang Road there were four bedrooms including the two that Mum never let us sleep in because they were saved for visitors. It was the sleep-out, built for workers who came and went over the years, that eventually gave me some independence from my three younger brothers. I moved into it when I was about eleven.

The old house on Kerang Road is still half there. The last time I inspected it, I checked out my little sleep-out and found the eye hooks still on the wall. They were there to guide a string from my bed to the switch at the door so I could turn off the light from the comfort of my own bed.

In 1959, Mum's dream brick-veneer home was built in Salisbury Street. Only a laneway, directly behind us, separated the old house and the new block of land. She named the new home Waroongai, meaning 'Our Home'. I was fourteen by then. Our old home was on a quarter-acre block but the new block was larger, over an acre in size. The move to Salisbury Street was just fantastic for us boys.

The new house was ultra modern at the time. Robin and Peter shared a room with twin single beds and so did Will and I. Both rooms had built-in cupboards and a study desk between the cupboards that we had to share. I don't remember ever using the desk. I used to delight my younger brothers by dressing up in Dad's overcoat and old hats and putting on a crazy show while they were in bed. Mum added a rumpus room outside the bedrooms that was big enough for a ping-pong table, hookey board and so on. The walls were painted in all those bright fifties colours that were popular at the time. Tangerine comes to mind. In the same room there was a complete wall of cupboards for storing preserved fruit. The new house was built on a small orchard of stone fruit trees so Mum had plenty of peaches and apricots to fill up her tall jars. We always had this fruit for dessert at night.

Mum and Dad's bedroom was at the other end of the house, alongside the beautiful visitors' room that was rarely used, as usual. The lounge and dining rooms were separated by a large sliding door to open up for parties. Mum loved to entertain. The heat from the slow combustion stove in the lounge room was channelled through to the rumpus room. For me, the best room was the kitchen. The eating area was like a cafe where we all would slide in on a bench seat (maybe this was to keep us all under control). I think Mum was ahead of the trend to have the kitchen as the main entrance to the house. Waroongai's official entrance near the visitors' bedroom was never used.

If I ever have the patience to build a house again on my land in south-east Queensland, I'd have the kitchen facing the morning sun with a patio outside and a breakfast table just like Mum had. If I ever buy another old house in the suburbs (which I never will) I would make sure the backyard had the morning sun where the kitchen is.

Why am I going into the details of this brick veneer house? To prove how restless Mum was. Six years after building her dream home, we were out of there and into an old homestead on Tralee in north-west New South Wales. By the time I was out of secondary school at Scotch College, Dad and his brother had divided up the blocks and dissolved the partnership. Dad and Mum produced five boys; Uncle Arthur and Aunty Doreen had three, all of who were keen to become farmers. Without Mum, I doubt that Dad would have left dear old Quambatook. It was her idea to move to Croppa Creek in 1965 and if we hadn't done that I may never have fallen in love with the variety of bush our country is blessed with. We left Quambatook lock, stock and barrel. That is, we left behind tractors, trucks and machinery.

Well I couldn't wait to walk
In my old man's shoes
And what more could I ask
To head off with my biscuit tin
Black tea in a thermos flask
To learn to plough a real straight line
And learn to be alone
In ever diminishing circles
Solve problems on my own

Now it's considered normal
To pass your acres down
But if you've got more children
Well you try to buy more ground
So you borrow heaps of money
Just to give your kids a go
After all that's said and done
You taught them all you know

(from 'The Farming Game' © 1994 Emusic Pty Ltd)

Chapter 6

TO WALK IN MY
OLD MAN'S SHOES

I guess I was a boy to Dad until he noticed one day there was a young man in a blue singlet standing in front of him. I remember him saying to Mum, 'John has become a man, eh?' I guess I was about nineteen but I must admit I was still pretty naive at that age. Dad never said out loud that he loved us boys but we felt it. When I had my own car, he would sometimes sneak off and fuel it up. It was probably his excuse to give it a run.

The new way of life in north-west New South Wales was what we all needed, in many ways. It certainly provided plenty of new opportunities for me now I'd finished school, including the gift of my first car: a brand new EH Holden ute. I had found studying at secondary school level really hard and failed matriculation miserably.

The move gave Mum the opportunity to think about her next dream home. The old weatherboard house on our property, Tralee, was lined on the inside only. The stud walls were exposed but surrounded by a gauzed-in veranda. Attached to the original little building was a huge breezeway, big enough for the large billiard table that came with the purchase of the property. The original kitchen was a scullery where the housekeeping and cooking were done out of sight of the man of the house; it had a separate walk-in pantry for preserves. In 1965, the state power hadn't reached our area so outside all of that was the power generator with a bank of batteries. The more modern kitchen had probably been added in the fifties. Initially there was plenty of room for Will and me to have our own bedrooms. Pete and Robin were still in boarding school and I can't remember where six-year-old Jeff slept. By today's standards it was pretty basic but Mum knew she would eventually have a new home to match what she'd had in Quamby.

♫

I was finally comfortable in my Aussie Rules position at half-back in Quambatook when I found myself in the land of rugby union and rugby league. No Aussie Rules. No girlfriend. No mates. What did I do? I learned to play rugby union. Or should I say I 'had a go' at playing rugby.

I eventually made fullback with the Moree All Blacks (now the Weebolla Bulls); I got by because I could catch and kick, but I never really learned the science of rugby. No one taught me how to side step or how to tackle. My specialty was to 'up and under'. That is, after catching the ball as fullback, I'd kick the ball high enough to reach it before it landed. Unfortunately, usually some no-neck from the opposition had other ideas and would shoulder me out of the way before I got there. I'm sure I probably up-and-undered too much.

I did run with the ball on occasions. After one such attempt, I woke up in the middle of the football ground, not knowing where I was. Suddenly the day was completely overexposed and someone's head had knocked my teeth through my cheek. I was actually 'knocked silly' – a saying I now know is real. I was carted off to Moree Hospital and checked out by the doctor to whom I made the most ridiculous drunken-like statements. My girlfriend at the time visited me briefly to see my face blown up like a dead cane toad's and she quietly snuck back to the rugby after-party. I was never quite right for her; I wasn't what you'd call the 'landed gentry' type.

♪

When we first moved, I took on milking a cow but gave that away quite quickly as I had no patience with an Ayrshire that had horns and an accurate kick. I tried tying her hind leg down but then she found a way to put her front leg in the milk bucket. She really was not amused at me stealing her calf's milk, but was quite willing to eat the oats I gave her.

I had more success with pigs. There are two ways to make money out of pigs: go big by buying food as well as building a proper sty for them with concrete floors in a shed, or keep it really small with lower overheads. I chose the latter and it was fun.

A 12-month-old pig was bringing $100 back in the sixties. Good beer money. So I cut two large belah tree poles and dragged and pushed them with the tractor until they were under the old foundations of the corrugated iron shearers' quarters. Then I managed to tow the five rooms of the quarters to the back of the homestead and turn the whole thing into a pigsty. I built five small steel mesh yards outside each door and I had a home for five sows. They usually gave birth to at least six piglets. I had a landrace boar that did the job for breeding purposes but he was very shy and I never caught him in the act.

The bonus was we had quite a lot of scrap wheat at the end of harvest to feed them. I just added blood and bone from the abattoirs at Moree. As the piglets grew, I let them out into a paddock surrounded by an electric fence. Pigs are quite intelligent and they have eyes just like us. I learned never to look a pig in the eye if it was to be yarded. It would know straight away what was going to happen if you looked at it, and would avoid coming anywhere near the yard.

♫

The year we moved to Tralee, we suffered the worst drought in recorded history. We had bought about 2000 sheep because we hadn't cleared all the scrub at the time. Those sheep were eventually sold for one-and-sixpence: skin value. This was after we'd had two stockmen take them around the stock routes in Queensland for months. By the time the sheep returned they were very poorly and many died. I don't have fond memories of sheep farming.

Dad had invited Jim Hanson and his family to move from Quambatook with us. Jim was like a big brother to me. Back in the Mallee, he'd taught me a lot once I was old enough to drive a tractor. Jim was still Dad's right-hand man when we moved and there was much to be done. So right next door we built a small house for Jim. Now it seems like a strange decision to build so close, but I guess it was to share the water tank that was filled by a windmill. I suppose Dad also thought it would be easier to connect the electricity when the power eventually arrived. It must have been a bit hard for Jim to see me, a first-year farmer when we moved, gradually become a manager. Dad slowly handed me the reins on Tralee and not long after, Jim took his family to Western Australia.

After a few years we bought nearby Backspear, about ten kilometres north but situated on the same Croppa Creek. Drought struck again. Backspear had been a beautiful sheep-breeding property but we'd paid wheat-farming prices and couldn't really survive on growing wool. The crows didn't help the situation; they were often caught picking out the eyes of lambs as they were being born. The ewe, at that moment, is unable to fend them off.

When we bought Backspear, most of it was not under plough and the man we employed to take care of the sheep used a horse. The young pony they gave me to ride knew straight away, of course, that he had a novice on his back. He was the boss. He would fight me heading away from the house and then I had to stop him galloping on the way back. We bought an agricultural Honda bike soon after. I'm glad I gave the horse away; there have been some tragic accidents on the bloody things. Mum was right all along.

When Mum and Dad moved to Backspear, Tralee became my property to run, and Will and I jointly owned it. Although Tralee and Backspear were separately owned, the two properties were still within the farming partnership. By law in New South Wales, Mum and Dad weren't allowed to own more than one property so, as we expanded, Peter became the owner of Nee Nee (and still is to this day) and Robin owned another property called Gil Gil. 'K and SE Williamson and Sons' ended up with about 14 000 acres of prime wheat country between Moree and Goondiwindi. All these expansion rules are a joke now as foreign corporates are buying up huge tracts of wheat farming land purely as investments, sometimes not even farming them, but just holding onto them.

Our best year ever was in the late sixties when we harvested 10 000 acres and produced 10 000 ton of wheat, most of which we harvested with our own headers and carted with our own trucks. Summer rain was the norm and we soon learned not to muck around up there. Sundays off at harvest time was unheard of in north-west New South Wales. We'd harvest into the night, even if we left some grain behind, just to get the crop off before the storms arrived. In the Mallee, we had rarely harvested once the air became moist in the evening.

With the purchase of the beautiful Backspear, at last Mum's dream of having another new home was possible. This time she renovated by hiring a dreadful Cape Cod conversion mob from Sydney. She had the house made into a two-storey home with a roof designed traditionally for snow country. It was most inappropriate and extremely hot upstairs! However, downstairs it had her trademark kitchen, living room and dining room, all attached to the carport and garden. It was a welcoming sight to come home to. A swimming pool was included and boy, was it a bonus in the summer. Like both our houses in Quamby, this one also had a visitors' room, rarely used, so we called it 'Ma's Room'. It was pink and white with awful mock-Regency period furniture.

You can imagine the impact Mum made on the farming community in the north-west of New South Wales. We had barely been there five years when she became a founder of Tulloona Ladies Club and the musical concerts began again. Mum produced the 'Backspear Burrcutters', a concert of skits and songs performed by locals. The show eventually became successful enough to be put on in Moree, and would sell out over a few nights. That was no mean feat in that town, I can assure you, but Mum knew that locals making fools of themselves on stage was immensely entertaining to their neighbours and mates. She had the backup of her own family. Willy made himself famous by miming Peter Allen's 'I Go to Rio' with piano, maracas and a hairy paunch. Robin always liked the drums. Peter, Mum often said, has a better voice than I have, and Jeff ... well you never knew what he would come up with. His favourite singer was Frank Zappa!

Send down the rain, Lord, if you don't mind
Send down the rain, lightning and thunder
It's just plain dirt but it's the world to me
I love all the birds … I love every tree

Send down the rain, Lord, if you don't mind
Send down the rain, lightning and thunder
I've never been known to pray, but it's worth a try
Lord, we're on our knees … it's so damn dry

Yes, send down the rain so I can stand in it
Send down the rain, just like cats 'n' dogs
Fill up the cracks, float a few logs down the river
Lord we're on our knees … it's so damn dry.

(from 'Send Down the Rain' © 1998 Emusic Pty Ltd)

Chapter 7

IT'S JUST PLAIN DIRT
BUT IT'S THE WORLD TO ME

I'm sure it was the move from the Mallee to north-west New South Wales that made me realise how wonderful the bush was. I was vaguely aware of the trees around Quambatook but it seemed at the time that there were river gums, swamp box and mallee and not a great deal more.

I'd been a bird lover since I was a little boy, so I was certainly aware of how important trees were for nesting. Kookaburras, owls, cockies and parrots, wood swallows and wood ducks all live in hollow branches mainly in gums and sometimes in fence posts. Pigeons, crows, magpies and honeyeaters make stick nests as high as they can. Blue wrens and finches use prickly bushes out of reach of cats and goannas. Mudlarks and cuckoo shrikes make sand nests mainly attached to high branches. Willy wagtails actually use hair and feathers and spiderwebs. They employ little spiders to help weave; I guess the spiders are rewarded with insects. Reed warblers build nests in the reeds on the edge of rivers alongside nests of grass built by the waterbirds, and on it goes.

I was astounded by the variety and individuality of the bush around our new home. I immediately spotted a variety of birdlife at Croppa Creek that I'd never seen in the Mallee. What a joy this discovery was! In fact, one day I was so amazed to see a red-winged parrot that I shot it with a pea rifle just to see how beautiful it was up close. It had a postbox-red slash on its wing with a combination of bright green and a bright blue rump. I am still ashamed today that I shot it and have never contemplated shooting a native bird again, except for the crows that ate the lambs' eyes.

Crows and ravens are very intelligent. They'll land behind the plough and eat the worms before they disappear. I was so annoyed with the crows at Tralee that, despite being a bird lover, some days I would carry a shotgun on the tractor. But do you think I'd ever see a crow on those days? Never!

We had an eagle's nest on Tralee in a tall brigalow tree. The eagles were easy to recognise in the sky, as they'd glide with their big wings spread in a slight V-shape. Most raptors glide with wings virtually flat. It felt like a privilege to have an eagle's nest in my paddock. There were also galahs, sulphur-crested cockatoos, wedge-tailed eagles, magpies and crows, as well as emus, 'lousy jacks' and 'twelve apostles', pale-headed rosellas, red-tailed black cockatoos and so on.

Around Croppa Creek, you could recognise the type of soil by what trees were growing on it. Thick belah forest meant rich black soil. Open belah and myall country usually meant sticky floodplain, which was not so high in nutrients. Then there was wilga country, which meant sandy loam. The softest, richest soil was indicated by thick brigalow forest. Brigalow is a large wattle but it's also a legume and produces nitrogen. Now ... find the land with a balanced mix of brigalow, belah and wilga and you have as good soil as anywhere in the world. If you drive down the county boundary road to Croppa Creek you will see some of it still untouched, amazingly!

The soil is so rich and friable that you can dig your boots into it up to your ankle. You can plough it with your boot. The soil is soft and easy on machinery, holds its moisture and is so rich at first that the wheat falls over. While the Mallee sandy loam would go quite hard after rain, the brigalow soil will actually crumble down in the rain and remain friable; it's soft to walk on. When the black soil gets dry, it cracks wide open. Then when big rains come, the soft mulch washes down into the cracks, so over a number of years the topsoil turns itself over. The topsoil can be a metre deep so you'll never buy a cheap farm in what we call 'The Golden Triangle'. I still drool over it whenever I go back there. Like my dad, I learned to grab two handfuls of soil and stick my nose in it to smell the sweet richness of the mulch. That soil has it all. The sadness is that more and more of it is becoming foreign owned, but that's another story.

Having said all that, I'd much rather we didn't rip up any more of the land. I'll never forget how bad the insects were at night when we first moved to Croppa Creek. But as the years passed, more and more bush was cleared and the insects disappeared along with the red-tailed black cockatoos and the red-winged parrots. There's very little of that bush left in New South Wales. If it's managed well, it provides the most magnificent sheep and cattle country. But how about leaving some just for the kangaroos, emus and wallabies and for bush lovers like me to wander through? And more importantly, for its own sake. Around Croppa Creek you'll still find whitewood, boonery, supplejack, beefwood, buddha wood, krui, bimble box and weeping myall on the precious stock routes. I have spotted all these trees in my travels through the outback, but not often all together to create such a paradise as the one in the north-west.

This amazing new bushland opened my eyes to the diversity of bush across Australia and changed the way I looked at our country forever. For many reasons I'm thankful for my childhood in Quambatook but, as a man, I found the real bush far more interesting. Prior to moving to Croppa Creek I noticed only eucalyptus trees. Now when I'm in Queensland around Esk or Toowoomba, for instance, I see bottle trees that are valued by some graziers while others dig them up to be transplanted to tourist resorts. What a tragedy it would be if there were no bottle trees left in their native habitat. I photographed a trio of them on a hill all by themselves years ago; they were like giant long-necked wine bottles standing maybe 18 metres tall. What a treasure!

Every town across Australia should celebrate the unique bush around them to open up the eyes of travellers to its glory. Some districts do this, but most don't. I think it would be wonderful to drive through the Great Divide and see signs describing the flooded gums, bangalow and cabbage tree palms as you go. Imagine having signs to indicate Coolibah Country, Desert Oak Country, Kurrajong Country, Snappy Gum Country, Silky Oak Country and so on? Or Angophora Country between Sydney and Newcastle, Spotted Gum and Blackbutt Country north of Newcastle, Scribbly Gum

Country on the way to Lithgow, Ironbark Country in the Pilliga and so on. And these are just a handful of the well-known varieties often planted in botanical gardens.

We left a couple of hundred acres of brigalow–belah country uncleared at the northern end of Backspear. I used to get up as the sun was rising and watch grey kangaroos sparring. I'd discover miniature bats in hollow tree trunks and follow goannas around. One particular morning I was mesmerised by the beauty and age of it all when I heard a high-pitched squawk and looked up to find a solo pelican right above me. It was as though it was saying, *Hey, watch me*. I did so, as the bird with its magnificent wingspan flew directly into the sunrise. It was spiritually uplifting. I felt the pelican was aware that I was in tune with the cosmos, that feeling of being a part of it all, as we are.

I still feel sad about all that Mitchell grass, crowsfoot grass and clover knee-deep that has been turned into fallow. Eighty years before our arrival in the north-west, the Chinese ringbarkers cleared the bush by hand and left trees for food and shade for the sheep. It was a wool-grower's paradise, but we were wheat farmers and that was what we knew.

There is very little of that paradise left out there now. Only the big properties that have been handed down through generations can afford to leave some of the land in its original bush state. But I guess beauty is in the eye of the beholder; after all, rolling wheat fields are something to admire and they feed a lot of people. Good wheat-growing soil in good rainfall areas is precious to Australia and the world.

♫

Moving to north-west New South Wales was exciting but we had to change the way we farmed the land. The kangaroo factor was a shock at first. Kangaroos had the potential to destroy our wheat crops just as rabbits had in the Mallee, where the sandy soil was ideal for them to burrow in. The soil was much heavier around Moree, so the rabbits could only nest in hollow logs, and therefore weren't a problem for farmers. Kangaroos had never been a big problem in the Mallee because the land was originally covered mostly by thick mallee scrub. But around Moree there was a lot of natural Mitchell grass on the black soil plains that was ideal for emus and kangaroos. They spread and bred as farmers cleared the surrounding brigalow, belah and wilga country for grazing and growing nice green wheat for them to eat. We turned it into plain country.

It wasn't long before I realised that we couldn't allow the roos to destroy our livelihood. Wheat farming is hard enough in bad seasons without a mob of roos wiping out your crops in a good one. Doug Makim, my neighbour over the creek on Graigue, knew what to do. We became good mates; we still are. As is turned out, he was a champion clay pigeon shooter, so he was an expert at shooting kangaroos. Doug could shoot a roo in the head on the run from the back of a moving ute. Apart from being a terrible shot, I wasn't all that keen on the job so I was quite happy to drive the ute. Being a revhead, driving suited me.

There was an occasion when we had a different 'roo drive'. On Doug's place, there were about a hundred acres of natural wilga country left for the sheep. Three or four of us yahooed and made a lot of noise so the roos would head towards the corner of the paddock where the shotgun champ was waiting. It was a terrible thing to have to do but, unfortunately, it was the roos or us; the kangaroo population had to be managed to a more comfortable level. It's called survival, and that's life. These days, Doug Makim is proud to have kangaroos and emus around.

We also used to enjoy the odd foxhunt in the wheat paddocks, spotlighting at night. I lost chooks to the bastards many a time at Croppa Creek. There were no beagles, horses or trumpets. No 'tally-ho, tally-ho'. Just two shotguns in the back of the ute. *There goes the bastard.* Those who think I'm a rabid greenie should know that I've seen things from both sides.

We couldn't believe how rich the soil was around our railway siding at Croppa Creek. It was so rich that our first years of growing wheat on brigalow country produced wheat with so much leaf that the crop would fall over. As time went on, it settled down and then we kept the nutrients up with superphosphate as we'd done in Victoria. The soil was so good in some areas, like the Sefton plain, that they probably still don't use fertiliser. The best practice, of course, is to alternate growing crops like peas and beans to replenish the nitrogen.

The hardest thing to take with wheat farming is a bumper crop being destroyed by a couple of nights of heavy frost. We generally sowed late, trying to avoid the late frosts. In September, the heads of wheat are beginning to fill with grain. A late heavy frost can freeze the stem and stop the grain from forming. The crop is destroyed and only useful for making straw bails. But late crops are never as good as early crops, so it's a catch-22.

One year, the heads on the wheat were three or four seeds across and long, just waiting for a September rain to fatten out the full grains, when the frosts came. We had about 3000 acres wiped out; a million dollars worth. We gritted our teeth and baled the lot, using our harvester as a mower. Then it rained and rained. We turned the bales over and over, stacked some in the shed (a bastard of a job) and eventually got next to nothing for them. That was when my thoughts of giving it away began.

There's a lot of heartache in dryland farming, especially with the unpredictability of the weather, but a lot of joy as well. There's a lot I still miss if I concentrate on the bright side of it. Being your own boss is a great way to live. For one, if you keep yourself working hard you'll hopefully get a good result in the long run. If you're lazy and piss all the profits down the hotel porcelain then you only have yourself to blame. It is certainly true in the farming area around Croppa Creek that hard work will pay off because the area is blessed with that good, dark-chocolate coloured, almost-black soil.

Sitting on a tractor for eight hours might sound boring, going round and round the paddock, but there's great pleasure in turning the rich soil. The smell of it is heavenly, the driving becomes second nature and you can virtually meditate as you go around. Before the modern laser systems, it was a challenge to plough a perfect straight line, especially if the paddock was near the road, where having straight lines was a way of showing off to the neighbours. More importantly, though, when you're sowing wheat you need it to be straight. If you wander off track, you'll end up with a long strip of weeds instead of wheat. That didn't impress my old man.

I think I finally felt like a wheat farmer when Dad left it up to me to sow all of Tralee, after he'd moved to Backspear. My mate Bernie Fing and I sowed about three thousand acres, nonstop. We had two Super 90 Chamberlain tractors hooked together, pulling two combines. We did it all in eight-hour shifts right through the day and night. During the eight hours, we had to stop the tractor and drive the truck to the barn, load it up with bags of seed wheat and drive back to the tractor. Instead of carrying bags weighing 80 kilograms on our backs to the combines (as I'd been doing for years), we used a platform along the top of the combines and wheeled the bags on trolleys to empty into the combines. Soon after I left the land, this was all done with bulk wheat and augers (machines for the purpose).

The worst thing about all this physical work was that you built up a sweat. The nights were frosty and I wore long johns, jeans, shirt and jumper all underneath my overalls. One minute you were sweating, the next minute you had ice forming on your lap. There were no air-conditioned cabins back then.

It was all worthwhile when you saw the wheat poking its head through the soil in August, revealing the long sweeping lines of green. And it was even more rewarding when spring arrived and the beautiful crop of wheat started waving in the wind and the heads started to form, sometimes four grains wide, with no contaminating black oats appearing above the crop. Then harvest time came when the header hardly got to the other side of the paddock before the bin was full. You'd throw a few grains in your mouth and it would soon form a lump of chewy in your mouth; prime hard premium wheat, perfect for spaghetti. This also makes your banker smile.

My main job was to get the wheat to the silos at Croppa Creek. One year, our yield was so good we couldn't cope with it unless we hired more trucks. So I went down to the silo and met a few city blokes who'd brought their converted gravel trucks to the area on spec. They were a pretty wild lot. One of them was always getting bogged or breaking down which meant we had to unload his truck, which became a bit of a pain in the arse. His grog bill at the Croppa Creek store was more than his fuel bill – that was the story anyway. That year, however, those blokes got us through.

We really celebrated a good, dry harvest. If it rained during harvest, it could mean disaster. Too much rain on the ripe wheat could bleach the grain and lessen its value. Worse than that, the grain would start to sprout roots. 'Shot and sprung' wheat is only useful for stock feed. When it did rain we'd all gather at the shearers' quarters and drink lots of beer. What else could we do?

Meanwhile, it was Mum's job to keep up the sandwich supply to the workers. I remember one harvest she hired an English girl, Jacqui, who was a great help, except she loved to walk around in a bikini. You can imagine how distracting that was for all the blokes. I'm quite sure she knew what she was doing.

♫

I'll always be thankful to my mother and her restlessness for my family's move from Quambatook to north-west New South Wales. Without it, perhaps I would never have realised that my country was so amazingly diverse. I realise now that we could have moved to a thousand other places in Australia and the surprise would have been just as inspiring.

I was a hard worker but far too lazy mentally to keep up with the technical side of it all. You can't make a living on the land by just loving it but thankfully, with songs, I have made a living out of that love. My vagueness has made me a songwriter, otherwise I think I might have struggled on the land. I'm far too romantic about the bush! And I'll go on trying to help people appreciate the beauty of it until I die.

There you were beneath the stars
My eyes could not believe
That was the night we fell in love
And it was on Christmas Eve

Chapter 8

THERE YOU WERE
BENEATH THE STARS

I met Mary Kay Price in 1969. She was sitting in another bloke's ute in Moree. Her beauty struck me immediately. Phil, who owned the ute, was a mate of Mary Kay's brothers. The next time I saw Phil I remarked that he'd better keep an eye on her, as she was beautiful. Not long after that, I saw Mary Kay at Yambulla, a neighbouring farm owned by the Shelton family who held the traditional Christmas party every year. I arrived with the English girl who Mum had hired to help with the cooking at harvest time. I found out later that Mary Kay thought the English girl was my date, and was very embarrassed when I gave her my full attention. Everyone else noticed, too, but I didn't care. I was spellbound.

Mary Kay was only seventeen and just out of boarding school. I was six years older. As you can imagine, tongues wagged. There I was, the oldest of five new boys in the district, a successful farmer; we had already bought two of the best properties around. I remember saying to her older brother, Tony, 'Geez, Droopy, where have you been hiding your little sister?' Later I caught Mary Kay's eye in the Croppa Creek store. I deliberately became interested in the same grocery shelf. It felt a bit like stalking that day but, as it turned out, she was warming to the idea that I was very keen to take her out.

My next move was to ring Mary Kay at Sefton, her family's property, and ask her to dinner and the movies in Moree. I'll never forget that evening when I arrived at Sefton. Mary Kay has a sister and four brothers and they were all inside the homestead playing the card game euchre. The Prices have always been mad about cards and they're very competitive and loud, but when I arrived the noise stopped as soon as I knocked on the door. It was a big moment. Mary Kay was very precious to them all and here was this older Victorian lad on their doorstep.

I was half an hour later than expected. Her dad, George, answered the door, and I said, 'Sorry I'm half an hour late, I got held up fueling the ute.' George turned and called, 'Mary Kay! He's here.' Then under his breath to the family, 'We've got a con artist here.' At the time I had no idea that the half-hour delay had caused a bit of tension. I can imagine the brothers saying, 'He's gone to water', or 'He's chickened out' or 'He's a bullshit artist'.

But I was determined, so none of this bothered me.

As I got to know George and his family, I understood it was par for the course to give everyone a hard time, all in good fun. The whole family had inherited George's sense of humour and irreverence, an amazing achievement for a man who hardly moved from the kitchen table with his racing form guide, a packet of fags and a box of Bex. Everyone in that family had a nickname and you could be excused for forgetting their real names after a while. George called me 'Dear Boy'. His adopted mother, Aunty Ducky, called me 'a dear boy' and I think it made him a little jealous. Out of earshot, the family referred to him as 'Pancho'. He did have a bit of an old Mexican look.

George had virtually retired by the time I met him in 1969. He was a soldier who escaped from Singapore when the Japanese invaded it. Apparently he managed to find a small boat, but somehow ended up in the water for quite some time waiting for a friendly ship to pick him up. It's all a bit sketchy. I don't think the family knows to this day exactly what to believe about the late George Price. He could get out of control on the Scotch but he was a loveable rogue and I guess that's all that mattered in the end.

Trucks and bulk-bins filled with rust
Boy leaves home to make a crust
A father's dreams reduced to dust
But he must go on

Tortured red gums – unashamed
Sunburnt country wisely named
Chisel-ploughed and wire-claimed
But never, never, never tamed

Whirlwind swirls a paper high
Same old news of further dry
Of broken clouds just passing by
That's my home

(from 'Galleries of Pink Galahs' © 1986 Emusic Pty Ltd)

Chapter 9

BOY LEAVES HOME
TO MAKE A CRUST

Everything was fine for our farming partnership until 1970. That was the year I left to follow my 'Old Man Emu' success.

Locally, I had became known as the one who could play guitar and sing around the fire with my bush and rugby mates, so I decided to try my hand at entertaining people at the Imperial Hotel in Moree, just for fun. Or to be more specific, at the 1810 Restaurant out the back. I'd already proved I could entertain at a coffee lounge in Moree. Max and Ernie Hitchins, who owned the hotel, paid me ten dollars, which just about covered a meal and drinks for two. I was singing mainly folk songs plus some Johnny Cash and Roger Miller, Harry Belafonte, and anything that people enjoyed. The Kingston Trio had shown me how to entertain people with good music. Plus I'd been singing George Formby songs on the ukulele at the age of nine. It was fun and gained me some friends. It didn't occur to me at the time that I could write my own songs.

In the sixties, I was blown away when I heard Rolf Harris's 'Tie Me Kangaroo Down'. *Wow, listen to that Aussie accent,*

I thought, *no hint of American style!* And he had a wobble board. *What a gimmick!* Everything was so original. And then came 'A Great Big Dog' with that breathing effect called 'eefin' and 'arfin'. On top of that, Rolf was a painter; he painted pictures as part of his show. Next came 'Jake the Peg'. I liked Rolf's real Aussie stuff and his ability to entertain.

Going round and round on a tractor gives you a lot of time to think. The bush around Tralee had been ringbarked a couple of generations before, leaving glorious open bush with knee-high Mitchell grass, clover and crowsfoot grass. It was prime wool country but times were changing. Properties were being transformed from sheep country to growing crops, which meant the land was ideal for kangaroos and emus. You'd watch the huge thunderclouds gather overhead, sometimes drawn together to create an isolated downpour and you'd think, *It might come over our place with a bit of luck.* 'Old Man Emu' was written while I was on the tractor. Emus and kangaroos at Tralee surrounded me so they became the main characters in the song. I never saw an emu racing a kangaroo and I still don't know which of them is the faster. My answer is always, 'Kangaroos don't run; they hop.'

My life as a songwriter really took off the night in the 1810 Restaurant when I first sang 'Old Man Emu'. The song was my attempt to write another 'Tie Me Kangaroo Down'; you can hear the Rolf Harris and Roger Miller influences in the zany lyrics. The small restaurant crowd, mainly rugby mates and their girlfriends, went off. It's the only time I've had to sing the same song three times in the one show in my entire musical career. That was enough to make me realise

I was on to something. And believe it or not, that was my intention in the first place: to write a hit.

Novel songs were the only kind of Aussie songs that radio stations would play back then. We weren't ready for serious songs with an Aussie accent, unless you liked the 'Hillbilly Hour' on Radio 3DB. We had been so used to hearing American hits that our own accent sounded embarrassing. All the quintessential Aussie songs of the 1960s and 1970s were humorous songs: 'Pub with No Beer', 'Redback on the Toilet Seat', 'I Hope Your Chooks Turn into Emus' and, of course, Rolf Harris's songs. That was the way to go. Chad Morgan was huge in those years because he virtually sent himself up as an Aussie in every song. Remember the first *Countdown* shows on TV? Good-looking young Aussies used to mime American hits. We've come a long way and I am so pleased now that I have been a part of changing that attitude.

♫

I was in a fortunate position back then. I had a useful family connection in Melbourne: Dad's first cousin Brian Rangott was Channel Nine's musical director. He was highly respected for his involvement in Graham Kennedy's *In Melbourne Tonight* and all musical events in the early days of Channel Nine. Brian had already helped me to purchase, at wholesale price, my first Maton guitar (made in Melbourne). It was a nylon string guitar. American folk singer Joan Baez played such a guitar and I wanted to play like her.

I played my very rough version of 'Old Man Emu' to Brian on my four-track reel-to-reel tape recorder. I had my guitar on

one side of the tape and my voice on the other. This was not
ideal; it needed to be mixed together on another machine. So
poor Brian had to flick the switch from one side to the other
to get some idea of the song. Fortunately he was impressed
enough to suggest I offer the song to the champion boxer
Lionel Rose. Lionel had a number one hit, 'I Thank You'.
My reaction was quite strong; I thought, *No way, I want to
record 'Old Man Emu' myself*. So Brian rang the producer
of Kevin Dennis's *New Faces* to come down immediately
and meet me. I was amazed at what power Brian had. I went
on *New Faces* that week. It normally took an audition and
months of waiting to get on that show.

I won the Victorian *New Faces* hands down. I was so
pleased I didn't let Brian down for his faith in me. I still
remember the cameramen bouncing up and down behind
their cameras. Once again it was an instant hit with everyone
and they gave me the Fred Award, a bright red, bearded,
cartoon-like head on a bakelite base, voted on by the crew.

Ron Tudor, a little bearded man I soon came to call
Rumpelstiltskin, was a sponsor of the show, and he always
hung around *New Faces* looking for new talent for Fable
Records. He offered me a recording deal straight away.
Naively, I signed a publishing contract with Tudor and gave
away my ownership of the recording. This means the original
recording is still being sold from one recording label to
another; I get artist royalties for the song but not mechanical
royalties. It's the only recording I don't have complete control
over to this day. Bugger! Not to worry, I've rerecorded it and
not too many people would know the difference. So 'Old Man
Emu' was released on Ron Tudor's independent Fable label.

I didn't win the national *New Faces*. I can't even remember who did. It always amuses me when I recall that John Collins, a judge on the national *New Faces*, predicted that 'Old Man Emu' wasn't good enough for television, so he marked me down. The Melbourne judge didn't agree with Collins. He was right. During 1970 I sang, and sometimes mimed, 'Old Man Emu' on every TV show available, and there were plenty back then. Even regional television channels had musical shows.

The song was a huge hit yet Fable didn't bother to send me the single. In fact, radio station 2VM in Moree received it before I'd heard the finished product; they rang and told me they were going to play it. I was out feeding my pigs early in the morning, my transistor sitting on a fence post in anticipation, when I first heard the song on radio. It was quite surreal. I sounded older than I'd imagined. I was only twenty-three. What a thrill – my voice on radio! I doubt that anything has blown me away as much as that in my forty-four year career.

For a while I kept the radio on all the time, hoping to hear my song again. At night I would tune in to 3UZ in Melbourne and could hear it creeping up the charts. It reached number one and was there for five weeks. It was played in New Zealand and even got a spin in California. The rest is history as they say. I knew then I could write a song. What I didn't know was that it would take so long to write another good one.

I took off from Tralee with my parents' blessing. The wheat farm would survive without me. It was time to see what was on offer with a number one hit.

I was on to my third EH Holden by that time. The ute waiting for me when I first left school had been destroyed in a prang with a header (wheat harvester). I then took over a farmhand's station wagon but ended up with a sedan by the time I left the farm. Travelling to rugby training in Moree and to games across the north-west took its toll on the car. Night driving back then was hazardous and there were roos everywhere. No car survived it, especially at night. I reckon there was a roo dent in every panel by the time I set off on my brilliant career.

My first stop was Tamworth. Mr Hoedown, John Minson, was king of Country Music Radio on 2TM at the time. I thought it was a good idea to call in and see him. Well, he was so pleased to see me that we spent the day together around the area. John's young son, Lawrie, tagged along with us. It's all a bit of blur but a few things I remember vividly. He took me out to the legendary bushranger Thunderbolt's cave. Perhaps he thought I would write about him. We also visited a house where three budding guitarists showed me their skills: the late Gary Brown, and the Emmanuel brothers, Tommy and Phil. I still made it to Sydney that day. That's when I first met radio personalities John Laws and Bob Rogers.

I was encouraged to go to Sydney for a Fable record launch. The Fable label was born out of an argument between radio stations and major record companies to do with royalties. Ron Tudor took the opportunity to sign artists to sing American covers and offer the songs to radio without worrying about royalties. Fable artists Matt Flinders, Liv Maessen and Bill and Boyd were going to be there. I was wide-eyed and green and everyone wanted to meet me, including the popular radio personality, John Laws. I didn't know who he was. His radio program wasn't broadcast to Moree back then and because I was originally from Victoria his fame hadn't reached me. We hit it off straight away and I remember Bill and Boyd telling me how fortunate I was that Lawsy had taken a shine to me. I now know Lawsy has a soft spot for bushies. I reckon it's because of their lack of bullshit. Lawsy had been a jackeroo around Mudgee and started his radio career in Bendigo. That helped, I guess. I certainly had no airs or graces with a badly dented EH parked outside!

After my visit to Sydney I continued on down the Hume Highway to Melbourne, cock-a-hoop, on top of the world and wearing a silly small-brimmed hat. A cop with dandruff all over his shoulders pulled me up on the old wooden bridge at Gundagai and booked me for having a damaged number plate. The yellow paint had worn off from driving through wheat stubble. I'm sure the cop just didn't like how I looked. The dented EH probably didn't impress him either. I felt like telling him to use a medicated shampoo.

I went on to record a whole album, simply titled *John Williamson*. They were all my own songs and except for 'Old Man Emu' they were very ordinary.

Now there were days we nearly sold
With frost and then a drought
Easier ways to make a quid
Would sort the young ones out
They say it builds your character
Good women and good men
Who turn around when the crop has failed
And sow it all again

(from 'The Farming Game © 1994 Emusic Pty Ltd)

Chapter 10

EASIER WAYS TO
MAKE A QUID

It so happened that my Mallee mate Murray Collins, who I'd met at a Presbo Fellowship Association in Boort (can you imagine?) also wanted to move to Melbourne. We rented a little house in Camberwell, which we called 'The Haystack'. I'm not sure why now – probably because we were 'hayseeds'. It was a two-bedroom weatherboard place owned by a fellow who was willing to mow the lawns for us.

At one stage we could hear footsteps down the hallway at night and thought it was haunted. However, being country lads we weren't easily fooled; we figured the noise was coming through the ground from a similar house next door. One night, Murray had a lady friend join us for dinner and we talked about the footsteps. She was a flamboyant actress type and leapt out of her chair and stomped up the hallway. 'You mean like this?' she asked, mockingly. Murray and I quickly grabbed the opportunity to disappear into thin air. By the time she returned, the table was unattended, three fresh meals were left steaming and a weird silence pervaded. We hid long enough for the lady to become quite shaken.

When we reappeared from our hiding places she said, 'You bastards!' in a tone that had a sense of relief.

During the year I spent in Melbourne after the release of 'Old Man Emu' I traded in my old Holden ute for a little Fiat that looked like a stretched beetle. It was gutless but fine for running around Melbourne. Murray was ahead of me when it came to cars. He bought a second-hand Volvo for its safety value. That would influence my choice of car in the future.

One of the things I amused myself with in Camberwell was discovering the old furniture stores and antique shops. I became fond of old brass kerosene lamps and bought a few beauties. You don't see too many of them now. I kick myself for not realising the potential of buying Australian-made collectibles. I've bought many things since but they would have been dirt cheap in 1970. Old Australiana is now almost extinct in such shops.

♪

With 'Old Man Emu' a number one hit nationally, the requests came flooding in, just to sing that song. I was driven around Brisbane one weekend by an overnight promoter and sang it on every live show. The Delltones were performing at a club in Redcliffe, a suburb in the Moreton Bay region of Brisbane, so I rocked up there, sang my hit song, and was driven like a maniac to three other live shows in one night. The driving that night was horrendous, speeding from one gig to the next. The promoter told me the next morning that his brakes had failed! I've been very arsey in my time. He was just one of the many fly-by-night promoters who capitalised on my hit.

I toured Queensland for the well-known promoter, Ivan Damon, on the strength of that one song. The tour was a shocker. It was done with cheap vehicles and we stayed in pubs. My 40-minute set was mainly folk songs with a bit of comedy, and hardly anyone turned up. I wasn't paid a cent. Ever since then, if I sense failure it takes me back to those years of shonky promoters, but I was learning fast.

Some of that year is a bit of a blur, but I remember being flown to Adelaide to perform on TV, as well as do a live show. I was playing my 12-string Maton guitar at the time (the one I used for 'Old Man Emu'). Twelve-string guitars have this habit of the high octave G string breaking and I was a bit savage on guitars. Halfway through my set in a pub in Adelaide, the damn G string broke again. I couldn't carry on so I just left the stage and changed the string while the local radio DJ bullshitted on to fill in. I haven't played 12-string guitars in my shows since! In fact I loaned that original 'Old Man Emu' 12-stringer to Maton to display in their Melbourne factory reception area.

Another memorable night that year was in Hobart. Once again, it was just a small set finishing with 'Old Man Emu'. The local DJ came out and introduced me as Frankie Davidson. Most of the mob realised his mistake, thank goodness. However, a fight broke out in the pub soon after I walked on stage. All I could say, when it settled down, was, 'Welcome to ringside with the wrestlers, folks!' I was already paying my dues and learning the tricks of the trade.

Once I'd decided that showbiz was going to be my life, it was time to get an agent or a manager. A rotund white-bearded fella named Jim Berinson was recommended. Jim specialised in voice-over clients. He had a rich speaking voice himself and was very good at silly voices. He managed the 'Marlboro man' at the time (a Gippsland horse-riding cattleman). Jim gave me the chance to be a cigarette-smoking character too, like Tony Barber and Paul Hogan, but I'd just given up smoking and I wasn't about to promote the evil nicotine habit. I decided it wouldn't be good for my singing career. How insane have we been sucking smoke into our lungs! I remember old Fred Farrell, a fencing contractor in Quambatook. He lit one cigarette from another; I doubt that he carried matches. That's like living your whole life in a bushfire.

Soon after, Jim handed over my career management to a younger fella, who really didn't do much except hang around when I went on television. He had a very difficult stutter. I'll never forget when I sang a pathetic thing I wrote (I can't really call it a song) on the Channel Nine television show, *Happening '70*. The presenter, Ross D Wyllie, asked him what song I was going to sing. My manager said 'W-W-W-Wallaby'. Not surprisingly, Ross announced the song as 'Wallaby', being aware of my manager's stutter. Unfortunately the terrible song *was* called 'W-W-W-Wallaby'. Oh, I hope the tapes are lost! At the time it seemed obvious to try to write a sequel to 'Old Man Emu', but of course another silly song about an Australian animal or bird was going to be an also-ran. That didn't stop me trying though. As an aside, another Quambatook boy was a regular on *Happening '70*: Molly Meldrum.

It didn't take me long to realise that Melbourne was a rock 'n' roll town. At that time, 1971, there were no licensed clubs. There was the odd cabaret room, like the Hilton, but

very few outlets for entertainers. In contrast, the Sydney club
scene was thriving. These clubs provided heaps of venues for
comedians, dancers and jugglers (even bad ones). Just about
every club put on weekend shows and had a resident band to
back singers. Virtually one hundred percent of vocalists sang
hits of yesterday and today.

Sydney seemed to be what I needed. I was a one-hit
screamer but I could entertain. I put medleys together of
Roger Miller, Johnny Cash, a bit of John Denver and threw in
some folk songs I'd heard by Joan Baez and Pete Seeger. 'Old
Man Emu' was always the highlight of my show and a silly
old folk ballad called 'Chastity Belt'. 'Whiskey in the Jar', an
Irish song, always went over well. I even sang 'Please Release
Me'. My voice was higher back then but I must admit I had
to push it a bit to sing in John Denver's range.

I was a huge fan of Roger Miller, a singer-songwriter with
a sense of humour, with songs such as 'You Can't Roller Skate
into a Buffalo Herd'. But it was 'Dang Me' that had mouth
guitar in it. *Reep peep peep peeper der dour dour dour.*
I was lucky enough, after 'Old Man Emu' was released, to
meet Roger Miller with John Laws and actually spent a few
hours in his room at the Hilton Hotel. I asked him how he
came up with the idea of 'reep peepin' along with his guitar.
He told me it was something he thought of on the spur of
the moment in the studio. I was interested in what Roger
had to say because I'd used a kind of mouth guitar on 'Old
Man Emu'.

Once I'd recorded my first album, what next? Mum and
Dad had both dreamed about careers as singers so they
could understand how I felt about wanting to pursue

my songwriting and performing career. Brian Rangott recommended I capitalise on 'Old Man Emu' for a year and then clear off back to the farm. He reckoned there were only a handful of people making a good living out of music back then. I guess he assumed I was doing alright farming. Maybe we *were* doing okay but it was bloody hard work and we'd had a heartbreaking drought and then a flood during the previous decade. So I ignored him.

Well, a dingo came around one day
Oom ba da little da da da
'Hey there, Emu, wanna play?'
But the Emu was too smart for him
Walked right up and kicked him in the shin

Well, the last time I saw Old Man Emu
He was chasing a female he knew
As he shot past I heard him say ...
'She can't fly, but I'm tellin' you
She can run the pants off a kangaroo'

Well there is a moral to this ditty ...
Thrush can sing, but he ain't pretty
Duck can swim, but he can't sing
Nor can the eagle on the wing
Emu can't fly, but I'm tellin' you
He can run the pants off a kangaroo

Well the kookaburra laughed
And he said 'It's true ... ha ha ha hoo
He can run the pants off a kangaroo
Ha ha ha ha ha ha ha ha!'

(from 'Old Man Emu', written by John Williamson, 1970)

Well the publican's a businessman
He don't care who you are
The only thing that makes him smile
Is three deep at the bar
Now look out for the funny drunk
A regular heart and soul
Always give him a little reign
But you gotta keep control

Working in the suburbs, working Parramatta
Working in the country, it really doesn't matter
Making people happy like singing at a party

(from 'Singing at a Party' © 1985 Emusic Pty Ltd)

Chapter 11

NOW LOOK OUT FOR
THE FUNNY DRUNK,
A REGULAR HEART AND SOUL

In 1971 I moved to Sydney. At the time, a friend of a friend was sharing a large flat overlooking the Pacific Ocean at Coogee. Luckily there was a spare room available so I moved in and quickly got to know 'the chines'. That is, a bunch of Western Sydney blokes who were all 'china plates', or mates, which became 'the chines'. They included a TAB manager, a Rothmans salesman, a taxi driver and an air steward. We all got on extremely well. There were never any squabbles over the contents of the fridge or tidiness. The Sydney-born fellas showed me the ropes of Sydney life.

Never the farm girl type, Mary Kay moved to Sydney to study nursing at Royal North Shore Hospital. It was a hugely social time for us. Wine bars had become the latest thing. We graduated from Cold Duck to Ben Ean Moselle. I've often wondered how the upper crust of Sydney society knew about the great still wines from the Barossa and Hunter while we were drinking such crap. But at least we had broken away from Lindeman's Sparkling Porphyry Pearl.

The only way to keep my career going was to find a club agent and work the cabaret circuit. In reality there was no circuit; it all came down to how many clubs your agent managed the entertainment for. If your agent managed ten clubs, it would give him or her leverage with another agent who looked after another ten clubs. So they would trade 'acts', as they called us. All I needed was a 40-minute show. There would always be a comedian as compere and maybe a performing act or jugglers or acrobats. Sometimes a club would have resident dancing girls to kick off the show. No pun intended. There was a regular club band to back your show and I generally had to use that band whether I liked it or not. Some of them were woeful imposters and some were the best musos in the country.

Working the clubs was bread and butter for hundreds of musicians, dancers, singers and performers. I'd go through the music charts with the band about half an hour before the show started, making sure they were aware of repeats and so on. Then I'd keep my fingers crossed. In fairness though, there were a few club bands that were excellent. I always knew the competent musicians by how much attention they paid to the run-through of the music charts. I soon learned that the less notice they took of what I was saying, the worse the musicians. It wasn't advisable to do original songs, so there were many standard songs that everyone sang. The bands usually guessed their way through the charts because they knew the songs anyway. I can't imagine what a mess they would have made of some of the songs I would go on to write, like 'Galleries of Pink Galahs' and 'Cootamundra Wattle'.

I wish I had stolen the sign in the dressing room at Manly Leagues Club. The sign read: 'The artist must thank the band at the end of the performance.' The old band leader there ruled the roost. Once again, the worse the band leader, the more arrogant he was. I was adding songs to my show that the bands had never heard of and that was a problem because they couldn't bluff their way through like they could with the many standard songs. So while this was a great period for me to learn to be an entertainer, musically it was quite debilitating. Agents just didn't want to know about original songs.

Dick Buchanan was a muso who was an expert at writing out charts that were very simple to follow using different colours on codas and repeat signs and so on. He was recommended to me, so I took my songs and medleys to him. I made up my own medleys but many artists used his charts so my best medley of Roger Miller or Johnny Cash songs ended up being used by other country singers. Such was the incestuous nature of the club scene.

Eventually I hired Allan Tomkins, a bass player, as my musical director. He would discuss the charts with the band and if they were hopeless, we could hold the show together on our own. It was always clear to me that the cabaret scene would eventually become 'same old, same old' and that it would die. If you did a cover song that was different it wouldn't be long before someone copied it.

One of my first shows in Sydney, after moving from Melbourne, was at the Coogee Bay Hotel. I was booked to sing for 40 minutes. This big, Chicago-type resident band was very helpful; they were a great bunch and very entertaining. The other guest artist was Maria Venuti. I was new on the scene with my one hit and Maria was very encouraging. I will never forget that and I've told Maria since. I remembered her act of kindness some years later when I felt it was my turn to encourage a new artist at the Chevron Hotel in Melbourne. A young Marcia Hines was just starting her solo career. What a contrast: 'Old Man Emu' following Marcia! I'll never forget how magic she was. Her whole body was in rhythm with the music and she sounded and looked gorgeous.

I remember being booked to sing at Balmain RSL Club in Sydney very early in this period. It was a Sunday 'smoko' morning: men only. I knew this was seen as an opportunity to be rude, foul, dirty – you name it! The comedian's first word that morning was 'fuck'. So I planned to do only my best songs and take the money. Anything rude I had was so mild in comparison that they would have ignored me. An old English folk song called 'Chastity Belt' was always a winner with a mixed audience, but it was bit 'Noddy and Big Ears' for this mob. Come to think of it, any of the risqué songs I've ever sung have always amused the women more than the men. 'The Vasectomy Song', which I wrote in the late eighties, always had the older women in breathless, raucous laughter. But even that one would've needed more foul language on *this* Balmain morning. My songs went over well enough; I was singing some John Denver, Roger Miller, Johnny Cash and the always-successful 'Old Man Emu'. The club manager that morning (I'll make up the names here) said, 'Well, this next young fella I'm going to bring on was recommended by Ronnie Paterson at Canterbury Leagues Club. So if he's no fucking good you can blame him!' Such was the beginning of my club experiences. They certainly taught me to expect the unexpected.

Another memorable occasion was at a club in the Hunter Valley. I had a bass player and a guitarist with me and I set up my own sound system. I sang a few songs, with 'Old Man Emu' being the highlight of the set. About halfway through, this silly old bugger stood up and yelled, 'I know what all those fancy boxes are (referring to the Bose speakers). They're playing the music. You're just miming.' The audience reacted by looking at me as if they thought this was true. So I immediately stopped singing, but still moved my lips as if I *was* miming. My musos cracked up behind me. Still playing the guitar, I walked over to the speaker, kicked it then started singing again. The audience woke up to the joke and pissed themselves. I recall being quite flattered that we must have sounded just like the recording.

Working in the clubs taught me how to handle smart arses and inattentive crowds. Often there would be one mug in an audience who just had to draw attention to himself. Most of the time it was better to ignore the prick because it usually only encouraged him to carry on. If it became so distracting, my first line (I borrowed it from somewhere) was to say, 'Listen mate, up here you're a clown, down there you're the village idiot!' This always got a laugh. If that didn't work, the next thing was to get serious and get the audience behind me. 'Listen, mate, if you don't want to listen, go home! These people have paid good money to come to the show.' This usually brought a good response from the crowd with, 'Yeah mate, sit down and shut up!' This, in turn, would cause a reaction from the club security guys, who would stand quite close hoping to get the chance to throw the prick out. You never want that to happen though as it's likely to stir support for the offender because security guys are rarely popular. The next thing you know, the idiot's mates will want to punch the security blokes and then it's chaos. It's very hard to bring the magic of the show back after all that. People go away talking about how this silly old drunk got thrown out and caused a fight and probably forget that, up to that point, I was entertaining them.

Back in those early days, I also had to deal with the rudeness of the club personnel themselves. It used to shit me how the club manager and about twenty of his friends usually occupied the biggest table at the front. Inevitably they were on freebies, all blowing smoke on me and often talking. One such lot at Queanbeyan Leagues Club invited me to sit with them for a beer after the show. The overweight manager noticed that I had cassettes for sale (I probably sold ten at the most on average). He said, 'Well, m'mate over here will have one, Mavis would like one and, hey Bill, you want one?' My hackles went up immediately. I calmly said 'Sorry, but I don't give my cassettes away.' 'Well you'll never work this club again, mate!' was his reaction. I don't think I *have* worked that club ever again because I've worked in many other venues in the Canberra area. Come to think of it, the last time I worked a club in Queanbeyan I filled the room on a door deal and was paid about half. Very dodgy agent. Very dodgy club. Sorry, Queanbeyan, it's not your fault.

In the old days it helped to piss in the pockets of managers and agents, but I wouldn't do it. My job has always been to put bums on seats. That's the way to win. The Mo Awards recognise achievements in live entertainment in Australia, and a category was introduced years ago for 'The Most

Successful Attraction of the Year'. I won it three years in a row, after which the award didn't exist. I called it the 'Bums on Seats Award' because the theatre and club managers voted on it. Oddly, I've never received an 'entertainer' award when I reckon *that* is the most important aspect of my career.

I went from club agent to club agent in the seventies. They had the scene locked up. Agents would look after each other's artists by doing deals among themselves and I reckon that's why the scene virtually died – the public became tired of the same acts coming to their club. In those early days, the shows were often free for members so the punters weren't always looking for value for money. Nowadays a club has to pay the artists to get quality. Either that, or we 'take the door'. I'd rather sing to an audience who want to listen any day. If they've paid money they won't tolerate others spoiling it for them.

We've come a long way since the days of competing with pokies in the same room as the show. Back then, many of the auditoriums still had poker machines at the back that made an awful racket. However, I have to admit that if it wasn't for the RSL, bowling, golf and leagues clubs in New South Wales, I might never have developed as an entertainer. The club scene was an eye-opener for this bush boy. That period of my career was about learning what you have to do to keep the audience's interest. It's the ability to entertain, along with originality, that keeps your head above others. You can have a great voice, great songs, but without the ability to stir the emotions of an audience you might as well sing in the shower.

You know there is much more to life
Than sky and endless plains
Your father told you stories of the war
Of Singapore and Paris, and how you long to go
But you are young, and stuck out on the dryland

Chapter 12

BUT YOU ARE YOUNG, AND
STUCK OUT ON THE DRYLAND

Sefton, the Price family's farm, was situated on a treeless plain at Tulloona Bore, west of the Newell Highway between Moree and Goondiwindi. The rich chocolate soil was lush and too deep for large trees to get a good hold. Apart from a few athel tamarisk trees planted near the back door, the homestead could not have been more vulnerable to wind and dust. In the winter it would have been icy as well.

I wrote 'Little Girl from the Dryland' about Mary Kay. She was allergic to horses and not impressed with the bush she was born to. Add to this an alcoholic father and a very strict Catholic mother and she began to hate the bush. She told me how she often tried to stop George from belting into her older brothers. She remembered sitting in the car many times outside the Boggabilla Pub while George brought out a shandy for her mother, Joan. George did join Alcoholics Anonymous but we don't believe he ever really stopped drinking. He mellowed though, and he was one of the most charming of men off the grog. If he *was* off the grog ...

George was always stirring me by saying, 'Do you wanna see me, Dear Boy?' The day I answered 'Well, yes, I do, George', he had no comeback at all. I left him a bit speechless when I asked for Mary Kay's hand in marriage. By this time I had been to Melbourne, won *New Faces*, recorded 'Old Man Emu', moved to Sydney and bought a terrace house in Emma Street, Leichhardt.

We were married back at Sefton in 1973. The homestead was spruced up for the day and it was a grand occasion. By then, I was compering the television show *Travlin' Out West* so the television cameras were there to film us in our wedding gear. I'll admit I was a bit of a wanker back then: I bought a white suit and wore a red bowtie. But don't forget it was the seventies – a God-awful period for clothes. Long hair, flares and all that stuff! Mary Kay, however, looked beautiful.

Our honeymoon at Nelson Bay was a little unromantic. Mary Kay had morning sickness. I had no idea she was pregnant. By the time we moved into the Leichhardt home, our first baby was on the way. The little two-storey semi in Emma Street was full of charm and we had great fun doing it up. It cost me $19 000 and I borrowed $13 000 of that. Paying twelve dollars a week rent at Coogee didn't make sense to me when it wasn't that much more to take out a loan. I saved a bit of my cash to knock out a wall. The damp in one wall was so bad I had the neighbour, who was a brickie, build a false sandstock brick wall inside it. There was no dampcourse and the bricks were easily available and cheap from demolition sites, because the Italians were completely destroying old houses in the inner city during that period. You just had to be prepared to knock off the lime mortar yourself. They were never meant to be a face brick but everyone went crazy for them. Some of them had convict symbols, like a heart or star, impressed into them. They were made of bad quality clay which created burnt splotches that had great character. You needed to seal them.

The outside front of the house downstairs was sandstone that I chipped back. The inside walls were just rubble held together by plaster. Back then I guess there were very few building regulations. Or if they existed, I didn't know about them. Had I not been so hell-bent on being a songwriter and entertainer I could have made a very good living out of buying, renovating and selling the old houses. There was no capital gains tax if you kept a house for three years. It was easy money.

Our daughter, Ami, arrived when I was on stage at Seven Hills RSL Club. The club manager jumped up and announced it to my audience. Ami Catherine Williamson measured 21 inches long. I remember that because it was another 'twenty-one' in my life. Both her grandfathers were born in 1921. I thought about buying a lottery ticket that week, but didn't. Later on, the address at our second home, in Epping, was number three (two and one) and the Epping postcode is 2121. And guess what, my city apartment today is number twenty-one. No, I didn't buy it because of the number. I'm not into numerology but I do enjoy coincidences.

I can hear you wondering why I wasn't at the hospital for Ami's birth. I don't think fathers were encouraged to be at the birth back in 1973. I suppose, also, that I couldn't afford to cancel a gig. Club agents were pretty tough in those days and, had I cancelled, I might not have worked for that agent or club again. Our second daughter, Georgie, was born only 13 months later and I decided to be at her birth but I don't know that my presence helped Mary Kay through it. At one stage she told me to fuck off when I offered her the gas. Georgie was a 14-hour labour so I could understand her mother's frustration. Amazing experience, watching your baby arrive. Boy, I'm glad I'm a man! I'll never understand why such a beautiful occasion has to be so painful.

I'm prepared to admit that I wasn't the perfect new-age father. At the time, a father's main job was to bring home the bacon. In my line of work it took a lot of determination but I certainly did that. Mary Kay, Ami and Georgie are all very comfortable in their own homes now, with plenty of yard for the three grandchildren and that's something I'm proud of.

I never accepted a job over Christmas so our family holidays were always special. Because both our families were on the land between Moree and Goondiwindi, most years we went up there and enjoyed all the activities the bush can provide. We would spend some nights camping on the Macintyre River. How good was that! We didn't catch many fish but that wasn't important. Camping, swimming, yabbying, hogging, playing euchre and five hundred, and, of course, sausages and cold beer. I was happy wandering around the bush, always in the knowledge that the Myall Blacks – who were an important part of local and national history – had camped there.

One year, the girls invited one of their school friends to come up there on holiday with us. She obviously didn't know much about camping. She quietly asked one of us what she should do to go to the toilet. She was told, 'Just take a shovel and walk out of sight behind a tree.' Twenty minutes later she arrived with poo on the shovel and asked, 'What do I do with it now?'

Some Christmas Days were 40 degrees in the shade out at Adavale, the property of Mary Kay's oldest brother. I remember observing how slowly everyone was moving around, a natural reaction to such heat. That way, you don't really notice how hot it is. It's a dry heat out there. My folks on Backspear had a pool and so did one of Mary Kay's brothers. That made the heat more bearable. All in all, you couldn't have asked for a more enjoyable Christmas for all the kids.

Oh this land is so big and so lonely
But a man can get away from it all …
So I'm tired of 'Kangaroo', he won't catch 'Old Man Emu'
For he's travelling this big country round …

Chapter 13

SO I'M TIRED OF 'KANGAROO', HE WON'T CATCH 'OLD MAN EMU'

As far as I was concerned, I was on top of the world in 1973. I'd got married, and I already had a TV show in Newcastle under my belt. Grundy Television had conned me into being the compere of *Travlin' Out West* for $150 per show, which was cheap even back then, but it kind of put me on the map. Trouble was, as the compere I don't think I was taken that seriously as a singer. I still hadn't written anything very good since 'Old Man Emu', although a song called 'Big Country Round' was used as the theme song for the program and 'Old Man Emu' was regularly played for the ad breaks. I received no royalties for those songs being used. I was very green but it didn't do me any harm.

To add to the wank I had enough money to buy a Volvo 1800ES Sportswagon to drive to Newcastle every fortnight. There were only five hundred of this model in Australia. It was a bit of a sheila's car, really, but I loved its design. I had traded in my V8 Falcon four-on-the-floor ute for it. By the time Ami and Georgie arrived, I had traded in the 1800 on a conventional 245 Volvo wagon in a clean swap with a Volvo dealer. No money changed hands. The bloke who bought the sports Volvo had one arm and the car didn't have power steering.

Travlin' Out West was really a variety show disguised as a country music show to entice country people to watch it. Cabaret artists like Sandy Scott and Col Joye and others always came on to promote their bush tours. It was hugely popular and watching it was almost a religion for two years in rural Australia. In fact, we recorded 72 programs over two years, initially in black and white and then in colour. But the program didn't screen in Melbourne or Sydney, much to Grundy's disappointment and ours, and that was possibly the reason it was eventually dropped. It was produced, I believe, to fulfil NBN Newcastle's Australian content requirement.

We even took *Travlin' Out West* on the road and what a success that was! The team comprised Tony Culliton as producer, Emma Hannah (Australia's Nana Mouskouri), brother and sister duo, Ricky and Tammy Osypenko, comedian Mal Malcolm, Jack Grimsley (ex-musical director of Channel Nine's *The Mike Walsh Show*) and yours truly. We sold out from Sydney to Cairns. All we had for sound were two columns of eight-inch speakers each side of the stage while our guitars went through our individual amplifiers. I've never forgotten what that taught me: no matter what the quality of the sound is, it's the content of the show that always wins. Having said that, I can't believe how well it all went considering the inferior equipment.

Back then I was known for wild suits and bowties! I avoided any clothing that might have pigeonholed me as 'country and western'. Looking back, I was getting ahead of myself, thinking I was on the way to much bigger things. It would take me sixteen years to really make it as a recording artist.

♪

During the 1970s, the shit hit the fan with our farming partnership. Will and Robin both got married which brought two more strong personalities into the equation. Unfortunately, friction developed between the wives. Will's wife, Virginia, and Robin's wife, Debbie, both thought Mum got too much of her own way as well. Although I was also married by 1973, I was well out of it all. Mary Kay had no attachment to the partnership; we had become Sydneysiders. Whether or not it would have been better if I'd stayed as a negotiator I'll never know. I think I might have tried to counteract Mum's dominating character and it would have become a complete shit fight.

Will and I sold Tralee fairly cheaply. I ended up with enough money to put a good deposit on an investment property in Epping, a suburb in Sydney's north-west. Will and Virginia took off to Toowoomba to blow it all in the eighties boom 'n' bust. Eventually they divorced and Will became a Ned Kelly tragic and returned to Victoria where his old schoolmates were. His experience on the land has made him a hard-working jack-of-all-trades and he still has a full-time job doing maintenance work at a wedding reception venue in Melbourne. He doesn't have Mum's restlessness.

Whether it was Rob or Debbie who became restless, I don't know, but they left the farm at Croppa Creek and headed back south in the mid-seventies. Debbie had also grown up in Victoria. Rob had a few management jobs on the land and built a house on the Murray River.

My youngest brother, Jeff, had the same upbringing as us four older brothers but was tarred with a different brush. You could say he is a dreamer but not a doer. Dad had to virtually kick him out of bed to get to work. Perhaps, by the time it came to the fifth son, Dad didn't give him the same attention along the way ... I don't know. Always a rebel at school, he might have turned out okay if it weren't for the big rock concerts he went to where substances were rife. As he got older, he seemed to reject the work ethic that the rest of us were quite comfortable with. Then he met a girl who only made things worse. Jeff has ended up in Mum and Dad's old house with his three children and seems to be a reasonable dad even if he has not taught them that you get out of life what you put in. The irony is he looks up to us older brothers. If he is truly paranoid schizophrenic then I blame the dope. There are some things in life that I just do not understand.

The exact opposite to Jeff is Peter, the only farming son left out there. He and his wife, Annie, are still on Nee Nee and perfectly suited to it. Peter is the most like Dad, having engineering talent. Annie was born on the land in the area; she is the perfect partner for him. Pete is looked upon by other farmers as an innovator. He also flies his own light aircraft in the tradition of Mum's family, and is even into aerobatics. These days it takes smart people like Pete and Annie to survive on the land.

I still believe Mum and Dad farmed in the glory days. I must say though, with vastly improved farming methods, such as 'no till' farming, my brother Pete has shown that a progressive farmer doesn't take the same risks that we used to. We used to sow after a good rain regardless of the lack of subsoil moisture. Pete doesn't do that now. Farmers are fully aware of the soil profile nowadays. The lower prices at least have made them better growers. We used to burn the stubble not realising how much it was sucking moisture out of the ground and killing good insects and micro-organisms. I was always proud of the cloud we would create with a good stubble fire. Der! That cloud was made of water from my soil.

♫

In 1976 Harvey Travel in Newcastle asked me to host a tour group to the Calgary Stampede in Canada. The tour included San Francisco and a Rocky Mountaineer train trip through the Rocky Mountains. I decided to take advantage of the trip to go to Nashville and Tulsa as well. Fortunately for me, I caught up with an American bloke who had visited us in my Coogee days and we drove to Tulsa in his classic E-Type Jag. We met up with an Aussie mate who was a contract welder and travelled to jobs all over the United States from his base in Tulsa. He was staying at a mobile caravan park. All the cabins were like the ones you see alongside roadwork construction, so they could be hooked up and moved. My mate had always been a dodgy sort and had made a lot of dodgy friends, a collection of hookers, dope dealers, conmen and burglars. All nice enough people on the surface but I learned not to trust them as far as I could throw them. One fella with an F-100 pick-up truck offered to steal me a Martin guitar. He knew a girl who had one. He was a handsome fella with a jovial personality but had no conscience about stealing from a friend. He had a mate who conned $500 out of me for some turquoise that was probably worth $200. Turquoise jewellery made by the American Indians was all the rage back then and the stuff is probably worth a lot these days as most of the turquoise you see now is fake. I couldn't tell you what happened to it all. I think the Aussie dollar was about 30 per cent more valuable than the greenback when I was there. This was before Paul Keating floated our dollar and brought us back to reality.

From Tulsa I headed to Nashville for a few days and found the place quite alien to what I was about. Just about everyone I met said I was mad worrying about Nashville when I was the compere of a television show in Australia. Nashville was full of would-be-if-you-could be people. I met a young bloke there who was looking after Johnny Cash's publishing. We hit it off and made a good team playing pool in the hotels and bars. He took me to 'The House of Cash', which was a mock-Southern cotton plantation style mansion with the big columns out the front. I vaguely remember walking in and seeing a secretary sitting behind a small desk in the middle of this huge entrance. Talk about over the top! I found out that Johnny Cash didn't steal songs from anyone; if he recorded one of your songs, you kept all the publishing rights, unlike Elvis, who kept all the royalties from his recordings and the songwriter got nothing. God, if only I'd had a suitable song to give him that day. My songwriting was at the fledgling stage back then so the best I could offer was a song called 'J C Bulginpockets', which ended up on *Humble Beginnings*. It was a very ordinary effort, about a rich man who rode roughshod over everyone. But how lucky was I to have had such a chance to be recorded by Cash? Nashville had songwriters on every street corner who could only dream of such a connection. I didn't meet Johnny on that occasion but years later I was his support artist in Tasmania.

While I was in Nashville I walked into a shirt shop and was blown away by the variety of singing cowboy outfits. I couldn't help myself and bought about four shirts. I hardly ever wore them back in Australia, except as part of my outfit to go with my song 'Comic Strip Cowboy'. Amazingly, I even wore a big black Yankee hat to go with it. What was I thinking? I was still so far from realising the Aussie way was the only way to go for me.

I thought my career would have been blossoming by the time I was 33, but in many ways it had only just started. I was yet to really pay my dues. I was struggling to work out where I was going. I could see that rock bands built their own following and popularity in the pubs. They could also be more original, unlike the club scene that was all about cover songs.

Tommy Emmanuel was my guitarist-cum-musical director. He was the best, so it wasn't hard to attract bass player Ralph Graham and drummer Shane Flew to create a band. Unfortunately, not long after we formed, Tommy took off on his solo career. So Ralph and Shane introduced me to a guitarist who had been in their band, Rainshine. This *really* changed the dynamics, as the guy was a small-time dope dealer. His customers were mainly musos so he was fairly harmless. Nevertheless, this meant that the small tours we did were like a Cheech and Chong movie: all about the dope smoking. I named the group JW and Crow. Our biggest tour was through the hippie country around Nimbin and Bellingen in New South Wales where the audiences were just as out there as we were. Later on we went to Armidale University in the Northern Tablelands where only one person turned up – obviously the 'JW' part of the band name didn't convey the message that it was me! We didn't play that night and the bloke helped us pack up and then had a beer with us. In fact, we tried a lot of venues with young audiences playing covers and some of my own songs, but I was lost. I really had no idea where all this would take me.

Eventually I was that desperate that I took the band (Ralph was the only original member by this time) all the way to Cairns to play at a disco for two weeks. Sydney to Cairns is a 2415-kilometre drive. I had a transit van and the drummer brought his old Holden. The tyres on the Holden blew before we got to Newcastle, barely two hours drive from Sydney. He had retreads on it, the idiot! Somewhere around Townsville, I broke an axle. I wasn't aware that the wheel had come off until I saw it flying past me, bouncing over a fence and coming to rest in an open paddock. Then ... *clunk, clunk, clunk, scrape ... scraaaape.* The old transit was well balanced thank goodness, otherwise we could have rolled, but the van's Falcon axle wasn't strong enough for the load of our sound gear.

We finally made it to Cairns and the sleazy disco brothers who booked us showed us to our accommodation. The two-storey derelict building had holes in the walls and rusty plumbing. I took one look and said, 'Either you find a better place or we're turning around and going back to Sydney.' The dickheads were a bit taken aback. Young rock bands obviously put up with all sorts of shit, just to get a job. I'd been around long enough to at least have some pride. I called their bluff because it was too late for them to get another band, so they found us somewhere else to stay. It wasn't the Ritz, but it was a lot better.

Well, the disco was an experience if nothing else! It turned out that my guitarist was gay (we didn't know) and he got his rocks off with the gay DJ. Our Kiwi–Irish drummer was quite obviously shocked by the whole experience; he'd led a sheltered life. But he got over it and we played on.

I can hardly remember what we played, but we got away with it. Each break, the DJ came on and played all the latest hits. Nowadays whenever I hear Elton John's 'Song for Guy', from his album *A Single Man,* or Pink Floyd's 'Dark Side of the Moon' I get the heebie-jeebies. What was I doing playing at a disco in Cairns? What was I doing all that way from my family? To this day I can't believe I was that desperate. Partly, I'm sure, I knew that I had to break the cabaret habit. The trip certainly did that.

The last night at the disco we were told by the dancing audience that it was a tradition to dress up. By then we'd made a few friends with the customers so we thought we'd dress up as clowns. I found a bowler hat, a red nose, a red-and-white striped shirt and some baggy pants. We'd also met a dope dealer on the edge of a cane field who sold us some sinsemilla (really strong marijuana). It helped the craziness of the clown outfits but it didn't help the music. But in that situation, who was going to notice? Everyone was mad there anyway. I remember one girl who came every night and danced with herself in the mirror. She always took herself home.

On the way back to Sydney I broke an axle again, not far from where it happened before. I looked for it for quite a while by climbing trees then discovered it had rolled over and stopped a few metres from where it came off. At least I knew where the nearest car-wrecking yard was and I'd become an expert at fitting axles. Thank goodness it was a Falcon axle; they were easy to find at the wreckers.

When I got home I decided to give this clown idea a go as a band. We named the band Sydney Radio. I tried to register 'Clowns' but I found out some smarty had already registered it, after I'd had our posters printed. I called myself Ludwig Leichhardt because I couldn't be JW dressed as a clown. Why Ludwig Leichhardt? Because the real one disappeared and so would this one before too long. I was still experimenting with possibilities. I bought a red-and-white striped canvas to use as a backdrop and updated the sound equipment but it was a waste of time. People didn't get it, and neither did I. I told the band to forget it and took care of the bills.

One thing I learned was that publicans and agents treated bands like shit. Whenever that happened, I revealed my true colours and set them straight.

♫

It was around this time that Phil Matthews gave me a call. Phil had just left Festival Records as their publishing manager and had decided to go solo as an independent music publisher. I already knew him, and Phil was aware of my songwriting potential although I hadn't really developed as a songwriter at this point. I wasn't sure I needed a publisher but he proved me wrong. He'd heard a couple of my original songs off an unsuccessful album and was impressed. Phil reckoned he could encourage my writing and give me good advice, which he did; his knowledge of publishing was invaluable. Even today, I'm still quite naive about the publishing side of the business. It's so boring as well as being quite complicated. It wasn't long before Phil arranged for me to regain 100 per cent ownership of my back catalogue of songs and recordings (except 'Old Man Emu', which Ron Tudor from Fable wouldn't sell me). In those early days I didn't realise I could take my catalogue with me from one recording company to another. It meant the new company could use all the existing songs to create a compilation album as well as release new albums. Now I lease my songs to the record company for the period of my contract but after that I can repackage them with a new company. I provide the recordings and artwork for an album and then the record company takes it from there. Well, that's a simplified explanation. It varies from deal to deal.

♪

Phil and his wife, Chris, eventually managed my entire career up until they retired in 2010. With Phil as my publisher, our first success was with the song 'The Breaker'. After being on the set for the movie *Breaker Morant*, I decided to write a song about the interesting character, Harry Morant. I'd read Kit Denton's book *The Breaker*, which had given me more ideas for the song. Phil had the music publishing rights for the movie and he suggested I give the song to Edward Woodward, an English stage and screen actor as well as a legitimate singer who played Harry Morant in the movie. But I didn't want to give the song away. I had met Charles 'Bud' Tingwell, the Australian actor, on the movie set and thought it would be good to have him as the prosecuting lawyer in my song. It was fun to record, including the gunshot and the marching sound I made by overdubbing a pair of hobnailed boots until it sounded like a platoon.

In the early eighties, Phil also encouraged me to go solo. I decided to forget the club scene for the time being. I was totally fed up with not doing my own thing and my songwriting was improving. Going back to my folk roots and singing 100 per cent Aussie songs seemed like the way to go. So I invented a little wheel-in stage with an old microphone clamped to a bit of sponge rubber under the top, beneath my feet. It was the size of a small restaurant table. My music needed a 'thump' if a pub crowd was going to take any notice. To get through the door it was designed to tip on its side and wheel along. I sat on an old drawer from the base of a wardrobe. This also doubled as the merchandise box to sell cassettes.

I needed a sound system, as I was about to offer my show to any pub that would take me. My motto was, 'give me a power point and I'll give you a good show'. So I purchased two Bose speakers and a mixing desk that I worked alongside me. Lighting was next. I rigged up four lights with white, amber, blue and red: white for bright songs, amber for ballads, red for the outback and blue for sad songs. I also worked these from my footbox.

In 1976 Mary Kay and I had moved to Epping. The Epping Hotel in Sydney was near home and became my first venue with this rig. I started with about ten friends who came along once a week on a Wednesday night and I saved the weekends for something better. It wasn't long before the crowd grew to standing room only ... maybe a hundred people. This success proved to me that I could do it, so I approached pubs and taverns all the way from Epping to Penrith in the west and to Wollongong in the south. They had rooms that previously had no entertainment booked in them. I took ten dollars on the door so the pubs had nothing to lose and everything to gain, especially on weeknights. Pennant Hills Inn and the Vicar of Wakefield at Dural, both suburbs in Sydney's north-west, soon proved to be perfect venues. In no time I added various pubs in western Sydney, a tavern in Parramatta, one in Smithfield, Blacktown and even the Collingwood Hotel in Liverpool, just to name a few. Further afield I added the North Wollongong Hotel. Now it seems amazing that I succeeded in some of these places.

I bit the bullet and concentrated on Aussie songs only. I started with old folk songs, some Stan Coster and Chad Morgan songs, along with my own. As time went on, I wrote more and more of my own to replace the covers. I guess the originality of my stomping set-up, which gave me the ease to work in any room, and the patriotism of my songs all came together and audiences related, everywhere I went. In fact this simple show worked them up so much at the end that after 'True Blue' I had to sing a calming-down song to send them off a little quieter. The support I received from my audiences sure helped my confidence. This period really was the start of my improved songwriting and the beginning of real success.

The Tamworth Golden Guitar Awards were gaining momentum and national recognition. I had been going to the

Tamworth Festival and performing my show in various clubs with their resident bands since 1972. I'd entered various songs in the awards to no avail. With new-found confidence from my one-man pub show, it seemed like the right time to take this show to the Tamworth Country Music Festival and set up at what they called the 'Talk of the Town' pub in Marius Street. I was feeling very cocky and had tarted up a white ex-taxi FJ Holden Special with a handrail attached behind the front seat that was notorious for breaking kids' front teeth. It had my original flag design on both sides of the car with the words 'I'm fair dinkum'. This was the title of a humorous song that came out of my suburbs show. I still have that FJ and it proudly bears many signatures of legends on the dashboard: Buddy Williams, Smoky Dawson, Slim Dusty, Lawsy (John Laws) and Chad Morgan – they're all there. I bought the DINKUM car number plate from the Roads and Traffic Authority and it's now on our Variety Bash ute.

I paraded the FJ at Tamworth, sitting on the bonnet with Karen Johns, who I recorded 'You've Gotta Be Fair Dinkum' with. That year, the Peel River flooded and my FJ was stranded on the north side of town. I'd met a young bloke nicknamed BJ at the pub who offered to drive the FJ back to Sydney for me. When he arrived I gave him a job as my roadie-cum-sound-and-lighting guy. He soon rigged a lighting set-up that he could operate with his feet as he fiddled with the sound mix. BJ stuck with me as my horizons expanded beyond the Sydney scene. By this time I was working at least four nights a week and building a street following. I'd progressed to a Commodore station wagon with a large Esky full of merchandise strapped to the roof. But I needed a much better rig.

Next step was an F-100 Ford, but with a safari conversion; in other words, a huge station wagon with a V8 tuned to roar. Look out Uluru, here we come! BJ and I took off to the outback, driving 14 000 kilometres through the heart of Australia. I was starting to wake up to the strength of being proud of who I was: an Aussie bushie.

The main thing mate is we're on the road, it's what we want to do
Headin' for the Alice with a dinkum show and crew,
With the ruggedest rig that we could find, no rattletrap would do,
Just learnin' how to live the life in the land of the kangaroo.

(from 'Alice Springs © 1985 Emusic Pty Ltd)

Chapter 14

HEADIN' FOR THE ALICE WITH A DINKUM SHOW AND CREW

On the way to Uluru I wrote 'Alice Springs' dedicated to the trip, the Todd River boat race (which is on sand – without water) and Ted Egan, King of Alice. I first met Ted in 1973 when he was a guest on *Travlin' Out West*. I'll never forget his engaging presence. I had no idea how influential he was back then and I don't remember the song he sang on the show. I vaguely remember that he encouraged Rolf Harris to record his hit 'Two Little Boys' about two mates in wartime.

I reckon Ted did a lot to bring the town of Alice Springs to national attention. He has been a teacher, a Northern Territory patrol officer and then Administrator of the Northern Territory, but most of all, he is a great believer in Australia. Ted and his wife, Nerys, are a great match. She is from Wales, loves to sing, and a singing husband is ideal for this Welsh woman. She was also a gracious wife of an Administrator. They lived in the lovely government house in Darwin for four years. Ted has gained a great deal of respect for his understanding of our white history and Aboriginal ways and his ability to describe life in the Red Centre.

Ted's song 'Drover's Boy' will go down in history as one of the greatest Australian songs. He proved to me years ago that a song would entertain as long as it has rhythm. For backing, Ted uses a beer carton as a hand drum and that's all. In fact, as soon as you introduce a musical instrument into 'Drover's Boy' I think it loses its power; the power of the quiet, lonely outback where a young Indigenous girl realises it is futile to scream while being raped ('broken in') and finds herself as a drover's boy, to be a guide and companion for the boss drover.

To pay due respect to Ted's song, I recorded it without a musical instrument – just a shovel in a bucket of gravel, a mulga stick and a bullroarer (a long thin piece of wood tied to a string and whirled in the air to make a roaring sound). At the Country Music Awards in 1990 I won the Heritage Award for 'Drover's Boy' and gave the Golden Guitar to Ted. He hadn't won a Golden Guitar at that stage. Back then, the songwriter wasn't recognised with an award, whereas today, both the singer and the songwriter are presented with a Golden Guitar. I asked him jovially more recently if he might like to give back my Golden Guitar. His response was, 'No bloody fear'. Oh well, maybe he'll leave it to me in his will. He's ten years older than I am.

For my first visit to Alice Springs, BJ and I set up at the now extinct Stuart Arms Hotel in Alice with a ten dollar door charge. I think we had about fifty people turn up. Ted and Nerys were there. That trip was all about writing songs and I wrote enough to produce the album *Road Thru the Heart*, released in 1985. 'You and My Guitar' was on that album, plus 'The Shed', 'Coober Pedy', 'See You Next Year

Mate' (about BJ's mate who we visited in Mt Isa) and 'The Dusty Road We Know'. My outback style of lyrics was on its way.

I wrote the words for 'Raining on the Rock' after visiting that powerful icon, but I was very unhappy with the music until I discovered tuning the low E string down to a D, giving a didgeridoo effect. The low string also gives a shimmering, hot, mirage kind of sound, I reckon. I used the same tuning on 'Galleries of Pink Galahs' and 'Cootamundra Wattle'. I remember trying out 'Galleries of Pink Galahs', 'Raining on the Rock' and 'True Blue' at Pennant Hills Inn. The latter very quickly became a sing-along but other songs, ones that later became the backbone of the *Mallee Boy* album, took a little longer to win the audience over.

Meanwhile, Phil Matthews was busy putting together a compilation album *Humble Beginnings* (released in 1985) which had my horrible songs from the early seventies, followed by *All the Best* (released in 1986). All of this was building towards me being 'discovered' as a songwriter more widely by Australians – after sixteen years.

♫

It was also around this time that I fully rejected the country and western image. I just wanted to be me. In fact, I performed in shorts at my first Tamworth Festival gig! It was stiflingly hot and they put up a small tent for me. Jeff came across from Moree and helped sell my T-shirts and cassettes. At last people began to take notice of me at the Tamworth Country Music Festival. It was a great boost. I had been reluctant to embrace the awards earlier on as I thought it would create friction between the artists. It *has* caused a degree of bitchiness but in the long run it's brought a lot more attention to Aussie country music and the camaraderie between the artists has grown and endured.

In 1985, nine years after the Golden Guitars were first awarded, I received my first Golden Guitar for 'Queen in the Sport of Kings'. It was released on the live album *The Smell of Gumleaves* in 1984. Funny thing is, I didn't even nominate it. Maybe they thought, *It's time to give Willo one!* By this time I'd figured that the judges liked either the Slim Dusty style or the American style and nothing in between. I have always searched for something that was uniquely Australian. 'Queen in the Sport of Kings' opened the gate for me, but the real Aussie stuff was yet to come, with songs such as 'Galleries of Pink Galahs', and 'Raining on the Rock'. These are songs, I believe, that cannot be tied to country music in the past. They represent a new kind of Australian country music; not traditional or American.

I guess that people in the bush related well to 'Queen in the Sport of Kings'. A fragile elderly lady, who used to shuffle past the front gate of our Leichhardt home, inspired it. I said hello to her one day and she immediately came alive and wanted to show me something. She'd possibly heard I was in showbiz. She invited me into her home, two doors down, to see pictures of winning trotting horses all the way down her hallway. I had no idea that there were stables still intact out the back. I also met the old bloke, who seemed a little grumpy but he ended up giving me an antique timer for pigeon racing and I bought an old kitchen dresser from them.

Her main reason for inviting me inside was so she could tell me she used to be a dancer in the famous dance theatre, the Tivoli, and she'd even flown to New Zealand on tour. That must have been very special for her at the time. The Tivoli back then was like the Opera House today. It wasn't long before it became obvious to me that she regretted being dragged away from her dancing career by her well-known trotting trainer husband. I could imagine him hobnobbing with his beautiful darling dancer at the races. The story blew me away. It just reminded me how you can never tell a book by its cover; don't believe that a quiet elderly person hasn't lived an exciting life. Her story also reminded me that you shouldn't allow someone else to dictate how to live your life.

I accepted my first Golden Guitar in 1985 in white jeans, T-shirt and sandshoes. As I've mellowed I've dressed more like I did on the land although T-shirts now look crap on my older bones. It's really the outfits resembling the American country music culture that I still reject.

True Blue
Is it me and you
Is it Mum and Dad
Is it a cockatoo
Is it standing by your mate
When he's in a fight
Or will she be right
True Blue
I'm asking you

Chapter 15

TRUE BLUE

I have no regrets that I didn't pursue the piano. I had the chance but I'm just not made that way. If I think about it, I reckon it probably would have taken me in a different direction. A guitar is much more practical for me as a performer. It's always been rhythm that turned me on. As a songwriter, it is often working on different rhythms that helps me vary my music. In my show, I am very aware of not performing two songs in a row with the same rhythm and feel. Pace and rhythm can determine the mood of a song as much as the key.

It's no wonder I use a stomp-box instead of a drummer. It means *I'm* in control of the beat and not someone else. Also, the rhythm of the lyrics is something I really work on. My guitar does what a drummer does with his hands. It can sound like a harp up the neck, but back at the bridge it can be a cymbal. I can tap it like a tom-tom or pick the strings like a high-hat. My whole body becomes a rhythm machine. I leave the solos to the guitarist and to my harmonica. The double bass enriches the bass strings on my guitar.

♫

Sometimes a project to write a song for a specific purpose can give me a surprise hit. This happened in 1982.

'Hey, Johnny.'

John Singleton always calls me Johnny, which I hate. I always feel belittled by it. It's like the way people used to talk about 'Little Johnny Howard'. Johnny, in other words, was a put down. But I always forgive Singo as I don't think he means it that way.

'I need a song about sticking up for y'mates; about fair dinkum Aussies. It's for my new TV show,' Singo said. '*True Blue Aussies.*'

As far as I can recall, I was given no more of a brief than that.

'Sure, Singo, I'll give it a go.'

Singo knew I could write on call because I'd written and produced a few jingles for his former advertising company SPASM. In fact, I usually wrote the jingles so quickly I had to hold on to them for a week or so to make out I had spent hours doing it. In the seventies, it seemed the more I charged for a jingle, the more likely I was to get the job!

As with all such projects, I got on with it straight away. I took a pen and paper out to the back lawn at Epping in Sydney, sat down at a wrought iron table and immediately wrote down 'True Blue, is it me and you' – terrible grammar but a start at least. What did 'true blue' mean? Real Australian, I guess. Actually, back in 1983, 'true blue' was a tag that was attached to really low-class secondhand car yards and daggy Australiana shops: not at all prestigious. So between Singo and me, I reckon we changed that.

'Is it Mum and Dad?' Well, they're definitely Aussies.

'Is it a cockatoo?' I'm a bird lover and despite the damage

they cause to farmers' crops, cockies in all their varieties are a great symbol of Australian nature and are part of our character: 'you silly galah'. I have never heard where the term 'wheat cockies' came from, but there we go, my song was on its way. The cockatoo is my plea to preserve the nature of Australia. I strongly believe that the original bush left untouched is one of our greatest assets, psychologically, morally and commercially. It's interesting that in South Africa the government has bought back private land to allow the old bush to grow, to expand safari resorts.

'Is it standing by y'mate when he's in a fight?' Thanks, Singo. That was his contribution. He was thinking about a bar brawl. I was thinking about when a mate is out of luck or sick.

'Or just Vegemite.' Now that's the line I regret, but it stuck, I'm afraid.

'Give it to me straight, face to face / Are you really disappearing, just another dying race.' I meant a dying style of character, where your word is your bond; going back to when you could leave your car door unlocked without fear of thieves who seem to be everywhere nowadays. I realised it meant virtually the same thing as 'fair dinkum', that is, you're trustworthy. I remembered all these things from living in the little bush town of Quambatook.

The second verse of 'True Blue' was influenced by the period when it was written. 'Tie it up with wire' referred to Aussie resilience in tough times, especially on the land. I know Singo believes in the Aussie character more than anything else, as I do, but *that* character, I reckon, comes from the way this ancient land creates 'the battler'. In 1982, we were about to deal with the belt-tightening of the Hawke government's economic reforms and Premier Joh Bjelke-Petersen was selling off Queensland coastal land to the Japanese for golf courses and condominiums. I wasn't impressed. So 'Sell us out like sponge cake, do we really care' came from that. Things haven't changed much, have they? It's the Chinese now.

And so the song progressed and I recorded it for the album titled *True Blue*, released in 1982. The bonus for me was that 'True Blue' was ideal for the 1986 'Australian Made' campaign. Once again Singo was on the phone.

'Hey mate, I wanna use "True Blue" for Bob Hawke's "Buy Australia" campaign.'

'No worries,' I said, 'but I'm gonna have to rerecord it. The original is very ordinary.'

The original recording was really only a demo. I was recording my album, *Mallee Boy,* at Trafalgar Studios at Annandale in Sydney at the time. So with my engineer Peter Walker's grungy Gibson guitar (through a VOX amp) we put down the hit version that had a lot to do with the success of *Mallee Boy*. I knew a lot more about the strength of the song by then because it had been very popular in the pubs I'd been performing in, especially the Pennant Hills Inn.

Bingo! I didn't charge the Australian Made campaign a cent for using it in their television commercial but it gave the song thousands of dollars worth of advertising for weeks. The song 'True Blue' was given unbelievable exposure on every free-to-air television channel, even on ABC TV. And it gave me a hit. But I was a mug for not getting a fee. No doubt Singo made heaps.

In 1986, Singo approached many of the Australian Made companies to contribute towards the campaign. By that time,

American food company Kraft owned Vegemite. Even though the song mentioned their quintessentially Australian product Vegemite, the company refused to donate towards the Buy Australia campaign. Singo was ropeable. So when I rerecorded it in late 2010 with the Sydney Symphony Orchestra, I replaced Vegemite with 'or will she be right?' which is more about Aussies being too complacent. Nowadays on stage I actually sing 'Or is it MightyMite?' MightyMite is a similar product produced by Three Threes, an Australian company run by the McAlpine family, under their label. I reckon MightyMite is better anyway and they make the best green olives, mustard pickles and pickled onions as well. I like to help an Aussie company like that. We have to keep Aussie products up there. The McAlpines are good sponsors for my New South Wales Variety Bash car, the old Holden ute with DINKUM number plates. What could be more true blue than that?

I'll never know what licence Phil Matthews gave Singo, but not long after the Buy Australia campaign, I appeared on a Harvey Norman advertisement on television singing 'True Blue' in front of a stack of white goods. I was in Mt Isa at the time and didn't see it but a couple of mates rang and told me about it. They knew I wouldn't have approved. Now I was ropeable! Fuck! It was the worst thing that could have happened to me to cheapen the song and also cheapen my image as an artist. I immediately told Singo that I hadn't given him permission to use if for anything other than the Buy Australia campaign. I spent $60 000 on a full-page advertisement in *The Sydney Morning Herald* saying that I didn't endorse the Harvey Norman advertisement. I was determined to save face.

Well, Singo couldn't believe I had the audacity to stand up to him. But I knew I had to do it. It had quite an impact on the advertising world and really embarrassed Singo, who said to me at a lawyers' meeting, 'Mate, I thought we were mates'.

I replied, 'No, Singo, my mates are the ones who rang me about the bloody embarrassing use of me and "True Blue" for Harvey Norman.'

From then on, Singo knew how much the song meant to me. I think he understands now. Radio presenter Alan Jones even had a go at me on air, referring to 'poor Gerry Harvey'. *Poor Gerry Harvey,* I thought, *what a joke!* I also seem to remember Singo saying something to me like, 'Who do you think you are? Paul McCartney?' I might not be a Beatle but I am very proud of my song. And so are our Wallabies rugby team and our Test cricket team.

I had no idea that 'True Blue' would be adopted for so many occasions. It has become an anthem to inspire Aussies to try a bit harder, to hang in there. It's often used to boost people's spirits in times of natural disasters. Steve Waugh, the Australian cricket captain, found it useful for inspiring the Australian cricket team. I'm pleased the words have other meanings to people, too. For instance, 'Don't say you've gone' means the song is often used for funerals. I can't count the number of times people have told me they buried their mum or dad or some other family member to the song. I hear it all the time and it's quite humbling that they want to share their stories with me.

It surprises me how many companies have offered me big dollars to use 'True Blue' to promote their product. Even more surprising is that they often think they are the first to come up with the idea. Talk about selling the goose that laid the golden egg. I've proved to quite a few people that money can't buy you everything. Any time I hear 'Waltzing Matilda' used to sell something I cringe. How dare they devalue a song that is more important than 'Advance Australia Fair'? And bloody hell! Kentucky Fried Chicken used 'Waltzing Matilda' during the 2014 Ashes Test to flog chicken. No one seems to give a shit! Some things have to be sacrosanct. While I'm living 'True Blue' is *my* calling card, not a song representing some national grocery store or food item. If 'True Blue' is to remain true blue it must never represent anything else. I will protect the song forever.

♫

Mixing with characters like Singo, I was bound to meet other interesting characters. During his break from advertising after he sold SPASM, Singo invited me to join him, together with Rod McKuen, the American singer-songwriter, and Australian author, Kathy Lette on a trip to the goldfields around Hill End near Bathurst in central New South Wales. It was for a television show about the history of gold mining. He thought I could write a song for the show. I wrote one called 'Two Little Fräuleins Sitting on Their Gold Mines' referring to prostitutes who made their fortunes by lifting their dresses rather than a pick and shovel. I have no memory of what happened to that documentary, but we sure had some fun mixing with the locals. I still have a brush hook that I found in the grass. It has a beautiful Sheffield blade and is as good as new. That's gold for me!

Now I could spend m' holidays on videos galore
Or lie on the beach gettin' sorry and sore
Or I could sail the ocean see another foreign shore
Well I took m' little Kelpie and I sailed the Nullarbor

And I saw the colour changes from Albany to Broome
A pair of white Corellas singin' out of tune
Wildflowers in bloom
And I saw the rusty Hamersleys from a dusty Wittenoom

(from 'Sail the Nullarbor' © 1987 Emusic Pty Ltd)

Chapter 16

WHY DON'T YOU TAKE
YOUR BEST MATE AND
SAIL THE NULLARBOR

I released two albums in 1986. The compilation album *All the Best* went gold quite quickly. It was followed later in the year by *Mallee Boy*, which went berserk! Number one on the general ARIA charts. *Mallee Boy* very quickly sold twice that of *All the Best* to go platinum at 70 000 copies and didn't stop until we released another 'best of' album. By then *Mallee Boy* had gone triple platinum and was still selling. I had arrived … and I'm still trying to equal it! Five songs from that album will always remain in my show: 'Mallee Boy', 'Cootamundra Wattle', 'Galleries of Pink Galahs', Raining on the Rock' and 'True Blue'. 'Cracker Night', 'The Budgie Song' and 'Paint Me a Wheelbarrow' are revisited now and again. I like to think that songs like that last for a long time because their themes are ageless. Love songs, however, unless they are *really* special, will date more easily. Look at 'Waltzing Matilda'. It describes things that will always be deep down in our Aussie psyche and will never die: the bush, the underdog, and the campfire. But, if my songs are all forgotten in fifty years time, I won't be around to know it. But where I would be with out 'True Blue'? I honestly don't know.

All of a sudden money came rolling in from record sales of *Mallee Boy*. Up until then I relied mainly on touring for a living. Phil had always said it would happen and it did, but not without a lot of hard work. I had left the easy life of doing 40-minute shows for the clubs and built a 'street audience'. That is, I had created venues throughout the Sydney suburbs west and south of Epping. There didn't seem to be much for me in the east or north. There had been many victories but also some humiliating experiences in pubs where people didn't seem to know, or want to know, what the world outside their suburb was like. It was quite freaky. At the Sefton Hotel, the locals didn't like the hippie types who followed me (mainly from the Dural area in Sydney's north-west). The publican didn't want me back … as if I wanted to return anyway. I figured if my one-man show worked at the Collingwood Hotel in Liverpool, the North Wollongong Hotel and the Blacktown Inn, I was on the right track. These were all pretty tough venues to play in, so bugger the odd pub that didn't get it.

♫

The next step was to expand and spread my wings. After my roadie, BJ, went back to Tamworth, Tim Kirkland and his mate Gary became my sound-and-lighting guys in the pubs. Then Tim married Marie and they formed a small agency. I gave them a good start by letting them become my agents. Tim and Marie Kirkland did a good job for a while but

I wanted to have everything under my own roof and they were determined to have an office in Parramatta. That didn't suit me. Phil Matthews then became more than my publisher, he became my manager. Tim and Marie, while very disappointed by my decision, went on to become successful agents and I hope they're still doing well with their promotions.

This was something I had to do. I bought a wonderful old Federation house in Rawson Street in Epping to be my office and built a six-car garage out the back. I also bought my own sound and lighting equipment. This meant slowly adding two more vehicles to the touring show I had. My fleet of vehicles had grown to an F100 and trailer, plus two Toyota Troop carriers. By now I not only carried the equipment, but a crew of three roadies and Carole Stannard who sold the merchandise. It was her suggestion to start a fan club. We called it 'The Fair Dinkum Club'.

It was time to really hit the road and sail the Nullarbor again – find a new audience and some new songs. We headed for the West, making the long road journey from Sydney to Western Australia, some 4000 kilometres. Phil wasn't going to let the opportunity to make a documentary slip by, so we hired a director (whose name I have forgotten on purpose), a cameraman and a sound guy to come as well. That documentary cost me $60 000 and all I got out of it was a bit of live performance footage and some useful stuff for advertising my shows. The documentary was unstructured and useless – none of us had a proper plan. However, my trip to the West was the beginning of my love affair with that great state. I didn't make money on the first trip but nowadays my shows sell out over there.

It was the Pilbara region in the north-west, on the way to Broome, that captivated me. So much so, that I painted a number of landscapes capturing the amazing red hills covered in golden spinifex, interrupted by the small, white, snappy gums. One of those paintings ended up on the back of the *Warragul* album. That trip also inspired three songs: 'Westown', 'Welcome All to Broome', and 'Sail the Nullarbor'.

Westown' describes the coastal town of Carnarvon. Back then, there was a very uneasy feeling about the place. We arrived at the motel to be met by the owner, who made it known that he hated 'black fellas'. So much so that he bragged about his bull terrier being trained to attack them. One of the crew had his camera stolen from the troopy, so that didn't help either. There were Indigenous fellas sitting around the streets with beer bottles. All in all, it didn't create a great impression. But there was also a mile-long jetty, which is still there today, that was a delight to walk along, right out into the ocean. I remember an old bloke with his leathery legs pushing an old pram full of fishing equipment along the jetty. I can't remember how the show went in Carnarvon but the town gave me a good song and I'm pleased to say that Carnarvon is a much better town today and quite a food bowl for the West.

Further north, we left the film crew in Karratha, then after a successful show at Port Hedland – the town covered in red dust – we continued on to Broome, a town full of surprises. I performed in a motel up there. During the day, Mary Kay and I were wandering around the town and met a local Indigenous girl who wasn't impressed with all the so-called progress that was proposed. 'Welcome All to Broome' was born. That night Mary Kay woke up to see a young Aboriginal kid in our room. By the time I woke up she had very forcefully told him to 'get out' and he banged his head on the window as he hurriedly made his escape. Nothing was stolen.

Boomerang Café was released in 1988. It was nowhere near as successful as *Mallee Boy* but, to me, the songs from Western Australia made it special.

> *There's nothing to do in Westown*
> *Sink a middy down the pub*
> *Take a woman home to your caravan*
> *But carry a Mulga club*
> *And watch where you walk in your wobbly boots*
> *Or the nights will rob ya blind*
> *In Westown ... In Westown ... In Westown*
>
> *Oh see the dance of the egret, pelican ponder*
> *Take a walk on wrinkled sand and wonder*
> *Hard to imagine floods 'n' summer thunder*
> *In Westown ... In Westown ... In Westown*
>
> *And there's nowhere to go in Westown*
> *Take a drive in a blistered car*
> *But you won't get away from yesterday*
> *They'll wanna know who you are*
> *Oh the shimmering heat will burn your mind*
> *It's wild and rusty red*
> *In Westown ... In Westown ... In Westown*

(from 'Westown' © 1987 Emusic Pty Ltd)

Now that I was fully self-contained and not relying on other sound or lighting systems, it was time to go back to the bigger venues of the clubs and theatres, with my own gear and a big backdrop. The club scene had dried up for many acts, because so many performers were just singing the same old covers. The incestuous system developed by the club agents virtually killed the scene, and the new drink-driving laws probably didn't help. I didn't charge the clubs, but simply took the door. The ticket sales were often dubious, but what could I do? If the club wanted to let their mates in for free, we couldn't do much about it. The good thing was that there was no theatre hire fee so that probably made up for it; theatres were expensive to hire. All in all I owe a lot to the licensed clubs for giving me so many venues to perform in.

Over the next ten years I tried all sorts of things to keep myself and the show fresh, other than the new songs I wrote, of course. Pixie Jenkins, the fiddler, came on board and influenced the sound of my concerts to a big degree, but more than that, he brought more comedy. He played the character of a naughty little boy, which gave us an Abbott-and-Costello effect with a lot of banter. 'Teach Me to Drive' on *The Family Album* has to be the best example of that. Then there was Paul Burton on upright bass and Giles Smith on fretless bass, and Garry Steel on piano accordion and keyboards. Then it got quite out of hand, taking on board Kelvin Nolan playing guitar and Randal on drums, and then another bass player, Lindsay Butler Jr.

I took that group to London in 1996 to give it a go. What a waste of money! I was much more successful in 1998 when I returned to England with my one-man show. I guess it was all about finding my limitations and learning from experience, but it was a costly exercise. In the end it proved that I am not inspired to write about other countries. I wrote a love song in London that has never been requested by my audience since it was released. And that's the litmus test. The soul of Australia is always a part of my best songs.

If you're livin' in a Lawsy town
You're better off than the rest
You're living in 'God's great garden'
You could even say you're blessed

Chapter 17

IF YOU'RE LIVIN' IN A LAWSY TOWN

To this day John Laws claims to have made 'Old Man Emu' a hit in Sydney. Bob Rogers claims the same. I'm thankful to both of them for their encouragement and support in those early days, and they have continued to support me now for more than forty years. Some say the song was going to be a hit anyway. 'Old Man Emu' still has something that is very hard to explain; I think it is the rhythm of the lyrics more than anything. Young children today love the song just as much as when it was first released.

In 2006 I agreed to travel to France for the Festival Interceltique de Lorient (Celtic Festival). Mary Kay loved any excuse to visit France, so off we went. It was at that festival that I realised the true power of 'Old Man Emu'.

I fancy myself that I can get by with a bit of French, enough to impress them that I'm trying, at least. At one of my concerts I was offered an interpreter to explain my introductory stories in French. An English person who could speak French was amused at the interpreter's French explanation to my song 'Diamantina Drover'. 'He told us in French,' she said to me, 'that a drover is a man who drives sheep!'

Most of the audience didn't understand the lyrics (how could they?) but they almost broke the portable wooden dance floor jumping up and down to 'Old Man Emu'. When the music stopped in the song and I said 'While the eagle's flying round and round, I keep my two feet on the ground, I can't fly but I'm telling you, I can run the pants off a kangaroo' they would all stop dancing and crouch until the music started again and then they would dance even more wildly. I understand now that there is something intrinsically Celtic in the rhythm of the words that triggers something very deep in the Celtic soul. I've never come close to reproducing that rhythm in another song. Weird isn't it – that song was my first attempt at writing!

♫

I don't recall exactly how the friendship developed from that first meeting with John Laws but I do remember catching up with Lawsy at Jumbo Jim's panelbeating shop in Sydney. Jumbo was like a big brother to Lawsy. He probably had the biggest American country music collection in Australia, if not the world; overseas record companies gave him all the new releases. In between smash repairs, Jumbo had regular barbecues where anyone famous connected to country music would go, including Johnny Cash, Roger Miller, Willie Nelson and, of course, Lawsy.

Phil Matthews encouraged my Lawsy connection and I decided to write a song about his show. The song was recorded at the Channel Seven television studio in Epping. It was called 'It's a Grab It While It's Going Kinda Life' – a terrible song about a floor tiler who listened to Lawsy every day. It was the beginning of some thirty jingles I wrote for Lawsy over the next forty years. Lawsy loved all the jingles and because he was so trusting he'd play them on air as soon as I handed a tape to him. Of course he would give every new single of mine a spin as well, but only once. If he didn't like the song or if it wasn't popular, that was it. He even played 'The Vasectomy Song' until it was banned, as well as 'Rip Rip Woodchip', which was controversial. Lawsy is no greenie so for him to play 'Rip Rip' proved to me he was a loyal mate. I think he only played it once, but it had an impact.

The most significant thing Lawsy has done for me has been to help people get used to hearing a normal Aussie accent in songs. I will never stop reminding people that this was a rare thing to hear on radio at that time. Between the 1950s and 1980s, radio announcers went from an Aussie version of a BBC accent to pseudo American–Aussie accents, like disc jockeys such as John Torv, to the normal everyday Aussie speech of today. Even Lawsy sounded a lot different then to the way he does now. In other words, we are no longer 'puttin' on the style' as they say. I wish I could say the same about all Australian country music artists today.

There is a bond between me and Lawsy that's not easy to explain. I think he feels most at home talking to people on air. I guess being physically among people is something I've become used to in my business. But it can be harder for radio announcers.

In December 2006, Lawsy actually said on air (and I happened to be listening at the time) that he and I should take a trip to the outback. I could tell straight away that it would probably be his last ride out in the bush. I guess he thought I would be the ideal company for such a trip. Luckily, I've never bothered working much in December; I regard that month as family time. He calls me 'his little brother', so I guess that fits. I soon found out through my good friend Jan Hayes from Ooraminna, south of Alice Springs, that we could link up bed-and-breakfast stations from the Flinders Ranges right through to Alice Springs. This suited Lawsy because we didn't have to socialise with many people that way. Actually, I don't blame Lawsy for being shy. I soon realised that punters find it hard to leave him alone. I'm wary of too much attention myself but I usually manage to slip around relatively unnoticed. Lawsy stands out like a neon sign, especially as he is so tall. On this trip he had a very bad back and was using a walking stick. That made him stand out even more.

I'll never forget when we needed a new tyre in Coober Pedy for his flash Lexus four-wheel drive. First we visited a recommended tyre dealer. Lawsy was impressed with the unassuming bloke who ran the shop but he didn't have the correct wheel size for the bloody Lexus. So we had to go to another bloke who had a reputation for ripping off tourists. We both stood at the tyre service counter and were ignored for a while. Then, when we asked about a tyre for the Lexus, the bloke's immediate reaction was, 'Oh that'll take a day or so to come from Adelaide.' So we stood there listening to this mongrel laying it on thick on the phone about the high price of the tyre and the delivery costs and so on. But somewhere during his bullshit the penny dropped and he realised it was Lawsy standing there. Well, I've never heard an attitude change mid-sentence like it, in my life! I had so much pleasure in watching him squirm as he told us to leave the Lexus, and a new tyre would be on it by eight o'clock the next morning. Lawsy was *huge* on radio out there. Imagine how much damage he could have done to the tyre dealer? What a great evening we had, chuckling about that in an underground restaurant surrounded by all the magnificent outback colours in the sandstone.

Rip, Rip, Woodchip turn it into paper
Throw it in the bin, no news today
Nightmare, dreaming, can't you hear the screaming?
Chainsaw, eyesore more decay

Remember the axe men, knew their timber
Cared about the way they brought it down
Cross-cut, blackbutt, tallow wood and cedar
Build another bungalow pioneer town

I am the bush and I am Koala
We are one, go hand in hand
I am the bush like Banjo and Henry
It's in my blood gonna make a stand

(From 'Rip Rip Woodchip' © 1989 Emusic Pty Ltd)

Chapter 18

IT'S IN MY BLOOD
GONNA MAKE A STAND

An old bloke once said, 'Every Aussie should live at least four hundred years, just to get a rough look at the place.' True. My kinship with our nature was developing when I was a wheat farmer, saving special trees on the farm instead of clearing everything. However, my real obsession with Australia's natural heritage was only just beginning. The greatest thing about touring Australia with my music has been to further my fascination with the bush.

I've said it before and this won't be the last time I say it, but I believe the Australian bush in its original state is the most valuable asset we have left. I have the privilege of owning a nice chunk of it in the Queensland hinterland. There are forty acres of old dairy country I regard as 'humanised' and therefore land that I can play with. The other larger area, although selectively logged before my time, I regard as sacred. I'm simply a guardian of it, to pass it on to others untouched. I rarely venture into it even though there is a sub-tropical wonderland in there. Bangalow palm forest, a waterfall, ancient strangler figs can all be found there.

The original diversity of flora and fauna I believe is still there. It's certainly dense enough to become completely lost in. Huge ancient trees you don't see until you're right upon them, an old vine that is as thick as a horse, that you can sit on and sway slightly, walking stick palms and macrozamias … they're all there. Nasty stinging trees are waiting to catch the unwary and even their dead leaves on the ground can give you a really painful welt. Some people are fatally allergic to them. A red cedar tree has been left in that forest because it wasn't tall and straight. If it was in an open paddock I reckon it would shade half an acre. I'm still not familiar with this forest, so it scares me. It lures me to venture deeper, like a cliff edge. It's the kind of country in which that brave man Bernard O'Reilly found a crashed Stinson plane and saved two men in 1937. He knew north, south, east and west by the moss on the trees. If I ventured deep into my forest I'd have to leave pink tape on the trees, like Hansel and Gretel's crumbs, to find my way back. It's all on a steep gradient to make you slip and slide if you're not careful; good training ground for the Kokoda Trail. I get turned around in a city so I'm not what you'd call a great bushman in this country.

The demonstrations protesting about the logging of old-growth forests in Tasmania made me aware of the devastation that was going on down there. How could we sell off our ancient hardwood forests to the Japanese, or any other nation, just to make chipboard or paper? Most Australians were just sitting back and letting it happen. I was astounded. *At least we should be making our own products out of it*, I thought at the time. But then I realised the extent of the devastation nationally. Every state was flogging off our timber and turning old-growth forests into wood farms, leaving seed trees of just one or two species. The native diversity of every kind was being destroyed in our ranges.

Back in the seventies, I realised that we might lose all the original bush in north-west New South Wales and I'd already written a couple of songs with this message. 'It's a Way of Life' protested about what the cotton industry was doing, and 'Trees Have Now Gone' was about the clearing of trees for broadacre farming. So 'Rip Rip Woodchip' was written as a protest song. The timber cutters couldn't believe it. John Williamson, an ex-farmer, country singer, on side with the greenies. Farmers were supposed to be right-wing conservatives. In fact, they thought I was singing for the Greens party but politics had nothing to do with it. I'm a one-man band. The irony is that I was brought up in the bush and, as a farmer, I fell in love with the bush. Something was telling me when we were clearing the brigalow, belah and wilga at Croppa Creek that we had to draw the line soon. Generations before me thought the bush was endless.

The woodchippers even invited me to the forest around Eden in south-east New South Wales because they genuinely couldn't understand my position. I told them I understood their point of view but they didn't see the big picture. The Australian bush was being destroyed wholesale all over the place. It wasn't just about New South Wales. I spoke to one contractor with his huge chainsaw and pointed out a 300-year-old eucalypt. 'You wouldn't cut her down, would you?' I asked. 'Bloody oath I would,' he replied. I could see that to him it was just a piece of timber, not a home to many species of birds and animals. They showed me that they were using a chequerboard system; that is, clear-felling 50-acre blocks instead of flattening the lot, which was supposed to give wildlife a chance. But this did not convince me that it would help in the long run, especially as the only seed trees they left were a couple of species, which they favoured for timber in the future. The forest would never be as diverse again. In fact, it would be cut away again before hollows for habitat would be formed. So the chequerboard idea only slowed down the habitat-destroying process. If someone can prove to me that I'm wrong, I'll listen.

The Victorian woodchippers offered me a helicopter trip over Gippsland. They must have thought they would easily sway this farm boy. I turned down their offer. I'm sure they would have been very nice to me but they had no idea how much I love our forests.

Some years later, in the nineties, I was talking on Perth radio about my objection to woodchipping the jarrah forests in Western Australia, when a woman phoned in. She said she was the wife of a woodchipper and declared proudly that she cared for injured animals. She had a couple of baby possums in her care. She didn't seem to realise how many thousands of birds and animals would have perished as a result of her husband's chainsaw. They were clear-felling over there. It's like bulldozing Melbourne and expecting all the people to fit into Sydney. I was left speechless by her remarks.

But no matter how much the woodchip industry tried to group me with the green movement, it didn't really stick. I was, and still am, an individual with my own beliefs. I refuse to become a member of any political party. I believe in the power of one. *That* has become a strength. No one can say I'm speaking for someone else or for an organisation. Sure, I am influenced by what I see, but as an ex-wheat farmer I can see both sides of the argument. However it is hard to look a third-generation timber family in the eye and suggest to them that their business is killing off the last of an endangered species in the world. They really don't want to understand. They are bound to get angry. In fact, ironically, an old logger from Western Australia was so disgusted by 'Rip Rip Woodchip' that he returned my first album to me in the mail. I was delighted because my only copy of it had been borrowed permanently.

One incident caused by the release of the song was a bomb threat in Taree, on the mid north coast of New South Wales. I was booked to sing in the high school hall. When we received the threat we thought we'd better notify the police. We didn't have to cancel the show in the end but the high school was thoroughly searched and I had many policemen and women standing side of stage enjoying my performance. It turned out to be a threat by some poor disturbed fellow. I could have turned it into some good publicity for the cause but I felt all along that it had to be a hoax. I wasn't out to denigrate the timber workers, just the Japanese companies that were tearing our old-growth habitat down. We were selling off our nature to profit another country. The Japanese must have been laughing.

♫

It was over the Tarkine wilderness protests in Tasmania in 1995 that I got to know Bob Brown, who later founded the Australian Greens. I'd met him before, but this time we spent some time together. Bob showed me a huge scar in the Tasmanian forest where it had been clear-felled. All over the ground were cubes of carrot dusted with 1080 poison. The vegetarian wildlife would eat the carrot, return to their homes and die a very slow and painful death. This practice was to stop them eating the young leaves on the regrowth for the timber industry, but the native animal population was being decimated.

My friendship with Bob Brown has not won me friends in the bush but I think he is one of the finest Australians. He's probably the only true greenie that I know. He genuinely feels for the earth. When I was inducted into the ARIA (Australian Recording Industry of Australia) Hall of Fame in 2010, I made it known that it was an honour to have Bob present my award. I am utterly convinced that without the green movement most of our future forests would have just two or three timber species and they would be no more than eighty years old before being logged. Forestry departments convert old-growth forests into tree farms.

In the long run, has my song been useful for the cause? Well, for one thing, I think I showed that you didn't have to be a hippie or a rabid greenie to stand up for our habitat. I'm known as an ex-farmer, and farmers all over Australia knew that when 'Rip Rip' was released.

There's an area of original bush near Nyngan in the centre of New South Wales named after the bushranger Ben Hall. I joined the cause to fight for its survival. The most effective ally we had was a bulldozer driver whose job it was to clear the forest for planting North American pine trees. One morning, he told us, he drove up to find gliders, possums and koalas clinging to his big yellow machine. That was just too much for the driver. He became a conservationist. He was no greenie. The Ben Hall stand of Aussie bush still remains. Too many people still take our bush and wildlife for granted. They have no idea how much we have lost. Yet I imagine most Aussies are proud of our kangaroos, emus and koalas and other native wildlife.

♫

I look out the window at Springbrook and see on the ridge, turpentine, stringy bark, brush box, blue gum, forest oak, blood wood, tallowood, hoop pine. Different trees provide different things for our wildlife. I don't mind selective logging in forestry, but not in national parks! I love good timber. It's a joy, but we must keep all the species sustainable. Why? Because we are caretakers of the land for future generations to enjoy. It is arrogant not to care or to think that if you own land you should be able to do with it what you will. The old Christian adage that 'Man shall have dominion over the earth' is bullshit, in my opinion. We are no longer ignorant of the damage we do, and have done. I'll change the words in the Bible: 'What natures gives us, nature can also take away'. If it's already farmed, then leave it in a better state than you found it. If it's still bush, it's probably too marginal to farm, so leave it be.

There is no bush like ours anywhere else in the world. Get to know it. Use the timber, but sustainably. Cut limbs for stock feed, but sustainably. Don't destroy it. Respect it. There's something deeply spiritual about it. Soak it up and listen to it. I can't live without it.

Oh pass the hat around between your friends
There's no time to contemplate
Maybe if we show some love
Maybe it's not too late

Chapter 19

MAYBE IT'S NOT TOO LATE

Our cuddly little koalas are given the most attention in this country, largely because they're a tourism drawcard. Despite their popularity, because most of these marsupials live around the Great Dividing Range and the coast, their habitat continues to be destroyed by residential development, the timber industry and bushfires. Koalas did inhabit west of the ranges too, but agriculture devastated much of these areas long before we realised what we were doing. It is a special thing to see them out there nowadays (mainly along creeks and rivers). So, it has become more and more important every year to protect koala habitat. Developers generally still don't care. The fight goes on.

Jean Starr, a gracious lady who lived in Port Macquarie (halfway up the New South Wales coast) encouraged me to see what she and a few others were doing to take in injured and diseased koalas. She had a local veterinary surgeon lending a hand. Considering what was at stake for the future of these iconic animals, I was moved to write a song called 'Goodbye Blinky Bill'. Blinky Bill and Nutsy are characters in a book by Australian children's author Dorothy Wall in the

1930s. I thought the message might be stronger if I used these familiar names. Imagine these and other children's books for future generations if the koalas became extinct. What would future generations think of us? That is the underlying question. But of course, koalas don't just exist for children's books. They belong to the world. Australians are responsible for ensuring that koalas are protected forever. I can't say that this is happening yet. Not by a long shot.

So my song encouraged people to pass around the hat to save koalas. The royalties from the song plus the generosity of my audiences in the 1980s raised in excess of $200 000. The money was used to build a brick wing, which houses six intensive care units, for the Koala Preservation Society in Port Macquarie, which is named the John Williamson Wing. I'm immensely proud of that, but also humbled, as Jean is the real hero, not me. The hospital has grown every year since then, but so has the number of koala patients. Jean Starr is not with us anymore. She passed away in October 2012, but her dedication back when very few people cared has inspired a nation.

♩

A National Koala Conference was held in Port Macquarie in May 2013. In attendance were some three hundred delegates: scientists from Sydney University and koala experts and researchers from around the world, including California, Europe, the United Kingdom and *National Geographic*. It was a sign of the growing concern for the plight of our favourite marsupial.

I attended the conference dinner as Patron of the Koala Preservation Society of New South Wales. There wasn't anything I could say that the guests didn't know, so I sang my song, which I dedicated to Jean Starr. I explained who Blinky Bill and Nutsy were for the overseas guests. After that I just listened and got sentimental and kept my fingers crossed that something meaningful would come out of it all.

My old mate Dr Jim Frazier was the keynote speaker at the conference dinner and he entertained us with his wildlife film, photography and commentary. Rightly or wrongly he also left us feeling that the planet is doomed unless the whole world's attitude changes now. While people like Rupert Murdoch give the green movement a hard time, I think Jim is right. There is no god when huge corporations corrupt governments all over the planet. Why don't humans realise that we are destroying the very thing that makes life bearable, that makes life beautiful? Did we evolve here or are we from another planet that we have already destroyed? Why do so few of us get it? If we are part of nature, why do we have so little respect for it? If we are in 'the image of God' then God must be truly disappointed at the result. We're like the mistletoe that lives on a tree until the tree dies and then the mistletoe dies. Like a plague of locusts. Like a cancer.

Jim made me think too much. Back at the hotel that night, I reflected on how positive it was to see and hear that the Port Macquarie-Hastings Council sponsored the three-day conference. I praised the mayor for his initiative and said they should promote Port Macquarie as 'Koala Central'. It would be good for the town's tourism and hopefully beneficial for the koalas.

I just want to enjoy my bush while it still exists. I have sung my heart out about it all. But big business is not listening. They're only interested in looking after shareholders. Who complains about what they do if their shares go up in value? Not the shareholders. The small shareholders can feel they're not responsible, but yes they are; they don't have to buy those shares. How could anyone buy BHP shares after what they did in Papua New Guinea? Greed, greed, greed. With all the money Kerry Packer made I bet he's most proud of what he did for the white rhino at Dubbo Zoo. What do we have to do to turn Rupert Murdoch's heart around? He has the power now to change the world and save the planet. Now that is power to be proud of. *That* would truly make him king. Come on, Rupert. One directive to all your newspapers and television stations and you would be truly loved by billions and feared only by the enemies of the earth. You could save the earth for your grandchildren! Give Jim Frazier some millions and he will create a symphony with all the animal sounds left on the planet and make a film that would rock the soul of the earth. My mate Jim has guaranteed it.

Goodbye Blinky Bill

Goodbye Bunyip Bluegum, goodbye Blinky Bill
And beautiful little Nutsie, I can't believe it
Our koalas are all dying, can it really be
A national disaster, a world catastrophe

Shiny little black nose and fluffy little ears
Furry little bundle soaking up the tears
Snugglepot and Cuddlepie are crying in the rain
And wombat's gone into his hole and won't come out

Oh pass the hat around between your friends
There's no time to contemplate
Maybe if we show some love
Maybe it's not too late

'Cause Blinky Bill is dying, cross him off the list
Knock on doors, ring the bell, save the eucalypts
I don't think I could stand the shame, knowing that I could
Have saved the world from losing something beautiful and good

One doctor on the job is hardly enough
One little hospital, wake up Australia
It's our corner of the world, time to pull our weight
What would we tell our children about our little mate

(© 1986 Emusic Pty Ltd)

Push a wheelbarrow to Broken Hill
Test your endurance, test your skill
With a pick and shovel and an old crowbar
And a billy wrapped up in a blanket

Put your men through the toughest test
Half a dozen of the very best
The team to beat is from the west

From Burra through to Broken Hill
You've gotta be fit or the heat will kill
The man with the flag and the paint on his shirt
Loves this town like his mother

Chapter 20

PUT YOUR MEN THROUGH
THE TOUGHEST TEST

My music has taken me from east to west and north to south in this amazing continent. Along the way it's often the people I've met who have given me the inspiration for my songs. They are as diverse and as interesting as the landscape itself.

In January 1985 I was booked to put on a show at Burra, an old copper and zinc mining town about 160 kilometres north of Adelaide in South Australia. It was to celebrate the beginning of the Wheelbarrow Push, a tortuous race over more than 300 kilometres from Burra to Broken Hill, the isolated mining town in far west New South Wales.

The event commemorated what the miners did when the mines closed down in Burra, while Broken Hill was just opening up as a mining town. These early miners piled their worldly possessions into a wheelbarrow and walked all the way to Broken Hill. So, the wheelbarrows in the race had what those old miners might have had in theirs – a pick 'n' shovel, a crowbar, a billy and a blanket – although the modern wheelbarrows had rubber tyres and the gear was all tied down with gaffer tape.

This is how it works. A team of six people share the pushing of the barrow. They push it at a three-quarter sprint pace and change over on the run. While the one with the barrow is running, the other five line up on a running board on the side of a small truck. From memory, each runner goes for about two hundred metres, hands over the barrow at breakneck pace and jumps back onto the truck at the end of the queue. This is no mean feat. I tried jumping off at half their pace and went arse over head, rolling over a couple of times then ending up on my feet with camera undamaged but my pride hurt. You really had to hit the ground running.

I got to know one of the teams, the Dampier Salt Shakers, from Western Australia, who were the unbeaten champions. They trained in Dampier on the salt fields. They were a great bunch of fellas. They gave me their wheelbarrow, crowbar and all, as a gift. The wheelbarrows in Western Australia aren't actually normal barrows but special racing versions. The team thought I should take it rather than them lugging it back to Western Australia. I kept it, unused, in my shed for years but temptation finally got the better of me and it is my current wood barrow at Springbrook. It's galvanised and very reliable. The team should be pleased to know that all the tools and billy have been put to good use. It still has the sponsors' stickers on it so I haven't forgotten where it came from. The team featured in my song, too. The prize money of $10 000 was given to the team's favourite charity. Apparently the races still exist in Western Australia but people eventually found the Burra Burra–Broken Hill race a bit too arduous.

Our famous Australian painter Pro Hart, from Broken Hill, traditionally started the race with the Australian flag.

This particular year, however, the honour went to me. The race was run over three days so I had to do it on each day. I was honoured to get to know Pro Hart on that trip. He took me for a ride in his big Rolls Royce to the local fish 'n' chip shop. It's incongruous to see a Rolls Royce in a place like Broken Hill. We bought yabbies instead of prawns. What a delight! The wheelbarrow race and Pro inspired me to write the song 'Paint Me a Wheelbarrow' which was on the *Mallee Boy* album. After the album was released, I sent a copy to Pro with a note to say that I was also a painter of sorts and that the song was dedicated to him. Soon after, in the mail, came a painting by Pro of the wheelbarrow race. What a treasure that is for me! I loved Pro.

Pro was an original in thought and talent. I remember how he supported the innocence of Lindy Chamberlain in the case of the death of her daughter Azaria and painted a haunting picture of her trial. I guess that painting would be worth a lot of money now. I saw it recently in his gallery at Broken Hill and was amazed that the gallery guide didn't even explain its significance. Pro portrayed Lindy as a little girl to underline the prejudice that surrounded her trial. She had little hope because of the power of the opinion of the general public at the time. It was quite different to his usual paintings of mallee trees. Pro had also invested a lot of money in painters such as Rembrandt. He was no fool. His gallery in Broken Hill is definitely worth a visit.

In March 2006, a week before Pro died, I visited him for the last time. He was unable to talk but he seemed to know who I was. I kissed him on the head and left his home in tears. He was a great Australian, and a generous soul.

Now the woman was a mighty cook – very wide across the bum
The station kids, black and white, were allowed to call her mum
Her kitchen was a bakery for an outback appetite
For big slabs of bully beef or good old Vegemite

Some of the men were bachelors – some of the men were not
It didn't worry the station cook, she'd feed the bloody lot
Visitors from the Isa or tourists in a bus
With a huge pot of strong tea and a minimum of fuss

Now the station pet was a Brahman bull,
you could pat him on the head
He'd never seen a saleyard – he was station bred
I tried to take his picture with a stockman and a gin
But they faded into the scenery with a drought resistant grin

To the famous Brunette Races – they'd head off for the fun
Where the beer flowed like a river, there was Coke and Bundy Rum
The station's boys were favourites to win the tug-o-war
The 'townies' weren't prepared to risk another broken jaw

It's the last of the outback stations owned by a family
Hard fought by a pioneer of the Northern Territory
I hope it won't be swallowed up by a public company
And fade into the heat haze of outback history

(from 'Station Cook' © 1989 Emusic Pty Ltd)

In 1989 I met a veterinary surgeon nicknamed 'Sundown Doug' at Mt Isa, a city in the Gulf Country region of Queensland. He offered me a seat in his Cessna to fly to Mallapunyah Springs where he had to test some cattle for tuberculosis. What an offer – to fly over the border between Queensland and the Northern Territory to a family-owned station! Our fuel stop was at Cape Crawford, where the pub is known as Heartbreak Hotel. The pub is over 100 kilometres south-west of Borroloola, at the junction of the Carpentaria and Tablelands highways. There I met a heli-muster pilot filling in time between jobs. Doug was quite prepared to wait at the pub and drink lemonade while the chopper pilot quickly whisked me out to what they call the Lost City. It is a natural phenomenon of columns of sandstone sculptured by time. From the air it looks like a miniature high-rise city. As usual with heli-muster pilots he had no fear, clipping the tops of bloodwood trees to get a very close view of the scenery. We landed at the Lost City and wandered around for about twenty minutes while the helicopter engine kept running.

'I don't want to stop it,' the pilot said, 'it might not start again!' I guess I'm a bit of a fatalist taking such rides. If the motor conks out, helicopters will float down from a good height as the blades will spin and soften the blow. But this was *not* a good height. Fortunately we returned to the Heartbreak Hotel in one piece.

Off we flew again to Mallapunyah Springs station. The Darcy brothers owned the station. Their father was one of the first carriers out that way with a big old truck transporting cattle and supplies for the stations. The cattle had all been yarded in preparation for Doug's arrival. What a sight from the air, cattle and men on horseback amidst the swirling dust!

'Here comes Sundown,' they were saying. Apparently they called him 'Sundown' because he was notorious for landing his plane on station landing strips when it was dangerously late. It's generally considered foolish to land when there are no landing lights on the airstrip because you could easily run into a kangaroo or a cow. I can understand how that might happen. But in those remote areas it's often hard to predict arrival times with the changeable weather conditions and fairly casual fuel stops, so if you mistime it, there's not much choice but to fly on.

The first thing we did when we landed was meet the stockmen. The black blokes sat with their saddles a short distance from the Darcys, all in good humour. The camp cook was one of the Darcy daughters, a woman in her sixties who had come home to help with the muster. I wish I'd asked her more about her life. I sat nearby, watching, amazed at her ability to cook corned beef and vegies over a dead tree burning at one end. She knew exactly how much hot coal everything needed. It was obvious she had done it all of her life. The atmosphere will always be with me and it gave me another song, 'Station Cook' for the *Warragul* album. I've seen many great stock campfires in my time and this was one of the best. At smoko, one of the Darcys (I think his nickname was Mugga) sipped on a mug of tea. I remarked that the enamel mug he was using was more like a saucepan, though in his huge hand it was quite in proportion. He said, 'Very handy when they're passin' around the rum, mate. Y'say, just a couple of fingers in the bottom will do, thanks.'

I stayed mainly out of the way at the stockyard, as the cattle were very annoyed at being yarded. They were not at all used to being so close to humans. If you weren't nimble, you could easily break a leg or arm or a rib if you got in their way. All day the men were lurching up onto the yard rails to avoid being crushed. When the cattle had all been tested and dabbed with silver paint, Doug and I headed back to the station to meet the other sister and her husband, George. George had his own little pad outside the kitchen and didn't seem to be a part of the working station. He certainly didn't look as useful as the big strapping brothers. His wife wasn't a small woman either, but she seemed almost insignificant standing in the huge kitchen, big enough to cater for a busload. We wandered out into the yard and met the family pet Brahman bull. The mango trees up there were the biggest I've seen, as tall as gum trees.

What an eventful day, and we had yet to fly back to the Barkly Homestead Roadhouse. The day was starting to dim and I began thinking about Doug's nickname. He'd gone fairly quiet when I decided to tap him on the shoulder (he had headphones on and I didn't) to ask him how much further it was. He literally nearly hit the roof with fright. *Shit!* I thought, he's worried about landing in the dark. Then he radioed the roadhouse to ask them to drive out onto the airstrip to guide him in and chase away any animals. When we landed I was out in a flash so he could immediately take off again and head back to the Isa.

♫

I made my first trip to Kakadu in the late eighties. It was truly amazing. We flew from Darwin over the jungle and landed on an airstrip cut into the thick scrub. A good bloke with a white beard was running a small holiday camp owned by a mob from an island off the coast. Apparently the Indigenous owners had had their own people running it but all they did was tear it up with four-wheel drives and not respect its value. I'll never forget what we were shown. There was a rocky outcrop in the water, completely white from bird shit, with nankeen night herons by the hundreds flying around it. That struck me as weird because they were night herons. We were shown a cave with a mummified corpse wrapped up inside it. It was an area that very few people get to see so I felt lucky to be there. That day we were also taken by boat through the swampy country. The little jacana birds with red heads hopping from one floating lily leaf to another were fascinating. Not to mention the sea eagle that swooped down and snatched a large snake from the water. Amazing!

The thing I remember most was meeting Long Peter. He arrived with an elder to have a barbecue and lots of beer. Long Peter was so ancient I could barely look at him in fear of the unknown. He really enjoyed a can of beer, which he called 'a green one': a VB (Victoria Bitter). At one stage he grabbed a piece of PVC pipe and played didgeridoo with it. I was dying to capture this portrait of him but his presence was so overwhelming that I was afraid he wouldn't approve. So I took a photo when he wasn't looking. I guess he was at least 200 centimetres (6 foot 7 inches) tall. He proved to me that some Indigenous people can handle grog, because when all the green ones were gone he asked for 'a red one' (a Melbourne Bitter). Our host was well prepared, as the beer kept flowing.

I woke the next morning with my tent mate complaining about my snoring. I'd drunk more beer than I should have, but nothing ever puts me off breakfast, no matter how crook I feel. Much to my amazement I saw Long Peter wandering around the bush with 'a blue one' in his hand. I thought, *Well I'll be buggered!*

On the same trip, the crew and I went up the Alligator River with some Asian Aborigines, who looked like Maoris, hoping to catch barramundi. The Alligator River is full of crocodiles, not alligators; I guess the early explorers didn't know the difference and I can't remember either. Is it something to do with the mouth? Anyway, we didn't catch any barra but we saw lots of crocs and drank plenty of 'green ones'. A few times the water was quite shallow so a couple of us got out and pushed the boat. That was quite exciting, as you can imagine!

♫

Another time at Kakadu, Mary Kay and I were invited to go buffalo hunting with a fella who believed he was the real Crocodile Dundee. Buffalos were on the increase so quite a few people made money out of buffalo meat. Rod Ansell was the fella's name; the Darwin police hunted him down a few years later as he'd gone a bit crazy. That was a tragedy as he had a beautiful wife and three great little kids who were prepared to live out their dad's fantasy of being the most bush 'bushie' on the planet. He was into survival and all that stuff. We sat round their table and had billy tea even though we weren't around a campfire. I remember we all went tearing down the road, side by side, to a mining road, to avoid the dust. We arrived at the swampy country and met his wild-looking mates. Dundee, as we called him, invited me into his open jeep and we drove to a spot on the water to admire the geese and pelicans and corellas flying across the Kakadu country. To my surprise he pulled out a joint. I thought, *Why not?*

We tore off with a buffalo catcher on the side and headed towards the buffalos. The catcher consisted of two steel prongs that were designed to catch the buffalo behind the ears. The buffalo we chased was elusive but we wore the poor bugger out and eventually he succumbed to the catcher. I thought it was quite cruel. The animal must have been almost dead with exhaustion by the time they tied a heavy rope around his horns and dragged him up the ramp into a truck by throwing the rope over the cabin of the truck through a pulley and the jeep did the rest. I've castrated calves and had to handle cattle and sheep on the land, so nothing surprises me, but I found this method of handling buffalos quite disturbing. However we were taken into some real Northern Territory bush where the birdlife was unbelievable. The Territory leaves a lasting impression on you. It's incredibly diverse. 'Amazing Day' came out of this trip. It gave me another song for *Warragul*.

♫

'Bill the Cat' also ended up on *Warragul*. While most of the songs on that album are inspired by my experiences in the bush, particularly in the Northern Territory, I've always thought that humour has a place on an album, if it's the right song. I have to thank Neil Young for this song.

I've always thought of Neil Young as a folk singer. He has a plaintive tenor voice that seems to give his songs drama, even if there is no drama in the lyrics. Neil Diamond does this too; he could make a wooden table sound monumental. I was delighted when I went to a Neil Young concert in the late eighties and he came out on stage, just him and his guitar, with his harmonica soaking in a cup of hot water to make the reeds bend more. He probably had musicians behind him but they didn't matter. He played his hits that could be described as 'white man blues'. During interval, all this scaffolding was erected; industrial noises were coming through the sound system. Then on came Neil with a heavy metal band. We were out of there like a shot. We came to hear the Neil Young we loved. I'm not into heavy metal especially sung by a folk singer. I'm not saying there is anything wrong with metal; it's just not my thing. I'm a bush boy. Metal is a city thing, I reckon.

That night when we got home, I slept on the couch. I'm not sure why. Perhaps I'd had a few drinks and I nodded off. When I woke I had a blues kind of melody in my head. It was definitely with a rhythm I'd heard Neil Young play the night before. God knows why, but I started writing 'Bill the Cat', one of my biggest novelty hits. There was definitely a purpose behind the lyrics. I get very annoyed about dogs having to be kept inside your suburban fence while cats have the privilege of roaming through the neighbourhood, killing birds at any opportunity. Feral cats are diminishing our native bush and animals, probably because people dump kittens in the bush.

They don't take responsibility for having the cats spayed or taking them to a cat protection centre (or dare I say it, knocking them on the head). My mother always had cats because she was petrified of snakes. She left it up to me to take care of the frequent kitty litters. I know a lot of people adore cats but I'm afraid I just don't understand the animal. On the land, of course, having dogs was the norm, but I won't have one now because it would chase the goannas and pademelons (very small wallabies) away from our cottage on the edge of the forest.

'Boogie with M'Baby' also found its way onto *Warragul* and both of these are still regularly requested at my shows. 'Boogie' comes and goes on the set list; many of my audience remember those old dance hall scenarios back in the fifties. 'Bill the Cat', I'm pleased to say, is well and truly back in my show now. It's the only blues song I play. I can play blues harp style on the harmonica and Col Watson can have fun on slide guitar. Even Dave Ellis plays a bit of blues on the bull fiddle (bass). It's been a great way to renew the song, approaching it from a different musical level. The audiences love it, especially the kids. It's funny how people love to really sing out 'balls' in the chorus.

I've played blues harp on many of my songs but the songs themselves aren't really blues. 'Buried in Her Bedclothes', 'Mates around the Fire' and 'I'm a Basher' are good examples of what I mean.

Just in case you don't understand how blues harp is played, I should explain. You use a harmonica in the key that is a third above the key the song is in. For example, in 'I'll Be Gone' I play an F harp for the key of C. If I'm in G,

I play a C harp. You'll find that most of the notes you need are when you're drawing on the harp (sucking). This allows you to restrict the air with your lips and force the reeds to bend. It's possible to get four notes out of one reed. That way you can slide the note like a trombone.

Warragul went triple Platinum in 1989, the year it was released, and reached number one on the general ARIA charts. It was also Album of the Year in 1990 at the Country Music Awards.

Do what you wanna do
Work when you wanna work
You're your own boss
Doin' it your own way
It's the last frontier
Away out here
Where dreamers and good old drifters go

Got a bit of red dirt with m'claim on it
An opal down there with m'name on it
A little bit of black with a flame on it, I see
It's a pipe dream
But it's the right dream for me

Do what you wanna do
Sleep when you wanna sleep
You're your own boss
Doin' it your own way
Yeah, and you'll get lost
Tie a ribbon 'round a Buddawood tree
A hundred dusty tracks all look the same

(from 'Pipe Dream' © 1997 Tony Dennett and Emusic Pty Ltd)

Chapter 21

WHERE DREAMERS AND
GOOD OLD DRIFTERS GO

I can't believe some of the silly risks I've taken in my career. I must have thought I was bulletproof when I decided to hire a DC3 aircraft and fly up to the Gulf of Carpentaria for two shows. To add to the expense I took a band – bass, drums, fiddle and guitar. Who did I think I was? Elvis? However, in the eighties I was on a roll and I knew there would be a song in it, and that can always make a trip worthwhile. So from Brisbane we boarded 'Papa Whisky November', the aircraft's call sign PWN, and headed towards Cooktown. Apparently PWN had been used for mapping and reconnaissance during the Second World War. Its war history was printed and framed inside the cabin.

I knew that we were in for an adventure when we were greeted by Sheila, the air hostess, who was decked out in a 1940s uniform in keeping with the era of the DC3 plane. The interior of the plane had not changed much since the war. It had a window that bubbled outwards so you could see the ground. The view below us was wonderful as DC3s were allowed to fly lower than the larger planes.

Our first stop was Cooktown, just over 2000 kilometres north of Brisbane, where we stayed overnight. Hot water flowed out of the cold tap in the shower at the hotel. I was stunned! It was only September. That night I was also aware of something going on between Sheila and Bill, the pilot, in the hotel corridor. The next day we flew to Weipa for our first show in the beer garden at the local golf club. We drew a crowd of about two hundred people. During the performance we were rudely interrupted by hundreds of flying foxes in the nearby mango tree, screeching and pooing as they flew over the audience. I was fascinated by the obvious romance between Sheila and Bill, who were trying not to show that they were in love. Bill was still married at the time so they were being a bit coy about it all. They now live on some island in the Pacific. I hear from then now and then. They're so happy. What a great love story.

From Weipa we flew to Nhulunbuy, the main mining town on the Gove Peninsula on the west coast of the Gulf of Carpentaria. I took a huge punt and put on a show at their showground. We went to the trouble of tying hessian around the area to avoid giving the locals a free show. It didn't help; there were still more people watching from their houses on stilts than we lured inside the hessian. I was given a necklace by a local Indigenous woman made from giddy giddy beans stuck into balls of spinifex wax. She told me they used the giddy giddy beans to poison their husbands. That left quite an impression on me!

The trip was certainly memorable and I hadn't visited that part of the country before. The flight back to Brisbane was spectacular, especially as we flew very low over the beautiful

Daintree Rainforest. As a bonus, the trip gave me another song for *Waratah Street*: 'Papa Whisky November'. The song is Dick Smith's favourite, because he's a pilot. Whenever he comes to my concerts, I just have to sing it.

Apart from *Mulga to Mangoes* (1994), most of the albums released between 1991's *Waratah Street* and 1998's *Pipe Dream* were either repackaged compilations of previous songs (such as *Love is a Good Woman*, an album of love songs) or retitled older albums.

♫

During this period I took the band to England and did the regular touring around Australia. This took up most of my song writing time. *Mulga to Mangoes* picked up a number of awards including a Golden Guitar for Best Selling Album in 1995, an APRA Award for the Most Performed Country Work and a Golden Guitar for Video of the Year for 'Tropical Fever'. The very talented Mark Jago produced that video clip. Over the years, Mark has become a great mate. I value his and his wife Caroline's friendship enormously. They have produced many videos for me over the years.

The time had come to head out bush again. This was where my real inspiration came from.

I first met Tony Dennett in 1984 when he approached me after a show at the Vicar of Wakefield Hotel. I'd virtually created this venue for myself by bringing my little stage into the lounge area. Eventually they built a separate room with a stage. Tony was a local orchardist from the Dural area in outer Sydney. He showed me a few pages of words for a song about his old mate who was a flower grower. The original words were very long, so I tightened them up and it was a beauty. It became 'Dad's Flowers'. He came up with an interesting line that his old mate used: he called Parramatta Road 'the varicose vein of Sydney'. That was the kind of line Tony was good at. In 'Crocodile Roll', which we wrote together, 'the little swine drank some wine and really pigged it out' was another one. 'All Australian Boys Need a Shed' was his best. The title had so much going for it, it was easy after that to write the rest of it. So when I was finding it a bit hard to come up with new songs for another album, I thought that Tony and I should go bush for some ideas. Tony knew a bloke who had a camp site at Grawin, a rustic little opal mining village in north-west New South Wales, about 60 kilometres from the nearest populated town of Lightning Ridge.

Opal mines in Australia will always be a great source for song material. They attract characters who are extremely individual in their attitudes to life. With the exception of Coober Pedy, the rule is that you are not allowed to build permanent accommodation on a mining lease. However, you *are* allowed to build accommodation out of scraps of iron and timber – a humpy, in other words, much like Aborigines did as fringe dwellers in the early days. This provides an amazing atmosphere that surely was very much like the gold mining villages of the nineteenth century. I absolutely love the ingenuity of this bush architecture. The way rusty sheets of iron, recycled boards and local rock are used has influenced what I do around our yard at Springbrook. I'm sure the opal miners appreciate the bush as much as I do. That's part of the attraction for them. It's ironic that similar humpies were bulldozed years ago when Indigenous people built them outside town.

Grawin was the perfect place to find a song or two. It was late spring so all we had to do was stretch a cable between two trees and draw a canvas over it and sleep in the open. I was taken fifteen metres underground to see what the mining was all about. You wouldn't want to be claustrophobic as there's not a lot of room down there and the ground is quite unstable. Men have been buried alive. Opal mining hardly disturbs the trees. After a couple of years of drought I was surprised how damp it was underneath the bimble box trees. No wonder these trees survive many years of the dry. In fact, that's why you can't live underground in that opal mining area. It's just too damp. It's a different story around the opal mining towns of White Cliffs and Coober Pedy.

I met Vegie Bill out at Grawin. He was a wonderful old fella who kept his life going by selling vegetables to the miners from his ute. I had a yarn to him on camera for the Seven Network television show *Bush Telegraph*, for which I was one of three presenters. I interviewed him at the Club in the Scrub, a very basic timber and iron construction boasting a nine-hole golf course with barely a blade of grass to be seen. While we talked inside the club, the patrons played billiards in the background. The billiard table had a lean and the pockets were missing so you had to fetch the balls off the floor. But we carried on while Bill talked about his life as a grader driver in the Kimberley, that northernmost region of Western Australia. Opal mining meant nothing to him except for the simple life it afforded him. He just longed to go back to the Kimberley.

He showed me a picture book about the Kimberley when they flooded Argyle Station to form the Argyle Dam. Bill told me he talked to a frogman diver who dived under the dam and checked out the old homestead. Bill said, 'The diver told me that the gates were still swinging.' I was very amused at this haunting image, imagining the chooks and dogs still swimming around under the water. He also told me how he was invited to the funeral of an Indigenous family member. Apparently they took the deceased back to their home country in the rear of a station wagon. It was a drive of several hundred kilometres, so the coffin was filled with ice. They needed to take meat for the barbecue afterwards, so they took full advantage of the situation. Yes, the sausages and steaks were stored in the coffin, along with the deceased relative. 'Well, it was a hot day,' he explained.

That trip was certainly worth it. I wrote 'Coolibah Blue' after driving through Bonville on the way to Grawin. Old Bill gave me another song, 'Vegie Bill', and the song 'Pipe Dream' was also inspired by the trip. 'Pipe Dream' really tells it as it was. It was very easy to get lost with so many tracks going in every direction and all the bushes looking the same. I have the affliction of losing my sense of direction at the best of times but Grawin was a nightmare. Despite *Pipe Dream* being the highest selling album for the year at the Country Music Awards, it failed to get a final nomination for any of the other categories. That was disappointing.

♪

The late Vegie Bill was right: the Kimberley is an amazing place. The limestone ridges that used to be coral reefs, the grand boab trees, and rock formations that you see from two roads are just a glimpse of what's on offer. I've been a couple of times but I've got to get back and spend much more time up there. It's like another country and I believe its value as a tourist attraction in Australia is still in its infancy. There are more songs out there.

By the time I was old enough to understand how big Australia is, I remember thinking about the Kimberley where our explorer Ludwig Leichhardt disappeared. I had the impression that only black fellas lived up there. Mum, Dad and Jeff went up there in a kombi van for the opening of the Ord River Project in 1963. I remember them telling me that the Aboriginal kids used to chase the vehicle out of curiosity. Mum brought me back a great didgeridoo, handpainted with red and yellow ochre. There were vast stations up there but not much else besides the three towns of Broome, Derby and Kununurra. There were also missions up there, including one that went back to the Spanish arrivals, I believe. Now there is a bitumen road between Broome and Darwin. The Gibb River Road has been left in gravel, so four-wheel drivers can experience the old days. Dad only needed an air-cooled kombi!

At the end of a tour in the nineties, I went out from Kununurra to see the Argyle Dam. Its construction has really opened up the Kimberley region. Someone had told me to catch up with Roy Walker, an old ringer who had camped on the spillway of the dam. His camp was as rough as you'd expect from an old ringer, but he was always pleased to see visitors, especially me, as it turned out, because he was a bush poet himself. He was eager to show me a small rock enclosure where he liked to recite his poems to visitors. One was a very romantic poem about rounding up the Milky Way when he died. Roy had a great passion for horses. He'd not long been married to a Swedish backpacker. She was a delight and obviously loved Roy. The local authorities had no problem with him squatting out there, thinking that he would be the last resident. I sang a couple of songs for them. I also put my freshly cut didgeridoo in his water trough so that it would season without cracking. I was quite sure I would be back.

The real bonus for me was that his old ringer mate Allan was staying with him. Allan was the toughest old bloke I've ever met. He reminded me of my dad's father, Lew. Square chin and a wide fist. And to add to the demeanour, he had an American pit bull terrier. After listening intently to both old ringers I couldn't believe my luck. What a story ... or two stories really.

Roy told me he was an orphan from Perth and took off as a teenager to become a ringer on Argyle Station. He told us that the only girls he met up there were Indigenous, apart from the station owner's wife. I can understand how a young bloke would soon befriend the local girls. Unfortunately for the young blokes, it was deemed illegal back then to mix with Aboriginal women. Of course it didn't stop them, and Roy told the story of being chained to a boab tree by the local constabulary as punishment. You'd think the only policeman in the area would have had more to do. Apparently the best-looking local girls were called 'studs' and were often employed by the station as housekeepers. These were the girls sought after by the station hands and ringers for company.

Above: In my Cyclops pedal car.

Left: Dressed as Donald Bradman, aged four. Little did I know that 52 years later I'd sing at Sir Don's memorial service.

Below: The only photo of me, right, with the ukulele.

Dad's parents, Lil and Lew, in the wheat, 1950s.

Dad and Mum in sorghum crop at 'Backspear',
Croppa Creek, late 1960s.

My mum, Shirley.

With Dad at Kerang Road.
L to R: Me, Robin, Peter and Will.

A fancy dress competition: Will, Robin, Peter and me
(with actual .22 rifle) in the front yard at Kerang Road.

The Avoca River was perfect for fishing: a redfin
fish I caught with my new rod and basket.

Aged 12, duck shooting on the water course
near Mungindi, New South Wales.

Our traditional two weeks' holiday after Christmas:
off to Lakes Entrance, mid-1950s.

.. Programme ..

No.		Section	Age
1.	Margaret Free & Dawn Williamson	Piano	(10, 10)
2.	Ian Meldrum—"Lazy Bones	Pops	(10)
3.	Kathleen Wall—"Vespers"	Recitation	(8)
4.	Glenys Kendell—"The Windmill Song"	Novelty	(9)
5.	Douglas Williamson	Piano	(8)
6.	Merle Adamthwaite—"Alice Blue Gown"	Vocal	(9)
7.	John Beard—"Lucky Old Sun"	Pops	(9)
8.	Margaret Free & Dawn Williamson—"I don't want to play in your yard."	Novelty	(10,10)
9.	Valerie Webb	Piano	(10)
10.	Dorothy Milic—"Loves Old Sweet Song"	Vocal	(13)
11.	Lynette Free—"Only Seven"	Recitation	(9)
12.	Marlene Whitehead—Dance	Novelty	(9)
13.	Lindsay Webb—"Arithmatic"	Recitation	(11)
14.	Lindsay Cameron & Ian Meldrum—"Daisy"	Novelty	(13, 10)
15.	John Williamson	Piano	(7)
16.	Margaret Free—"Piper From over the Way"	Vocal	(10)
17.	Giro Milic—"Bavarian Folk Song & Dance"	Novelty	(9)
18.	Alice Free—"Half as Much"	Pops	(11)
19.	Gerald Williamson—"I couldn't help it, Could I"	Recitation	(7)
20.	Valerie Webb—"In a Golden Coach"	Pops	(10)
21.	Glenda Tuohey	Piano	(9)
22.	Marlene Whitehead & John Beard—"Where are you going to my pretty maid."	Vocal	(9,9)
23.	Dawn Williamson—"Christopher Robin"	Vocal	(10)
24.	Gwenda Free—"Lost"	Recitation	(7)
25.	Hajo Milic—"Hello Bluebird"	Pops	(11)
26.	Barry Lonergan—Mouth Organ	Novelty	(10)
27.	Lynette Free—"Doggie in the Window"	Pops	(9)
28.	Douglas & John Williamson—"Tell me a Story"	Novelty	(8, 7)

— INTERVAL —

CONCERT TO FOLLOW

Program with Ian 'Molly' Meldrum and me, 1953.

Above: Working as a truck
driver at Croppa Creek during
harvest time, late 1960s. This
is before 'Old Man Emu'.

Opposite: At a talent quest on
the Gold Coast, Christmas 1963.
I won a bottle of champagne for
singing 'Whiskey in the Jar'.

With the John D Four
at Scotch College, aged 17.
I'm on the right.

With Fable Records owner, Ron Tudor, September 1970.

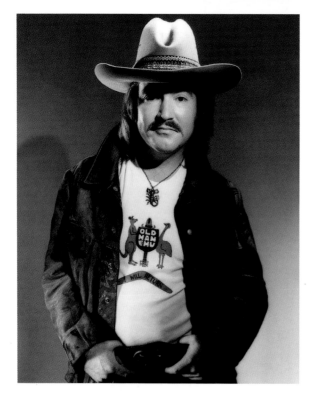

Left: First promotional photo, 1973.

Opposite: Album photo for the back cover of my first record, 'Old Man Emu', taken outside Moree. This Maton 12-string guitar now hangs in the foyer of Maton in Melbourne.

The Haystack
in Camberwell,
Melbourne.

All the brothers together on the family farm, 'Backspear'.
L to R: (back) Will and me; (front) Robin, Peter and Jeff.

Performing as
Merv Currawong.

Presenting Lawsy with a song written about him called
'It's a Grab It While It's Goin' Kind of Life' in the late 1970s.

Pub period in Sydney, early 1980s.

With Bullamakanka in the 1980s. Rex Radonich, who died
in a car accident, is second from the left, next to me.

Singing 'Waltzing Matilda' on my smallest ever stage:
a 44-gallon drum. Combo Waterhole is believed to be
where Banjo was inspired to write the song.

Gough Whitlam presenting me with the
Songmaker Award at Tamworth, 1986.

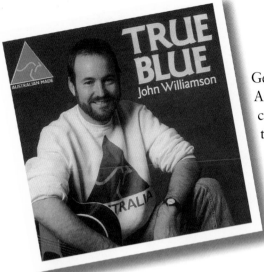

Getting behind the
Australian Made
campaign in
the mid-1980s.

My original
'fair dinkum'
flag design
stuck
on both sides
of an FJ
Holden Special.

(Courtesy of
Paul Harris)

With Mary Kay, and Golden Guitar awards for Album of
the Year (*Mallee Boy*) and Male Vocalist of the Year, 1987.

With Anne Kirkpatrick
and Slim Dusty, early 1990s.

With Smoky Dawson, late 1980s.

Giving my award for 'Drover's Boy' to Ted Egan, 1990.
(Courtesy of June Underwood)

With Slim Dusty in 1990.
(Courtesy of June Underwood)

Singing 'All Australian Boys Need a Shed' at the
opening of the new Parliament House, 1988.

The touring fleet that carried our own sound, lighting, four-piece band and crew of five.

The Great Wheelbarrow Race, 1985, which inspired the song 'Paint Me a Wheelbarrow' on *Mallee Boy*.

Above: Bottle trees near Toowoomba, Queensland, in their native habitat. If I had my way, they would be heritage listed.

Following spread:
Celebrating the Australian cricket team World
Cup victory singing 'The Baggy Green', 1999.

This is Your Life with John Laws and Mike Munro in 1995.

Singing 'Waltzing Matilda' at the Sydney Olympics, 2000.
(Courtesy of Dave Hunt/AAP Newswire)

With Steve and Terri Irwin. Steve and I were both
besotted with the Aussie habitat in its original state.
(Courtesy of Australia Zoo/Wildlife Warriors)

Singing 'True Blue' at the Steve Irwin memorial at Australia
Zoo in 2006. Steve epitomised the meaning of the words.
(Courtesy of Dave Hunt/AFP)

Typical set list.

Mates on the road:
Pixie Jenkins (left) and Warren H Williams.

My greatest joy has been in creating things, whether it's building projects up at our mountain hideaway or making a toy truck for my grandsons. (Photos top and bottom courtesy of Paul Harris)

With long-time manager
Phil Matthews.

With current manager
David 'Woody' Woodward,
and Meg in Fiji, 2010.

With Meg at a
Variety lunch at
Woolloomooloo,
2009.

Meg and I married in March 2013.
(Wedding photos courtesy of Lisa Maree Williams)

With Ami (left) and Georgie.

I'm always drawing, especially when I'm waiting around somewhere.

Dad (Keith) at 93, playing his old banjo. This was taken just
four months before he passed away in March 2014.

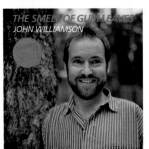
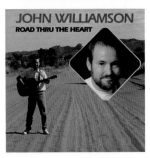
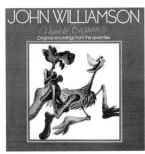

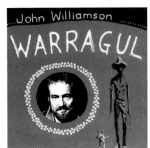

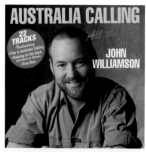

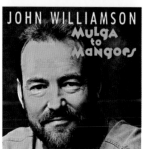

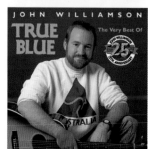

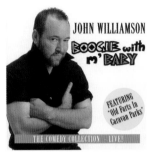

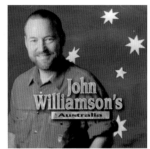

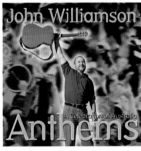

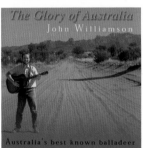

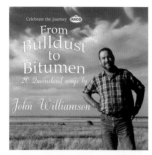

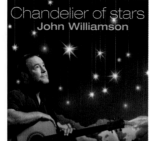

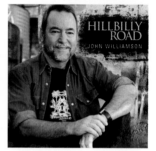

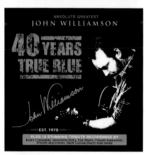

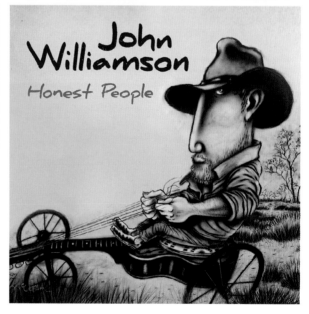

Allan's story was even more interesting. Apart from working on Argyle Downs, the cattle station, he said he was a troubleshooter for the mining companies. He was employed to sort out unionists who were troublemakers. He didn't mind bragging about how good he was at his job. He also said he was the quickest ringer to kill a stray bullock on the side of the road and whack it in the freezer. Allan's most fascinating story was that he married a 'stud'. He reckoned he was responsible for getting the law forbidding such marriages changed in Perth. 'The Prettiest Girl in the Kimberley' came out of these two men's combined stories and is one of the best songs on the *Pipe Dream* album. I regularly get requests to sing that one.

I'd been telling this story on ABC radio in Darwin, some time after I'd left the Kimberley, when one of Allan's sons rang the station and said he hated his father. He said that Allan was always making out that he was like Wild Bill Hickok but he had a dark side. Apparently the police were after Allan at the time we met; he was under suspicion of something involving his own daughter. No wonder he was visiting his old mate Roy; the police would never have found him out there. My mental picture of old, tough Allan and his pit bull terrier is a bit different now. My song is not specifically about him but more about our attitudes eighty years ago.

'There's a new world order!' the leaders all shout
And everyone's frantic they're gonna miss out
And the red, white and blues are still marching about
Oh we must have a flag of our own

'Cause this is Australia and that's where we're from
We're not Yankee side-kicks or second class Poms
And tell the Frogs what they can do with their bombs
Oh we must have a flag of our own

(from 'A Flag of our Own' © 1991 Emusic Pty Ltd)

Chapter 22

WE MUST HAVE A
FLAG OF OUR OWN

I love the style of home they call the Queensland bungalow, especially the houses that are built well off the ground for coolness. The further north you go in Queensland, the more of them you will see. The foundations are about three metres high, enough to use the area under the house as a garage to hold a ute, a trailer, a billiard table and, of course, a fridge full of beer. In other words, a man's shed. I have an old mate Ron Hodges who lives in Ayr, a little town south of Townsville. His mate Eddie – known as Skidmark – owned one of these bungalows in the middle of a cane field. Skidmark was renowned, as you might have guessed, for his frequent passing of wind. I was a privileged guest (tongue-in-cheek) at this man's shed to partake of as much beer and as much mud crab as I could consume. The crabs had been caught in the nearby mangroves by yet another mate. Skidmark's wife, very sensibly, didn't come down the stairs while we were there other than to hang out the washing.

I really don't like to get sick from drinking too much so I probably drank about a quarter of what the rest of them guzzled. I always pace myself when drinking beer. We certainly had a lot of laughs and enjoyed plenty of fresh crab, along with the beer. My autograph is on the exposed sewerage pipe to prove I was there. Funny, though, I don't remember when Ron and I got home. But I do remember at least three bodies passed out on the floor. Skidmark was on the trailer. The under-house shed had a concrete floor so it was easy to hose the smelly prawn shells and spilt beer out the door the next morning. I imagined Skidmark's wife hosing the bodies out the door as well!

♫

Channel Nine's *60 Minutes* has always been a good show, especially in the early days when it had no real competition on a Sunday night. Charles Wooley, one of their presenters, was interested in my push for a new national flag and a republic back in the eighties. My song 'A Flag of Our Own' had caused a bit of controversy at Inverell RSL back then. An English committee member demanded that I be banned from the club after reading an article in the local newspaper after my show. He didn't even see the performance. The publicity I received from that was invaluable.

So a *60 Minutes* crew came on my short tour around south-west Queensland. Charles drummed up the controversy, naturally, by contacting leading monarchists in the town of Warwick. They were quite willing to talk about how misled and mistaken I was. One woman claimed I was brainwashing kids against the Queen. That was almost laughable, considering how I was taught as a kid at school myself that the Queen sat on the right-hand side of God. Every school classroom at that time had a picture of Queen Elizabeth above the blackboard. The saying was 'For God, Queen and Country' in that order. Australia was last on the list! We sang the English anthem 'God Save the Queen' every morning. And boy, was I excited to go to Bendigo just to see the Queen and Prince Phillip drive by in 1954! The little old monarchist was the one who was brainwashed! She told *60 Minutes* I should be tarred and feathered and run out of town for singing 'A Flag of Our Own'.

Charles and I wandered around the fairground at the Gatton Show and Charles asked one lady what she thought of republicans. She said, 'Oh, they're okay. The one publican at our local drinks a bit, but he's okay.' She didn't even know what a republican was! I have to say that my push for a new flag has done me little harm. I reckon many people agree with me, but a lot of Aussies are afraid to step out of line on this issue mainly because of the two World Wars, and the flag our soldiers fought under. None of us want to offend the Diggers or their families. But I get offended every time I see the Union Jack on our flag when we win gold medals at the Olympic Games. It must make the Poms proud that one of their other countries is doing well. It also pisses me off to see the stupid boxing kangaroo fly because people feel our national flag doesn't do the job for them. If the kangaroo fits, we should do it properly. It's not seen as a joke by the Air Force or Qantas, or for the Kangaroos rugby league team. And we also call our national rugby team the Wallabies. These days at the Ashes cricket Tests we see England supporters in the crowd flying the St George cross flag. Even they have an independent flag separating them from the Union Jack. How ironic is that?

Charles Wooley and I became mates on that tour. We've made two more segments for *60 Minutes* since then. One was in Tasmania about the woodchip industry and the other was about my songwriting around Alice Springs. It was his producer who linked me up with the Hayes family on Undoolya, a 1200-square-kilometre cattle station virtually surrounding the east side of Alice. Jim and Gail Hayes and their three sons were more than happy for us to come out to the station. It opened my eyes even more to the beauty of the MacDonnell Ranges country. The landscape is vast and variable. It is indeed another world, another country almost.

Undoolya is so extensive that during cattle muster it was much easier for Jim and the boys to camp out. So we sat around the campfire with them, sharing the billy. I could see the swags were spread out ready for sleeping after sundown. It wasn't until Mary Kay and I were on the Plenty Highway heading east to the coast that I asked her to write down some words: 'I'm into cattle, my father was too, From great-great grandfather all the way through'.

I'm a relaxed driver, especially in the bush. It's a good time to reflect on the people we meet and the stories that come out of the journey. Jim Hayes told me how proud he was that his three boys had all come home to Undoolya. He encouraged them to learn other skills in Adelaide, then after that they could return to the station if they wanted to. With farming and grazing becoming more difficult to prosper these days, the children often don't return. The three Hayes boys from Undoolya are married now and carrying on in the Hayes tradition.

The song 'Three Sons' is about Jimmy and his boys and Undoolya Station. I won a Golden Guitar for it as Bush Ballad of the Year in 2000. The album on which it was released, *The Way It Is,* won another Golden Guitar for Best Selling Album of the Year and went platinum in that same year. 'Queensland Bungalow' was also on that album.

It is understandable how attached the Hayes boys have become to their land. It's very similar, surely, to how the Indigenous Aranda mobs out there are a part of the landscape. I understand completely how it becomes who you are.

The lines 'If you take me from my land, you leave me with no soul' from 'Keeper of the Stones' says it all. I feel that way not only about Springbrook but about the whole nature of Australia. Each time we destroy habitat we destroy a piece of ourselves. I can't imagine how empty I would be if I didn't feel that attachment to our original bush. I guess that's when people try to fill that void with manmade material possessions like sports cars, boats and mansions. Okay, I like to have a good car too, but not without first having some real Australian bush to take care of and to experience; to be part of. For me, it is endlessly satisfying, endlessly inspirational and exciting.

Well a kookaburra tries to laugh
As a tin pot trailer falls in half
Your darlin' wife has had enough
Of using a bucket for a bath
But you're hardly even half way there
It took you ages to prepare
In desperation to make it square
You promise her overseas somewhere

Now there's cattlemen in bare feet
Big spare ribs with not much meat
Even in June you feel the heat
So you give that crocodile a treat
Yeah, jump in the Jacky Jacky creek
If that's the kind of thrill you seek
Hardly a sport for the meek
They lost a retriever there last week

(from 'Cape York Peninsula' © 2001 Emusic Pty Ltd)

Chapter 23

THE KOOKABURRA TRIES TO LAUGH AS THE TIN-POT TRAILER FALLS IN HALF

I've endeavoured to pen songs that feature Australia's natural iconic places such as Uluru. This was the main reason I decided to go camping, in 2001, all the way from Cairns to Frangipani Bay – to experience Cape York Peninsula. I'd met a man named Darcy Gallop in 2000, at an Indigenous dance festival at Laura in northern Queensland. At the time he was the Administrator of Cape York and was representing the Queensland State Government at the festival. I was a guest singer at the festival and very soon gravitated to this character who had pitched a tent on site. It was a dry festival (meaning there was no alcohol allowed) but Darcy didn't let that stop him having a quiet one in his tent where we had a yarn.

Darcy was very proud of that fact that his father was an engineer and had had a bridge along the main road named after him when the Cape York roads were created. Darcy seemed to know the Cape like the back of his hand and was quite familiar with the characters along the way. He had a humble little cottage, just north of Cooktown, where he lived

with his partner, Jacqui, who had produced documentaries
for the ABC. They had a few acres surrounding the house
where Darcy struggled to grow an array of tropical fruit.
From what I gathered, it was hardly worth the effort, but it
kept Darcy interested. I'm guessing he is in his late seventies
by now so it was good for him to have something to get up for.
He had two huge mastiff dogs to keep him on his toes as well.

Darcy offered to be our guide on our camping trip. He
was into bush poetry so he liked my songs. So six of us headed
off from Cooktown: me and Mary Kay, Mary Kay's brother
Steve (nicknamed Runt) and his wife, Sherry, and Darcy
and Jacqui. With Darcy's local knowledge we set off with
no fears. He soon proved to be a better four-wheel driver
than I. On some of those tracks you really need to know
where your wheels are, so I got us bogged a couple of times.
But I had a winch on the troopy so it was never too much of
a disaster. That is, as long as there was a tree to latch onto
within fifty metres.

Jacqui suggested we hire a couple of cameramen to join us
along the way. She reckoned we could make a documentary for
the ABC about my songwriting discovery trip, so I promised
I'd attempt to write a song. I wrote 'Cape York Peninsula'
during the filming so they could actually see me writing. By
the end of that trip I had also written 'Frangipani Bay' and
'Granny's Little Gunyah'.

When we reached a national park north of Coen, we met
an Aboriginal ranger. He was a good-looking young fella and
very amiable. Jacqui decided it would be a great opportunity
for me to interview him about the unusual anthills in the area.
I was particularly interested in why they seemed to face the

same way. They call them 'cathedral anthills' but apparently that's technically incorrect; they're 'mounds'. Anyway, these cathedral anthills looked like little Westminster Abbeys. Fortunately the ranger knew the scientific answer as well as the myths that have been passed on by the old bush people.

As we were filming, a couple of tourist buses pulled up maybe 200 metres away. The older ones in the bus got out and stretched their legs and seemed to be watching what we were doing with great curiosity. As I finished interviewing the ranger, I was beckoned by the people to come over and say g'day. So I checked I had a signing pen in my pocket and off I went, thinking, *You never know when you might meet an interesting character*. There could be a song in this as well. I thought, *I'm pretty roughly dressed but they probably recognise me, but aren't sure*. After 40 years in the business I'm pretty used to that kind of thing.

When I got to the buses I could tell they were arguing about something. One old bloke and his wife thanked me for coming over. 'You'll be able to settle an argument for us,' he said. *Here we go again,* I thought. 'Can you tell us? Is that Ernie Dingo over there that you've been talking to?' he muttered. I was a bit taken aback at first, and felt like saying, *No, mate, but they all look the same don't they, these Aborigines?* But I soon saw the funny side of it and realised I had a great story to tell in my show along with all the other funny ways that Aussies approach me when they recognise me, or think they do.

On another occasion a young girl behind a bar in Sydney said to me, 'Have you any idea how much you look like John Williamson?' I thought for a change I'd have some fun with it and said, 'Yeah, it actually gives me the shits. People are always saying that to me.' To which she replied, 'I know how you feel. Everyone reckons I look like Meryl Streep.' Then I said, 'Geez, I reckon I look a lot more like John Williamson than you do Meryl Streep.' She looked at me as if she was thinking, *This guy's a bit strange*. Before my mates and I left the pub I pulled out a True Blue sticker and left it on the bar, signed 'Love to Meryl, from John'.

I loved the camping side of that trip. Because I snored loudly, I left Mary Kay in the ute while I took my swag and slept under the stars. We were in crocodile country so I was a bit wary about where I slept. I had this theory that if I placed my swag on the bush side of a big log and not on the riverside I would be safe. I've never seen any footage of a croc jumping over or going around a big log to attack anything. Quite confident of my theory, one Australia Day I mentioned this to Steve Irwin and he said 'Yeah, but they can come from the bush as well!' So much for that theory!

One place we camped was the scene of an amazing story not long afterwards. A bloke woke up in his swag with a big croc lying on top of him. Keeping his breakfast warm, I presume.

It always amazes me how vast this country is. We met the most wonderful characters halfway up the Peninsula Development Road: Dawn and Billy Jackson. Darcy, of course, knew them. They lived on Wolverton Station, one of the most northern stations in Australia and a distance of 1890 kilometres north-west of Brisbane. Their galvanised iron station house was more like an old woolshed. It had no lining inside the walls and the floor seemed to be laid straight on top of the earth floor. If there was concrete underneath, it was far from level. The floor waved up and down underneath their bare feet. The inside was completely painted with silver paint. The kitchen was almost completely black from the well-used fuel stove they'd got from some old pub.

Billy and Dawn would have to be the most unassuming couple I've ever met. They never wore shoes. I've discovered over the years since that this was the norm up there in the wet tropics. I can imagine how much trouble you would have with feet in socks in such a hot damp climate. A huge mango tree overhung their roof, covering the house with rotting mangoes. I don't know why Billy didn't cut it down because he hated mangoes. He said they just attracted the wild pigs. (My neighbours at Springbrook hate them too because the mangoes attract flying foxes.) I love mangoes; I'd soon have a net over the tree if it was mine. But isn't it always the way? You never appreciate something that comes easily.

My song 'Granny's Little Gunyah' captures something of the atmosphere up there at Wolverton Station. Dawn had this warmth that drew her grandkids to her. She's no longer with us and Billy has retired to live in Cairns. The next generation, at the time living in another house within a stone's throw of the 'gunyah', has taken over the property now. I do hope someone is living in the old place. It's a museum piece; the real Saltbush Bill dwelling just as the cartoonist Eric Jolliffe used to draw in his comic books. I've never seen another farmhouse quite like it. I am so thankful that Darcy introduced me to them. People such as Billy and Dawn are typical of the salt of the earth characters who keep me going as a songwriter. We all love hard working, down-to-earth, honest people.

Tomorrow we'll be wooing another little town
We'll always keep it up even when we're down
Mates on the road, happy to be
Born to play music 'til we die

Chapter 24

LIKE A BOOMERANG, WE SHALL RETURN, WITH ANOTHER STORY AND SONG

One of the most agonising aspects of touring a show is finding a good road crew and keeping it all together. In the old days, invariably I found there was one bad apple that spread rot over the whole organisation. I heard Joan Baez say on the television that she reached the age of sixty before she found the perfect team. It's been much the same for me. More often than not it was marijuana or alcohol that caused the problem. And a musician often caused it. If one of them couldn't score a deal he became quite agitated and hard to deal with. This often led to tantrums or the truck being driven hundreds of kilometres out of the way to meet a dealer. Of course, quite a few of us had fun with dope in the early eighties but once things got serious it was a thorn in the side. Out of that period a few became addicted.

There are many issues involved here. I've always had a policy that anyone touring with me could do what they liked after a show but there was to be no alcohol or drugs while on the job. First and foremost it was a safety issue. One lighting guy thought he could smoke dope and still climb ladders. Even when he knew the rules, he persisted. I could smell the stuff from a mile away, so that was the end of him. Shame, as he was quite good at his job. I once had a guitarist who insisted that he have a bourbon on stage. Well, he obeyed the rules for a while but then became sneaky. This started to corrupt the show. One night in Mudgee, I realised by the time I sang 'True Blue' that he was absolutely pissed. His playing was all over the place. We went off stage while the audience cheered for more and I sacked him on the spot. He didn't ever return to my stage.

Secondly, my reputation is at stake. Now that I realise that marijuana can cause huge psychological problems, among other things, I'm the last to encourage young people to smoke it. It might be useful to some people who are in pain and if it were used medicinally that wouldn't bother me. I watched a documentary about a Tibetan monk years ago. He was using quite desperate measures to cure young men of addiction to all sorts of drugs. As the monk was being interviewed, I remember seeing a line of young men sitting on the ground in the background, drinking water until they threw up. The journalist asked him what was the worst drug. Surprisingly he said marijuana, because it damages your nerves. That was enough for me to back off in 1996, even though I was only a very occasional user. It made me aware that my nerves would jump sometimes when I was asleep. It doesn't happen now. My other observations are that I think dope slows down the process of maturity, especially for teenagers. I reckon if you want a natural high, get up at sunrise and walk along a beach or along a bush track and be aware of the beauty around you. That's what your nose, ears and eyes are for.

In the pub days of the eighties, I referred to dope in a few humorous songs like 'The Shed', but now I refuse to sing that material. Recently the Men's Shed Association wanted to use the song and I suggested that I modify the lyrics but they didn't want to know. It's probably nostalgic for the old buggers who also came through the eighties. I've also had a number of people at my shows recently who want to know why it's not on my latest best-of album, *A Hell of a Career*. You now have the answer.

I don't know how I got away with some things that happened in the early days. I had one so-called sound engineer who really had very little idea what to do if something went wrong. A good sound engineer understands electricity as well as the wiring for sound. But once the gear is set up, they need a good ear. It's a luxury to have an actual recording engineer, but they usually won't lug or won't tour or are too expensive or too arrogant, and on it goes ... the ongoing problem of having a good team. I envy someone like Kenny Rogers who has had most of his team forever, apparently. The market and audiences are so much bigger in the United States that he can afford to keep a good band and crew financially happy and in work. I'm sure, from an artistic perspective, I can keep an outfit happy. They've always been proud to work with me and the crew I have now is fantastic. Mike Chandler, Dan Webbe and Heath Moore are true professionals.

One year we took two Toyota Troop Carriers and the six-tonne truck across Bass Straight to Tasmania. I'd just hired this young fella as a lugger. He always wore army fatigues; those camouflaged army trousers. I remember how he used to brag about being into karate. That was a worry to start with! Anyway, the night after the Burnie show, two of the crew went down to the beach, lit a fire and opened a bottle of Jack Daniels. The Karate Kid joined them. Apparently they consumed the whole bottle of JD. Next thing, the other lads were knocking on my motel room door, as the sun was coming up, whispering, 'He has a rifle'. I let them in and they explained about the JD and how the Karate Kid had disappeared then come back to a sand dune near where they were. They could hear him saying 'Gotcha! (*Click, click.*) Gotcha!' But now he was back in his motel room playing with the rifle. *Oh god*, I thought, and immediately rang the police. It was a very tricky situation. Did he have any bullets? Apparently he had karate-kicked in a large door at the army storehouse down the road and procured an army issue M16 rifle.

Well, the Burnie Police behaved like Keystone Cops. Instead of driving quietly in and sneaking up on the lad's room, they tore in with sirens blaring. Bloody hell! If he was really out of his tree he could have easily mowed them down. Fortunately he had no bullets and the cops managed to make him throw the rifle out the door. So the Karate Kid was taken downtown and shortly after, I drove to the police station and explained that he had no father. He was, by now, feeling sober and apologetic. His fingerprints were taken and they left me with the problem to solve. I took responsibility, gave him a hundred dollars and flew him back to his mother. I hope I didn't release a maniac on the public. The lad in question might have straightened himself out, but I hope he never touches Jack Daniels again. I'd be relieved if his mother reads this book. Maybe she could let me know that he has turned out okay.

I've always tried to treat everyone on the road as equals, even though some of them needed to be brought down a cog or two. One night off, one of the luggers was big-noting to all the ladies in the pub and being quite an embarrassment to the rest of us. A couple of the girls he was chatting up were looking our way and I foolishly said, 'Don't worry about him, he's just one of the shitkickers!' Well, the next day the truck was not washed and had 'shitkickers' written in the dust all over it. I had to sit the crew down at the next theatre and explain the context, and I apologised. I then demanded that the truck be washed.

Generally, though, I haven't had too much go wrong. I've always had reliable vehicles. I bought a brand new Hino truck, which we took on the road for about twenty years, back in the days when you had to take your own full sound and lighting everywhere. The troopies were bought for their toughness and I still own two of them. You can't wear them out and they have hardly any rust. One of them is my main farm vehicle at Springbrook. The other has been decommissioned but I'll turn it into a camper one day when I become a grey nomad.

Actually, there's hardly ever been a need for a four-wheel drive vehicle while touring. These days the sound and lighting systems are much more compact and most venues have what we need. The old bulky sound gear is waiting in my shed for the day when I do a private gig up north. The truck that's now too rusty to register will make an ideal stage. In the meantime it's been ideal for storage and has become another bedroom with a king-sized bed for a recent family Christmas gathering. Waste not, want not.

♫

I rarely take on overseas gigs. Firstly, my goal has always been to write for Australians and therefore I never imagined my music would mean that much anywhere else in the world. I know it appeals to tourists who have visited Australia, as a memory of their trip, and that audience continues to grow for me. But my music is parochial so I don't expect ever to make a mark on the international stage. It bugs me sometimes that it seems important to Aussies that you are world famous. It would be nice financially for me to be world famous, but deep down I am always happy to be well known in my own country and appreciated for writing songs that have a lasting meaning to my own people. I certainly don't want for anything.

All this doesn't mean I can't entertain people overseas though. After all, Australia is an interesting place and there are many Brits who dream of coming to live in our country. It was those people, I guess, who came to my concerts in the 1990s in England. My first of three trips over there was in 1996, where I had performances in London and Dublin. The whole band was with me. I took my stage backdrop of ghost gums, my footbox and stool and all the stage gear. One night the crew left the van outside their accommodation with all the stage gear inside. Next morning we woke to find it had all been stolen except my precious Maton guitar. That was unbelievable. The lid to my guitar case was open and all. The thieves were either disturbed or felt sorry for me. Perhaps they were musicians and it was the honourable thing to do! The sound equipment could be replaced but never my beautiful little 1991 Maton BG808.

That guitar is *my* sound and it's still my favourite. Maton gave it to me back in 1991. Billy May, who started Maton, made me a steel-string guitar in the seventies with a wide neck. I was used to the wide fret board after the classical and 12-string guitars I'd been playing. Unfortunately a man pretending to be an airline porter in a white coat in Los Angeles stole that guitar. I had another Maton, white coloured, stolen by a TAA employee. Linda and Neville Kitchen (Billy May's daughter and son-in-law) who now own Maton have been generous to me and given me several guitars including a beautiful Messiah that is still drying out and getting richer every year. I have many guitars. If I write a song on a particular guitar it deserves to be looked after and I'll never sell it.

I was devastated at the loss of my backdrop of ghost gums too. It was irreplaceable over there. We received a lot of publicity about the robbery of the Aussie gum trees and guess what? It was left in the doorway of a newsagency in Worcestershire. We were able to retrieve that precious suitcase with the backdrop intact. Honourable thieves, as I said. I felt a bit like Lucky Gander, Donald Duck's cousin. I'm certainly not a gambler but I consider I've been extremely lucky throughout my career. That was one of those times.

I returned to England again in 1998 for a solo tour and again in 2000 for another solo tour of ten concerts in London, Edinburgh and the Midlands. My dear friend Ed Doolan, an ex-pat Aussie radio presenter on the BBC in Birmingham was a huge promoter of my music and my concerts over there. In fact, for many of them he was the MC and introduced me on stage. Not only that, he introduced me to many important people. From London to Birmingham I entertained theatre audiences of three to five hundred people. I guess if I lived in England I would have been happy with that but I can do better at home where I really do prefer to be. The gloomy English weather would get me down after a month. I think it makes the people a bit gloomy too. Perhaps if I somehow produced a hit song in the United Kingdom it might have been different. But my music, as I expected, was regarded as a novelty and not taken that seriously.

I gave it enough of a go to convince myself that it's not what I want. It has been my crusade to write songs that make us proud of who we are and to encourage people not to take this country for granted. I've never written anything outside Australia that was very good, except 'A Number on My Back', which I wrote in New Zealand after a Wallabies' defeat. It is Australia that inspires me in so many ways.

When I think of all the men that played
That took the knocks and made the grade
The legends that the game has made
I can't believe I'm here.

I'll wear the gold with a sleeve of green
It makes me strong it makes me keen
And I'll go forward like a steel machine
'Til cracks in the foe appear.

Could it be a dream
My father's son that's me
Humbled by the truth I am
A Golden Wallaby

And I will seize the day
'Cause it belongs to me
I have a number on my back
I am a Wallaby.

And if the ball won't roll my way
No matter how I try that day
I won't let my temper fray
I'll fight on 'til the end

(from 'A Number on My Back' (The Wallaby Anthem)
© 1999 Emusic Pty Ltd)

Pastel red to burgundy and spinifex to gold
Just come out of the Mulga where the plains forever roll
And Albert Namatjira has painted all the scenes
And a shower has changed the lustre of our land

And it's raining on the Rock in a beautiful country
And I'm proud to travel this big land as an Aborigine
And it's raining on the Rock what an almighty sight to see
And I'm wishing and I'm dreaming that you were here with me

Everlasting daisies and a beautiful desert rose
Where does their beauty come from heaven knows
I could ask the wedge-tail but he's away too high
I wonder if he understands it's wonderful to fly

It cannot be described with a picture
The mesmerising colours of the Olgas
Or the grandeur of the Rock
Uluru is power

(from 'It's Raining on the Rock' © 1986 Emusic Pty Ltd)

Chapter 25

IT'S RAINING ON THE ROCK,
WHAT AN ALMIGHTY SIGHT TO SEE

I don't often record with other artists or take them on the road, but ten years after I recorded 'Raining on the Rock' I had a phone call from Graham Archer, who was working on CAAMA radio (Central Australian Aboriginal Media Association) in Alice Springs. Graham, originally from New Zealand, had become quite fond of Alice Springs and was impressed by the talent among the local Indigenous Aranda mob. Alice is traditionally Aranda, or Arunta country. The mobs are Central, North, South, East and Western Aranda. Albert Namatjira, our famous water colourist, was Western Aranda.

'I'm managing a talented young fella named Warren H Williams,' Graham said. 'I'm encouraging him to record duets with well-known country artists. He would love to record "Raining on the Rock" with you. He is Western Aranda.'

Well, I have always been a huge admirer of Albert Namatjira. I think he is the only artist who really captured the colours of the centre of Australia in the early days. In fact, I reckon he opened our eyes to the many pastel hues out there in the landscape. He was the first Aboriginal artist to paint landscapes in the way Europeans had done and he seemed to do it with the greatest of ease. So I was especially delighted when I found out that Warren is Albert Namatjira's great-nephew. Warren doesn't paint but he can really sing, play guitar and write songs so I agreed to record the song with him.

When Warren arrived at Trafalgar Studios in Annandale in Sydney, he was quite shy. Firstly, I discovered his voice was in a completely different range to mine so I had to change the key of 'Raining on the Rock' so we could sing an octave apart. Warren has quite a high, husky voice that is very appealing. I felt a bit on the spot recording a song with the genuine article, so to speak, so I offered him the chance to change the lyrics if anything bothered him. He said 'Uluru *is* power, not Uluru has power.' I changed it immediately. Also I knew we had to sing the same words together so 'like an Aborigine' became 'as an Aborigine'.

I wasn't at all happy with the studio version we recorded but then something magic happened. I invited Warren to sing the song with me at the Golden Guitar Awards night in Tamworth. It was held at the showground in those days, when the awards really felt 'country', with sawdust on the floor in a huge tent. Steve Newton, my recording engineer, recorded the rehearsal and then the performance as well. I had Pixie Jenkins playing music sticks and Giles Smith playing bass guitar. It was one memorable moment! The crowd roared and gave us a standing ovation. Everyone wanted to embrace Warren and our Indigenous culture that night. Steve captured the moment by stitching together the rehearsal and the performance. The awards night performance left Warren a bit awestruck and a little incoherent, so we managed to find the sections we needed from the rehearsal recording. I don't think it mattered. The magic was there. That recording received the most airplay for a country song that year, gaining us an APRA award. We were also awarded Best Single at the Deadly Sounds Indigenous Awards in 1998. I gave the award to Warren to take home; he deserved it. Now I wish I had a replica as the award meant a lot to me. Sadly, it didn't get a gong at Tamworth.

Warren, along with Pixie Jenkins, the fiddle player, came on the road with me for quite a while. It was great fun. My show took on a mixture of humour, pathos, culture and Aussie pride. The three of us jokingly called ourselves the 'the greenie, the black fella and the poof', imagining that's how some of the old club managers would refer to us.

After a few years we all went our separate ways but while I was in England on a solo tour I felt the urge to go back to the trio. The True Blue Reunion tour got underway in 2003 and that period was a highlight in all our careers. We recorded the live show in 2004 and this became the *Mates on the Road* CD and DVD.

After quite a lot of encouragement from folk in the USA I decided to take the show over there in 2004, along with Pixie Jenkins and Warren H Williams. I knew I wasn't well known but Phil Matthews and I figured it was worth the effort. We decided to put on two shows only: one in Springfield in Missouri, and one in Ventura, a small beach town near Los Angeles. The idea was to see if my small number of fans would travel to see my shows. So we concentrated the advertising on those two venues, mainly through my website.

We landed at an airport in the middle of the night and straight away I had to drive on the wrong side of the road in slush and snow, with enormous trucks intimidating me from behind. Being an old mud-runner from the black soil plains, I found it a fun challenge but Pixie was shitting himself in the back seat. As the sun came up we stopped for breakfast at the most unbelievable diner with a variety of beasts' heads on the walls. I have a feeling it was not something many tourists would see out in the middle of the States. Springfield was also an eye-opener, with enormous, barn-like shops and restaurants along the highway. Huge billboards promoting sex shops sat alongside billboards for Jesus. I thought at the time, *Is this the way the world is going?* The township had no heart or centre. Now I see it happening in Australia.

In Springfield we drew about six hundred people in a theatre that held around two thousand. I wouldn't have enjoyed the trip if it weren't for a few dedicated fans who not only helped us with booking venues and accommodation but they were keen to show us around and introduce us to people at radio stations. The radio people seemed to be quite interested in my songs. We visited a couple of schools where Pixie proved to be king of the kids by playing up as the naughty little fiddle player. He was also quite a hit with a gay cop we encountered in a restaurant a little way along Route 66. But that's another story! I still have American fans who ask when I am going back there. I must admit the experience was worth it but I have no intention of returning. I found country Americans quite different. God knows why so many Aussie country singers want to live there. Give me Canada any day. Canadians seem much more like us.

While Pixie and Warren and I had some great times on the road together, after a while I felt like I was losing control of my own destiny and was happy to let Warren and Pixie pursue their own solo careers once more. However, in 2007 Warren joined me again for extensive touring throughout Australia until he remarried and had a baby and the pressures of being away from home became too much. Both Warren and Pixie have concerts on their own now, which they couldn't develop as part of my show.

It was also time for a change for me.

If you take me from my land
You leave me with no soul, I am like a tree
Everything I am is rooted in the soil
Or I am just a stick to burn

I see you my brother
In your desert shining
With your hand of gentle welcome
You're looking for my sense of humour
I wonder how you do it
Carryin' a heavy load

And I am proud to know you
The Keeper of the Stones
Elder of your tribe
The truth is turning slowly
I feel it in my bones
Rising on a beautiful day

(from 'The Keeper of the Stones' © 2005 Emusic Pty Ltd)

Chapter 26

AND I AM PROUD TO KNOW YOU, THE KEEPER OF THE STONES

What did I learn from becoming an Aranda man's mate? Initially, I got the feeling that this lad, Warren H Williams, born at the Hermannsburg Aboriginal mission, 113 kilometres south-west of Alice Springs, was quite used to having things taken care of by others. Once he cottoned on to how us white fellas operated, it was all fine. After all, one of his grandfathers was a Scotsman and that's where his 'Williams' surname came from. As it turned out, Warren is a respected elder of the Hermannsburg mob. He told me he was the 'keeper of the stones'. This meant he was like his uncle's lawyer. Family structures are quite difficult to grasp out there. Traditionally his uncle was more responsible for Warren than Warren's own father, Gus. I asked Warren to introduce me to his uncle so he could show me the stones that had been handed down for centuries. Warren said he would.

So one year when I was in Alice, he drove me many kilometres from civilisation and there was his uncle living as simply as you could imagine. His gunyah was just a bit of scrap iron, just like you find around the opal mining towns.

Warren asked him in language if I could see the stones. Of course, I'm not initiated into the Aranda mob so I wasn't surprised that the uncle said the stones were somewhere else, at a corroboree. I worked it out after a while that Warren would never say 'no' directly to me. He would say 'no' in other ways. This was Aranda style good manners, I suspect, and I respect that now.

On another occasion I visited Warren at Hermannsburg as part of a story for *60 Minutes* with Charles Wooley. He said the best place to camp was on what he called his 'grandfather's country', a little further west. It was a beautiful area. You would swear that man had planted the desert oak trees, as they are spread out so evenly over the red sand dunes. I suspect each tree needs that much space to survive. I was told that the oaks are so hard that when you fell one, if you don't cut it up almost immediately, by the following day a saw will make no impression on it. They were often used to make cattle yards.

We camped under a desert oak on a sand dune with Mount Sonder (known as the Sleeping Lubra to the Aranda people) in the background. Charles camped with us. The first evening we lit a campfire using ironwood and I placed a few deck chairs around. Warren and his wife joined us but they didn't want to know about the chairs. They immediately sat on the ground. Straight away I felt like a white idiot. The red sand dunes are no different to the white sandy beaches on the coast. We sit on towels and don't think anything of it. I also thought, *No wonder my knees get stiff when we rely so much on chairs*. I never really bend my knees much. So I joined them and pushed the deck chair aside. As the sun went down, the bush flies stopped annoying us. Warren made the comment that the flies love the oak trees. *Thanks for telling me now, Warren!*

It was while we were out there on another occasion, filming for Channel Seven's *Bush Telegraph,* that we managed to produce a video clip for 'Raining on the Rock'. A young fella named Chris Tangey (Tange, as I now call him) was hanging around us with his fairly basic little video camera and asked would anyone mind if he filmed alongside the *Bush Telegraph* crew. I'd met Tange when he was sponsored by Qantas to accompany Warren to Trafalgar Studios to film the original studio recording in 1996. We set up as the sun was going down near a big rock formation on Aranda land. It was far too difficult to get permission to use Uluru. Unfortunately there was a huge cloud bank veiling the sun, but just as the sun hit the horizon a wonderful beam of red light smashed against us and it was perfect. Not only did Tange put together a great clip but it was also the start of a great mateship. He is now a very successful cinematographer with his own media production company. He lives just outside of Alice, next to the MacDonnell Ranges and is the man to contact if you need direction or footage of the amazing heart of Australia. He and his wife, Annie, after many patient years trying to conceive, adopted three adorable children from Ethiopia who are all siblings; they call me Uncle John. Whenever we go to Alice we love to stay with the family. They are great lovers of this country, as we are. And Tange feels the same as I do about not losing the tradition of singing its song.

As part of this visit to Hermannsburg we were shown a small workshop where the women were sitting on the ground

making a kind of batik printed fabric. It was obvious then
that the women were the backbone of the town. They held
a lot of power. My guess is that it's the women who will
bring many of the Indigenous mobs forward. It reminded
me of the time when I was asked to perform at Uluru at a
ceremony organised by the Australia Day Council with
the aim of bringing together all the cultures of Australia
in the heart of the country. Steve Waugh was there to
represent the contribution of sport to our nation. There
was a representative of the Afghans, in recognition of their
significant assistance in building the original railway line
for The Ghan, plus representatives from several Aboriginal
tribes. A wonderful fella from the local mob sang 'Waltzing
Matilda' in his language. Warren and I performed 'Raining
on the Rock' together. As the ceremony progressed, I noticed
Warren standing up the back of the audience and asked him
why. He replied, 'You don't stand in front of the women.'

Hermannsburg was a bit of a shock when I first went out
there. The beautiful little whitewashed Lutheran church was
a delight, as were the grounds around it. But the town had
plastic shopping bags floating around in the hot breeze that
caught on every fence and bush. Alcohol is prohibited but the
inevitable Coke cans were everywhere. My mate Ted Egan
said to me once that the mob always threw things on the
ground after using them and it didn't matter. That was when
wood, stone or bones belonged to their landscape. The night
we stayed in the town they put us up in a two-storey unit.
A three-metre fence surrounded the building and the gate was
locked. This was to keep the petrol sniffers from stealing our
petrol. Even though our vehicle ran on diesel, Gus Williams,
Warren's dad, thought it best.

It was an honour to get to know Gus. What a warm and highly respected personality he was. He knocked on our door that night, and all of a sudden I realised I had a cylinder on the table with 'Black Label Scotch' printed on it. I never got around to explaining that it was full of cutlery. Gus was from the Slim Dusty period and had become quite a country music singer himself and he gave me an album of his to listen to. I often wondered what he thought about Warren's success. I like to think he appreciated the opportunities I created for his son.

I ran into Gus again at the Drovers Camp at Camooweal. Each year the Drovers Camp Festival celebrates the life of stockmen and women. Horse riding events are held. It's a different world out there. Legends come and go unnoticed by most Australians. But these men and women are dedicated to the art of being good cattlemen and women. It was 'Big Country stuff'. I felt a little out of place but at least being from the land I have bred a few cattle and sheep and could also sing some songs that they related to. I remember giving Gus a big hug that night and telling him I loved him, which I did. He had a genuine warmth that was handed on to his son. When Gus passed, the Western Aranda mob lost a great elder.

One of the most interesting things I learned about Indigenous people from Warren was when we were in Kakadu. Warren quite obviously felt out of place. He told me that the Kakadu mob were complete foreigners to Aranda people so he was quite uncomfortable, almost embarrassed to be there. But he wouldn't have said 'I don't want to go there.' Ever since that day I have realised that we are really ignorant to consider Aborigines as one mob, or to put them all in the same box. It would be like putting the Germans and the French in the same bag. Even Warren's mob and the mob west of Hermannsburg are still enemies. There is a deep-seated antagonism between them that stems back hundreds of years, according to Warren. In Alice Springs, which is Central Aranda, there is ongoing strife at the pubs mainly because of the mobs other than Aranda coming into town. Pitjantjara, for instance, come from further south. Actually it's all too complicated for me, but there are people who study it and know why different skins don't mix.

One day I walked six kilometres from the caravan park at Kings Canyon (about a two-hour drive south-west of Hermannsburg) across the plain. I came across a claypan and thought, *What an ideal place to sit, for kids to run around.* It was a perfect place for an Indigenous picnic. I really felt a strong urge that something would turn up and sure enough it did. I trod on a perfect, round grindstone shaped like a flying saucer, actually buried in the sand. Either I was in contact with the old people or there is that much stuff out there that I was bound to step on it. One thing is for sure, the more respect we show to the wise ones among Indigenous groups, the better off Australia will be. When you think of at least 40 000 years of survival there would be some great wisdom handed down. It could be very useful information for all Australians. We have capitalised on their art. Why not their wisdom?

(Yes) I'll be going Waltzing Matilda
And I'll travel up the road to Gundagai
But I'll be steering clear of that pub with no beer
When I'm travelling this big country round

Oh there's red rock and dust in this land of romance
Where the river banks will bust without warning
And I had to leave my girl on the shores of the ocean
To travel this big country round

Now you may call me a jolly swagman
But I don't regret a thing I've done …
So click go the shears, and I'll be gone for years
Travelling this big country round

Oh this land is so big and so lonely
But a man can get away from it all
So I'm tired of 'Kangaroo', he won't catch 'Old Man Emu'
For he's travelling this big country round

Forty years been drovin', no woman by my side
No one gives me orders on this dusty road I ride
But the flies can drive you crazy and the wind can get you down
But you won't find me lingerin' or hanging round this town

Channel country, gibber plains, tablelands I know
And then there's gentle sand dunes where little Mallees grow
There's a friendly campfire everywhere I go
I'll play another drovin' song the white owl wouldn't know

So see you later Birdsville, you're far too flash for me
While the beer was cold and yummy from here it's Billy Tea
The mob is keen on movin' and that sounds good to me
Good feed they reckon southbound, we're heading for Marree

(from 'Skinny Dingoes' © 2004 Emusic Pty Ltd)

Chapter 27

SEE Y'LATER BIRDSVILLE,
YOU'RE FAR TOO FLASH FOR ME

In 2002 Australia embraced the Year of the Outback. The first Great Australian Outback Cattle Drive was held that year as part of the celebrations. Birdsville is the Alice Springs of Queensland; it's part of the legend of the heart of Australia. The Birdsville Track is probably even more famous: the road between Birdsville and Maree in South Australia. The 517-kilometre track is famous for the legend of driving cattle north to south and south to north depending on the availability of grass. In fact it was the celebration of droving cattle over that track that brought me to Birdsville in the first place. I was asked to perform on the back of a semi-trailer with Warren H Williams on the evening before the cattle drive left.

As we flew from Sydney in a light aircraft over the desert country I could feel a song coming into my head. Not long before this I had been on a trip in north-west New South Wales supporting the push to save the stock routes through the state. They were under pressure to be sold off to farmers and graziers. My support was for the stock routes to be kept, as they also provided corridors for wildlife and native plant stock throughout the state. On that trip I met a traditional sheep drover with his caravan and dogs. He told me he had never married and it suited him fine to be his own boss. He enjoyed his independence. With this in mind I started writing the song 'Skinny Dingoes' in my head. By the time I landed in Birdsville I thought the drover in 'Skinny Dingoes' should be on the legendary Birdsville Track.

I made a point of meeting Eric Oldfield, who was there to lead the tourist cattle drive along with his experienced mates. Eric had been the boss drover for the final cattle drive in 1972, before road trains took over the job of traditional droving. He knew the Birdsville Track like the back of his hand. I met Eric and his wife when I was doing a sound check and settling in to the motel at the Birdsville Pub. That brief moment was enough to ask him about the topography of the track. He rattled it off: treeless gibber plains, channel country with coolibahs and sand dunes with mallee trees. It was enough for me to finish the song. So that evening I sang 'Skinny Dingoes' for the audience. I don't think I've ever written a song and performed it publicly the same day before, or since. It went over like a charm, perfect for the occasion.

After I sang the song, Eric Oldfield passed the stage stumbling a little, saying, 'That was a bloody good song, John.' Right behind him was his wife saying, 'Where are you going, Eric?' When the show was over, I was very keen to have a yarn with Eric. A few enquiries later I found him over behind one of the cattle trucks. He was sitting on a 44-gallon drum, enjoying a few beers with his droving mates.

I said to Eric, 'You look like you've been having a good time, mate.'

'Yeah,' he said. 'I'd be havin' an even better one if Old Handbrake wasn't following me around!'

I wondered how he'd be the next day in control of the cattle! Apparently he was fine. I guess he was toughened to it.

That day was a joy. There was a parade of the real stockmen on their horses, all of them keen to represent the legend of the Birdsville Track. It was such a memorable moment. This was no Clint Eastwood movie ... these men and horses were indeed magnificent and proud and I felt extremely proud too.

'Skinny Dingoes' was released on the *Chandelier of Stars* album in 2005, along with 'Keeper of the Stones', about Warren, and 'The Camel Boy', my tribute to the great artist and Warren's great uncle Albert Namatjira. The album picked up another three Golden Guitars to add to the mantelpiece.

♫

On my second visit to Birdsville I had a chance to sit on the edge of its famous Diamantina River and admire the wonderful birdlife. I also had another chance to wander over the gibber plain and discover amazing shiny baked red stones in all shapes and sizes. If I lived there I'd make use of those stones for sure. There are so many artistic resources in the outback. Like the rock-hard hollow logs of coolibah; these could be sanded down and would make beautiful pots. All that is needed is time for contemplation to let imagination take over.

Well here I am on city street dancin'
To fashion drums and rushing feet
Drownin' in a freeway stream
Stuck inside my four-wheel dream
Now I know you like the comfort zone, woman
Don't want to leave you all alone
Piggin' out on chocolate frogs
Paying bills and walkin' dogs
Checkin' out the butcher's bum
Listening to my nagging mum

Oh I've gotta cross that Anzac Bridge
Climb the Great Dividing Ridge
Roll out through the wheat and sheep
Way out where a man can sleep
Underneath the chandelier of stars
We can fly for hours and hours
Laid out on the jolly swag it's free
Come with me … woman
Come with me … woman
Out into the Big Red
Out into the Big Red
Out into the Big Red

The best Australiana museum I've ever seen was in Birdsville. The large shed was open this time. It would be impossible to estimate the value of the collection. Enamel signs, farm implements, toys, posters; I was in awe the entire time I was there, as I'm a bit of a collector of such things. Sadly, the next time I was in Birdsville I learned that John Menzies, the owner, had been trying to sell the museum and its contents as a single purchase for four years but had no takers. So in 2011 he simply shut the doors and took everything away to be auctioned. I wish I'd known about it. I thought the museum was a huge tourist attraction for the small town that has a population of less than three hundred people.

My most recent visit to Birdsville was in July 2013 for a marathon event called The Big Red Run to raise money for type 1 diabetes. It was a coincidence that my latest album was called *The Big Red*, a name I use to relate generally to the red outback. I guess that was the trigger for the organisers to ask me to put on a concert on top of Birdsville's Big Red, the massive 40-metre mountain of red sand dune, 30 kilometres west of the town.

On the drive out to the sand dune, several police vehicles were stopping the stream of cars heading for the sand dune. Out came the breathalysers. Some of the cops had come all the way from Mt Isa, more than 700 kilometres away, as the local Birdsville police station is a one-man show. The breathalysers were a warning to people of the police presence and of the perils of drink-driving. The boys in blue enjoyed a free show on the dune and were among the many fans who wanted a photo with me afterwards. They weren't breathalysing people after the show, which showed good judgement on their part, I thought. It was a family day out, not a rock concert.

The sand dune overlooks a salt lake surrounded by swampland covered in dead coolibah trees. It reminded me of what inspired my song 'Galleries of Pink Galahs' as several of the dead trees that day were completely covered in white, like large almond trees covered in blossom, and others in pink. These were no flowers – the trees were covered with corellas and galahs. What a sight this was from high above!

My guitarist, Col Watson, and I were driven up the sand dune with our guitars for a sound check about an hour before the show was to commence at sunset. The crew had painstakingly set up a stage on top of the dune. It had never been attempted before even though it was an ideal amphitheatre. Already there were hundreds of people settling in and snuggling up in readiness for a cool, breezy evening. Families had come from all over Australia to be there. It was a delight to perform my songs for them in such an iconic setting. After all, they were all campers and travellers and completely in tune with the songs I sang; songs that really came alive in that setting. It felt like the songs *belonged* there. Heath Moore, my lighting technician, had cleverly lit up the crest of the sand dune behind the stage. He could make it blue, green, red. You can imagine how magic that looked as I sang my outback songs, opening with my anthem 'Island of Oceans', followed by 'Skinny Dingoes', 'The Big Red', Redgum's 'Diamantina Drover' (I wish I'd written that one). The audience was ours for over two hours. They still wanted more despite the fact that the desert temperature was decreasing rapidly as it grew darker. It was an unforgettable night and I'm honoured to have been the first person to put on such a concert on the Big Red.

Afterwards, the cops invited us for a drink around the fire behind the courthouse back in town. Years ago, I accepted a similar offer in Mt Isa and had to sing 'True Blue' for them, of course. They reminded me of this night and reckon there's still a photo in their underground clubhouse from that evening. I told them I'd consider their invitation but we ended up not going. I didn't want to finish up the same way I did the last time in Mt Isa. That is, three sheets to the wind! We had twelve hours of flying ahead of us the following day. In fact by the time we landed in Sydney, we had visited seven airports: Birdsville, Windorah, Quilpie, Charleville, Toowoomba, Brisbane and finally Sydney. In Sydney the next day, no wonder I felt knackered and needed a nanna nap before singing 'True Blue' at a function for Steve Waugh at his foundation's charity event.

See the crest resembles me and you
The green and gold, of course, the emu and the roo
Just to feel the felt sends a shiver down your spine
You pinch yourself, you can't believe it's really mine

First session every Test the Aussies can be seen
To show their pride, pay respect and 'Don' the Baggy Green
And all the Aussies on the street who understand the game
Know that if they wore the cap they would feel the same

Chapter 28

TO SHOW THEIR PRIDE, PAY RESPECT AND 'DON' THE BAGGY GREEN

I've been asked to sing at some momentous occasions because of my career, occasions that have become part of our history. But it was a surprise to be asked to sing at the opening of the new Parliament House in 1988. Bob Hawke was the prime minister at the time and one of his staff thought it would be both amusing and appropriate to sing 'All Australian Boys Need a Shed'. I can't say I thought it was appropriate at all, especially with its reference to marijuana! But I couldn't knock back the opportunity to be a part of such an important date in our history. So I agreed to sing 'The Shed' as long as they would let me sing 'Raining on the Rock' for the Indigenous people of the Tent Embassy.

The Indigenous mob and their supporters were right in front of me as I sang, the pond behind me, looking down Remembrance Drive towards the Australian War Memorial. It was quite a day. Of course I was very annoyed that Queen Elizabeth had to be there as our head of state. I thought, *Two parliament houses later and we still don't have an Aussie as our head of state.* It amazes me even today that monarchists will say things like, 'Can you imagine Quentin Bryce as our head of state?' Well, yes I can. What is it with these people? Is it the tall poppy syndrome? Why the hell do they look up to a descendant of a family with a Germanic background as more appropriate than an Australian? A family with a murderous history of greed, plunder, promiscuity … need I go on? I'm not afraid to say these things. They are not gods. We lay our trust in this lot over an Australian who, if selected by both sides of parliament, would be intelligent, squeaky clean (hopefully) and well versed in the law of the land. But above all, they'd have great passion for Australia. Don't tell me the Queen does to the same extent. She is probably tired of the whole debate and wishes we'd get on with being truly independent. We can still call ourselves the Commonwealth of Australia, not the Republic of Australia. We can still have the same ties with England.

I'm not an extreme nationalist to the point where I can't see beyond this country but I do think you have to be proud of your own backyard before you can respect other nations. However, I am *very* one-eyed when it comes to our national sporting teams. I will lend my support to any one of them if it will help their spirit and will to win. If you ever have the misfortune to sit next to me during a Wallabies game you'll find that I become terribly anxious when things go wrong. And I go crazy when we score. And at home I get loud and jump around the room in rage or with excitement. I can't sit still. My passion can be quite annoying and embarrassing.

So when Phil Matthews and I read in the newspaper in the late 1990s that Steve Waugh was using 'True Blue' to inspire the Australian cricket team, I was rapt. And what a team we had then, with the likes of Shane Warne, Adam Gilchrist, Glenn McGrath, Darren Lehmann, and Mark Waugh ... So I made it my business to contact Steve and tell him how much I appreciated it. It turned out that all his family were big fans. In fact his mum and dad came to my concerts at Revesby Workers' on a number of occasions. Steve and I became mates. Not that we saw much of each other. If I wasn't on the road, he was. But if we ever run into each other, the friendship is still going strong. Steve also kindly accepted the invitation to be part of my *This Is Your Life* on Channel Nine in 1995. I was stoked he was there.

In 1996 I was contracted by Foxtel to do a 13-part series called *True Blue Aussies*, where I interviewed famous Aussie sportsmen, and Steve was one. It was a highlight to talk with him at the Sydney Cricket Ground and to go through all the emotions of a big game. He reckoned my batting style wasn't bad at all when I demonstrated it out in the middle of the ground. I think he was being generous! The SCG was empty of course. He showed me where everyone sat in the dressing shed and explained a few of the blokes' foibles.

While Steve and his team were overseas beating everyone in the 1999 World Cup, he and fellow team member Gavin Robertson sent me some lyrics called 'The Baggy Green'. It was a little rough around the edges, but it didn't take a lot of tidying up to make it flow. However, I still didn't have a tune for it when I was invited to be a surprise guest at a 'welcome home' function for the Aussie team's triumphant return to Australia. The function was held at Crown in Melbourne. The who's who of the Melbourne sporting fraternity was there, including representatives from all the television channels. Meanwhile I was stuck out the back in the dressing room twiddling my thumbs and warming up my voice to sing 'True Blue'. I had the refined lyrics of 'The Baggy Green' with me in case they might be handy. Just messing about with the lyrics on my guitar, I discovered that Gavin Robertson, wittingly or unwittingly, had co-written the lyrics to fit 'Click Go the Shears'. *You beauty*, I thought, *I can do something with this tonight.* There's a verse about always wearing the baggy green during the first session of a Test match that was ideal for Steve to sing. I knew he was tone deaf but he could just read it. Who cares – it was Steve Waugh!

After I sang 'True Blue', much to Eddie McGuire's surprise I had 'The Baggy Green' ready to sing. I'd written the words to the chorus for all the lads in the team and handed Steve the words to his verse. The crowd loved it and so did the lads. Molly Meldrum was there, networking as usual, and that night he had to have a photo with Steve and me and the World Cup. All of a sudden Molly was another Mallee boy from Quambatook, which he was, even though he had never admitted to it back in my struggling days. Eddie McGuire was so taken by the song he had me sing it on *The Footy Show* on Channel Nine the next evening.

I also was given the absolute honour of dining with the team at Crown that night. It was then that I realised how young they all were. I'd barely got through my entrée when 'my old mate Molly' was over my shoulder telling me that *we* had to record that baggy green song the next day. I actually said, 'Fuck off, Molly!' That didn't put him off because he rang me again when I was at Channel Nine the following night. Eddie said, 'Hey John, Molly is on the phone'. I don't think Eddie understood my reaction. 'Tell us how you feel, John,' he laughed.

It wasn't long before we had Steve and Gavin in a recording studio in Sydney with young lads from Steve's old school team in Bankstown singing 'The Baggy Green'. It was great fun recording it. We added a bit of Allan McGilvray's ABC commentary on Don Bradman. I think it gave it character. I also think it very fitting that there's a 'baggy green' song and I'm proud to have helped my mate Steve Waugh achieve a dream. He, more than anyone, has kept the pride of the cap going by reintroducing the tradition of wearing it during the first session of every Test match. He doesn't say much but when he speaks it's definitely true blue. Although he sings about as well as I could return a ball bowled by Mitchell Johnson. I wouldn't even see it!

♬

The absolute highlight of my friendship with Steve was when he invited me to be a guest in his corporate box on his final day of Test cricket. The Australian Cricket Board asked if I'd sing 'True Blue' especially for Steve. 'Is it me and you, is it Mum and Dad, is it Steve Waugh too'. I also sang the national anthem that day. There I was, out on the Sydney Cricket Ground saying g'day to Sachin Tendulkar from the Indian team waiting for the Aussies to come out onto the field. It nearly makes me cry just recalling it. The Australian team walked right past me in single file and every one of them shook my hand. Wow! What an honour! I don't think I've ever felt more proud. Steve finished his career that day with one hundred runs, not out. Not even Sir Don could do that. Good on you, Steve! And today the boys wear the baggy green much more often than only in the first session.

Thanks to Steve Waugh, 'True Blue' has remained part of our Test team's victory celebration. I love following the cricket, just as my grandpa did. He preferred listening to it on the radio but the television coverage is amazing these days. Being a big fan of Michael Hussey, I was determined to fly down from Queensland for his final Test match in Sydney. I let the team know that I would love to see Michael Clarke, the captain, after the game. Clarke welcomed me with open arms when I turned up with my guitar and sang 'True Blue' for the team, but especially for Mike Hussey. That was the night he handed over the job of singing 'Under the Southern Cross' to Nathan Lyon. 'Under the Southern Cross' is their sacred chant to scream after a victory.

What a night that turned out to be. First I sang 'True Blue' with the guitar, and Michael Clarke said, 'No wetting John's guitar.' *Oh, oh,* I thought, *what are those bottles of champagne at Mike Hussey's feet for?* The coach told me to put away my guitar and pull on a training shirt. Huss invited me into the circle to sing 'True Blue' again while the entire team joined in. Then came the champagne and the beer. I was initiated into the team (or should I say anointed) that night. Well and truly! I couldn't see for about ten minutes and I doubt anyone else could either. It blew me away that some of them were fans of my music.

It got even better. After enjoying the 4–0 victory of the Aussie cricket team in the 2014 Ashes series, I made sure

I was in Sydney for the final days. Once again, I offered my services to sing for the boys, especially if they finished with a whitewash of 5–0. We went to the first two days at the Sydney Cricket Ground but stayed at home on the third day, thinking we would go again on the fourth day. But our boys finished the Poms off by the end of the third day. What a thrashing! I'd told Gavin Dovey, the team manager, I'd be on call for whenever they wanted me. I arrived at the shed about 9 p.m.

First I ran into Darren Lehmann, the new successful Aussie team coach. We'd met before when he was part of the team under Steve Waugh's captaincy. A couple of the lads told me that Darren had taught them to relax and enjoy themselves on the ground. I always thought he was a top bloke and a real Aussie. What a job he's done! I met a number of the English team too. They hung around until about 10 p.m. They were good blokes.

I had to sing 'True Blue' twice that night, as well as 'Home Among the Gum Trees' and even 'Old Man Emu'. The boys had a great time singing along. Then came 'Under the Southern Cross' led by Nathan Lyon followed by a ten-minute shower of champagne and beer. I was ready this time. I had a fresh shirt in my guitar case. In these circumstances I'm just a punter like everyone else and these experiences make me feel wonderful. I met a couple of new players who weren't in the team on the Mike Hussey day. And I was surprised and absolutely delighted to learn that Shane Watson and his family were big fans and so were Ryan Harris and George Bailey. No Aussie could enjoy this more than me. I just feel blessed. Fuck being a world star! It doesn't get any better than this.

♫

When Ray Martin approached me in 1998 to write a tribute to Sir Donald Bradman, I was keen to do it. I never mind a project or a commission to write a song for a purpose, especially a cause or charity that I believe in like the 'Goodbye Blinky Bill' song to raise much-needed funds for the Koala Preservation Society in Port Macquarie. Ray had at last secured a rare interview with 'the Don' to be televised on Channel Nine. This was huge for Ray, as Bradman hadn't been interviewed on television before. Ray has always been a great supporter of my music so I wanted to write something special about our cricket hero for the occasion.

My first step for such a project was to ask Ray for maybe twelve things about Sir Don in order of importance. 'Wizard of the willow' was one saying that came up. I already knew a fair bit about the great man and especially what he meant to Australians and to cricket. I also remembered Mary Kay saying that her 'Auntie Duckie danced with Donald Bradman'. Her great aunt, as you can imagine, dined on the fact all her life. Apparently it was when Sir Don went on a rare promotional tour for the Mick Simmons Sports Store. It was at some club that the dear lady had the privilege of doing the foxtrot with this world famous man. Well, that was all I needed to kick off the song. The next line was 'She said it was the highlight of her life'. I knew that such a down-to-earth, humble emotion would grab the listeners. What woman wouldn't be blown away by the privilege of being held by Sir Don in his heyday? My daughter Ami was at the Conservatorium of Music studying opera at the time so I thought, *She'll know some fine young singers to sing some lines to add a youthfulness to the song.* It worked a treat in the studio.

First I had to sing the song, simply called' Sir Don', on *The Ray Martin Show*. Thank goodness Ray and the audience loved it. But, you know, I never did get to meet Sir Don. His son, John, told me later on that his father never liked the old song 'Our Don Bradman' but he liked mine. God! I wish I had written to him at the time and asked him what he thought. But that felt a bit pushy.

When Sir Donald Bradman left us for the cricket ground in the sky in 2001, I was absolutely humbled to be asked to sing the song at his memorial service in Adelaide. The service was held in the St Peter's Cathedral and was televised live. An estimated 60 million viewers tuned in to watch it. Sir Don had made a huge impression on cricket fans around the world, so viewers in Australia, India, Pakistan and England tuned in to pay their respects to the great man.

I'm not good at memorials or funerals so I kept myself well away from the cathedral until I was required. The television crew was outside the vestry. With makeup on and microphone stuck up my shirt, I tried to remain calm, telling myself I'm singing this for his family, forget about it being live to 60 million people.

My time for the song arrived. The television crew directed me to the side door of the cathedral. The pageboys were on their way over to me to lead me to the microphone and stool. I'm nervous again just thinking about it now. I was quite numb. The security person at the door said g'day and told me that my fly was open! My first reaction was, *Good one, mate, ha ha,* but I checked … and sure enough, my fly *was* open! It was because I had to undo my belt to slip the microphone up my shirt and hadn't realised it had caused the zipper to slip down. I was so relieved, thinking I would never have lived it down. Imagine performing to 60 million people with my fly open! What a close one! After that it all went like a breeze. Ever since that day I have a habit of saying *fly check* to myself before I walk on stage. Unfortunately, as I get older and more vague I find I'm occasionally very pleased that I *do* check!

After the memorial service there was tea and bickies in the pavilion. Prime Minister John Howard was there having the time of his life among so many cricket legends, like Bill Lawry and Tony Greig. I ended up at the bar of our hotel with Greg Chappell, who surprised me with lots of 'f ... ing' comments about all sorts of 'f ... ing' things. He was much more down to earth than I expected. It amused me because he was such a refined batsman. I was absolutely delighted to have a yarn with him.

Sir Don

When Aunty Duckie danced with Donald Bradman
She said it was the highlight of her life
That wizard of the willow swept her off her feet
Along with all Australians, every man on the street
Sir Don you gave us pride in ourselves
Please come out for just one more parade

Sir Don we're still in awe of your name
We know you'll shy away
But we'll honour you just the same
Born a country boy and we are proud

You built upon your legend with the power of your blade
You fought against the odds and put others in the shade
Let us tickertape your cavalcade
Please come out for just one more parade

Hero of heroes, bold of the bold
You dignified the uniform
You blessed the green and gold
Let us tickertape your cavalcade
Please come out for just one more parade
Please come out for just one more parade

(© 1996 Emusic Pty Ltd)

Yeah we'll cruise one more time down the Murray
Don't wave the river gums goodbye
Just thank 'em for the shade and the stories
Tomorrow there'll be time to cry

Chapter 29

TOMORROW THERE'LL
BE TIME TO CRY

Nerves can be awful things. After 44 years I rarely suffer too badly now, but in the past there have been occasions when it has ruined my performance. It's usually happened on live television, with just one song to perform and no time to warm up. Often there's no audience, just me stuck in the middle of a television studio like a prize parrot on a perch. The television crews are usually oblivious to what you're doing so the atmosphere can be quite cold, despite the hot lights.

In the seventies, it seemed to be important to sing to the camera that had the red light on. There were always three cameras and the floor manager would point to the camera that was on. Sandy Scott was the expert, gliding gracefully from one camera to the other. Looking at the right camera and putting on a pathetic smile used to throw me and sometimes brought me unstuck. The adrenalin would start in my stomach and creep up to my head and my brain would go into a panic then the brain would shut down. I usually got away with it; you learn to fake the words but it would depress me for days afterwards. One thing I've never done is resort to alcohol before a show or event to help me relax. Many entertainers I've known over the years have used alcohol to calm the nerves. 'Just a nip' to start with but so often the nips got bigger and it became a crutch. Others use drugs. There's nothing like a beer after the show but I've been wary of the trap of Dutch courage as they call it. Eventually I realised that you just forget about which camera is on except when you really want to emphasise a line. For instance I would sing 'Is your heart still here' into the camera. And you don't have to smile; just think about the words you're singing. I let the director follow me, rather than the other way around. It has often annoyed me how frequently they point the camera at the neck of the guitar or on my foot when I'm singing meaningful lyrics.

♫

I was watching *Adam Hills Tonight* on TV when Adam asked Bernard Fanning (from the rock band Powderfinger) how he handled singing about his late father and brother without becoming too emotional. I related to his question in regard to 'Salisbury Street' and my late brother, Robin. Robin was the third of us five boys: the middle brother, always the little mongrel. You might remember that as a young boy he loved to pull the little rubber tyres off my micro-model cars. Robin grew up to be quite the respectable country bloke. He was determined to know more about farming and studied at Dookie Agricultural College. The only difference it made that I could see was that he learned to slaughter sheep. That was a relief for Dad and me as we ate our own sheep.

Rob and Debbie were living on the Murray River with
their three kids. Rob loved waterskiing and together with
his brother-in-law had built a houseboat. In 1998 the small
cancer on his back that had been cut out reared its ugly
head again and took over his body. He tried to be positive
about it and experimented with diet and alternative methods
of treatment. He didn't want any kind of sympathy. It's
understandable he would spend his last days on the Murray.
The houseboat was beautifully built. The last time we saw
each other was on the houseboat. I couldn't help thinking
what it must be like, admiring the ancient gum trees, knowing
that before long you won't see them ever again. Rob was only
47 when he died.

I wrote 'Salisbury Street' initially as a poem to read at
Rob's public funeral. Rob's mother-in-law insisted that the
burial be a private affair. Mum and Dad didn't seem to have
a say in it. I had a go at reading the poem but I was hopeless.
I started okay, but the emotions completely took hold of me
and I wished someone else had read it. Since first reading it
at Rob's funeral, I've regarded the song as a tribute to his
positive attitude during the six months he faded away with
cancer. It brings back memories of our childhood and it is also
a Murray River song. The red gums, the sunset, the scenery
on that magnificent river all combine to pass on how Rob
felt about the Murray. The song is how I think I would feel if
I had to contemplate not seeing the Australian bush anymore.

Straight after the funeral, my daughter Ami and I flew
to Melbourne to appear on Channel Nine's *Hey Hey It's
Saturday*. I know Rob would have understood that you have
to carry on with life. I was quite numb about his passing for a

while. It took some time to realise he was not here anymore. We hadn't seen that much of each other in those last few years so it's not as though I missed his presence. He's with me, however, every time I sing 'Salisbury Street' and I'm pleased that the song is popular, for his family's sake especially. I will sing it forever.

Of all my brothers Rob was probably the biggest fan of my music. Rob was good at whatever job he took on yet I don't think he ever really felt fulfilled. Perhaps he regretted leaving the north-west and his brothers. I'm sure our friendship would've developed a lot more if we'd lived closer. Rob was a great father to two beautiful girls and a fine son and when those three children and Debbie are at my concert I know 'Salisbury Street' makes them proud.

It took me a long time to realise how much stronger the song is when I sing it quite laidback. I think having Dave Ellis playing the bull fiddle is the reason this works. When the sound on stage is fuller it seems to give me more time to relax into the rhythm. But perhaps it comes with maturity as well.

Chandelier of Stars

When m' travellin' days are done
Will you still be with me?
When all the songs have been sung
Standin' right beside me
Watchin' the grandkids grow
I've got everything but nothing without you

I've got mountains, I've got rivers
I've got a chandelier of stars
Got blossoms on the bloodwoods
Friends all 'round the country
And a heart as good as new
I've got everything but nothing without you

Too much time for thinking
It's gonna drive me mad
I walk along the river
I watch a motel movie
But lovers make me sad
I've got everything but nothing without you

So when this life that binds me
Turns me loose
Lets me rest on m' laurels
Will you put y' head on m' shoulder
And share the peaceful years
I've got everything but nothing without you

It's time to stop the slaughter of our native land
No more telling lies, drawing lines in the sand
Maybe we didn't know but surely now it's underhand
No more crocodile tears, did he die in vain
Did he make us cry, did he suffer all his pain
So we could knock it down again and again and again

Chapter 30

YEAH, C'MON WATTLE SOLDIERS,
WILDLIFE WARRIORS GET ANGRY

For some years I was aware that Steve Irwin and his mum and dad were into my music. No doubt 'Rip Rip Woodchip' would have been right up Steve's alley. I'm sure 'Goodbye Blinky Bill' would have resonated with him as well. When I discovered that he was buying brigalow land in Queensland just to save it, I knew we had similar dreams and a lot in common. We were both besotted with the Aussie habitat in its original state.

Steve first contacted me when he had finished building his stadium at Australia Zoo at Beerwah on the Sunshine Coast in Queensland. Steve asked me to sing at the opening on Australia Day 2003. He called the stadium area 'The Crocoseum'; it holds 5000 people and has a crocodile pool in the middle. The stage set-up that is there now was built on my advice. I've performed on that stage nearly every Australia Day since it first opened.

That first day, he introduced me to one of my favourite birds – the wedge-tailed eagle. I was able to hold this magnificent creature on my arm. It was heavy, but I persevered because of the privilege. I held my face as close to the bird as I could and looked into her eyes. It was like looking into another world of pale blue as I told her how much I loved her. I think she got my vibe and didn't hook her powerful beak into my nose. It brings tears to my eyes thinking about it. Those eagle eyes can spot a rat on the ground from thousands of feet above in the sky. I am so proud of our eagle and what a joy it is when a pair of them fly past at eye level at Springbrook. You never hear them, so you have to keep your eyes open. We have an eagle's view from the cottage.

The daily crocodile and bird show is quite something to watch and is still continued by Steve's great mate and director of the zoo, Wes Mannion, along with other staff. Being a bird lover, the bird show to me is even more spectacular than the crocodile show. While Steve was alive he always made sure he would be around to do the croc show on Australia Day when I was there. I can tell you that he was the exactly the same off-camera as he was on television. His bright eyes shone with an infectious enthusiasm. He was absolutely the real deal; always a big kid at heart and that never changed. As famous as he became, he still liked to be up at sparrow fart and drive the quad bike around the zoo. Like me, he thought there was nothing better than being in the bush in the early morning. I reckon he had to force himself to become a star, just to get his conservation message across.

It was really only on those Australia Days that I came to know Steve and his family. We always had sandwiches and a chinwag after the show. Steve loved to include me in his crocodile performance, with plenty of his staff croc handlers around me for safety! It was a memorable day when he introduced Bindi and little Bob to me. Bindi was unbelievably polite and loveable. Little Bob, who was showing off by wrestling a stuffed toy crocodile on the couch, was encouraged to show me his ukulele. Young children often present me with ukuleles to sign after my shows so I was prepared for this. I said to Bob, 'I'll play a very simple song for you on your ukulele that my dad taught me. It has two chords only.' So I tuned his ukulele and sang, 'On my ukulele, I keep strumming gaily, On my ...'

Little Bob grabbed the uke back and said, 'It's not your ukulele, it's *my* ukulele.' He was quite suspicious of me after that. Then Steve gave me a small carpet snake to hold. Well, Bob wasn't to be outdone by this ukulele stealer, so he put the snake around his own neck. Steve and Terri were delighted. 'That's the first time little Bob has handled a snake,' they said. I think I brought out Bob's competitive nature. When he's as famous as his dad I'll remind him of that one day.

♫

Where was I when Steve died? Like most Aussies, I remember it well. On 4 September 2006, I was in Leonora in Western Australia. The little mining town was having a small festival to revitalise its spirit. I'm not sure why I took the risk of doing a show in such a small town; only 150 people had booked. My manager, Phil, rang me in the afternoon and, very emotional, said, 'Steve Irwin has died ... he was killed by a stingray.' It was *very* hard to believe. Not Steve! Suddenly I didn't give a hoot about the small audience numbers. I told the festival organisers to tell the town that the show was now free, that

I would do a special performance in memory of Steve Irwin. You know, it was mainly the local Aboriginals who filled the remaining seats in the hall. They also knew and loved Steve, more proof of his broad appeal.

The songs poured out of me that night. I chose every song I could think of that related to the spirit of the land and its beauty. The crowd was right with me in understanding my emotions.

It was soon after that night I was asked to sing at Australia Zoo for Steve's memorial service to be televised live around the world. I knew I had to do it, as hard as it would be. 'True Blue', of course, was a song that could have been written for Steve. As far as I'm concerned, he epitomised the meaning of the words.

I'd recorded an orchestral version of 'True Blue' not long before Steve died, so I decided to use the orchestra backing track, but I would play the guitar live and sing live. Thank goodness they asked me to sing 'Home Among the Gum Trees' first. It gave us all a short breather from our emotions. That settled my nerves a bit and the crowd helped by singing along. Everyone seems to remember me singing 'True Blue' at Steve Irwin's memorial service. I found strength from realising it wasn't *my* luxury to cry. My job was to sing for Steve's family and his mates. I needed to be strong for them. But when they brought Steve's Toyota ute into the Crocosseum, loaded it up with his swags and possessions, and all his close mates and the staff from the zoo lined up in front of me, boy was it hard to keep it together. I think it would have been quite weak and selfish of me to break down. Steve was a mate but I wasn't as close to him as those around me that day, and his family was sitting above me in the stadium. I'm usually quite pathetic at funerals, but this was an honour and I wasn't going to spoil it. I got through it but not as easily as it may have appeared on television.

I'm proud to have sung for such a great Aussie hero. Initially I was inundated with emails and messages of praise from all around the world, and to this day they still occasionally come in from overseas after all these years. It seems that fans all over the world understood what my words meant. It's probably the most international thing I'll ever be recognised for. Steve's legacy, of course, carries on through Terri, Bindi, young Robert and Wes, Steve's mate. The zoo also purchased a large area in the north of Cape York Peninsula and is battling to keep mining out of it. The Australia Zoo is still progressing with new ways to enlighten our kids about the need to save habitat for the world's wildlife. To me, an untouched area of Aussie bush is more valuable than any museum of Australian history. And such bush is becoming more rare. To walk through country that has been disturbed only by Aboriginal people is very spiritual and a privilege. I'm sure Steve felt the same and I hope the generous spirit of our hero is never lost.

It was an obvious idea to write a song in memory of Steve. But rather than write an opportunistic song just about him, I thought it was more appropriate to write something to support his charity, Wildlife Warriors. I'm sure Steve would have preferred that. So the song I wrote, 'Wildlife Warriors', went on an album of the same name. Money from that album was donated to his charity. It gave me a chance to compile an album of all the songs I knew Steve would have approved of, songs that were about the nature of Australia.

I'll never retire John, old mate
This stage I'll never leave
I'll push out another song, old mate
As long as I can breathe
As long as there's a sunrise
I'll always tune me throat
As long as the fish are biting, mate
I'll never leave the boat

Ah that's what it's like to be a country balladeer
It'll never up and leave you lonely
There's nothing new about it
It's like old Uluru
So don't you go changing, mate
I'll thump you if you do

(from 'Aussie Balladeer' © 1994 Emusic Pty Ltd)

Chapter 31

AH THAT'S WHAT IT'S LIKE TO BE A COUNTRY BALLADEER

I'm sure it was my sense of entertainment that got me through the first sixteen years of my career. My original songs weren't that good, apart from 'Old Man Emu', and neither was my voice. Ever since I fell about laughing as a kid at the Deaf and Dumb and Blind charity concerts (as they were called back then) that came to Quambatook I was always aware of the importance of entertainment. I'm sure they only came to small towns like ours in the 1950s. I guess they were the tail end of the vaudeville days: jugglers, acrobats, amusing songs and, best of all, the old comedians. Somebody always did a routine with a selection of hats that were on a small table. Every hat matched up with a silly dance. It was not unlike John Cleese's routine of silly walks. My mates and I couldn't get enough of this kind of thing. Of course we didn't have television in those days and funny movies were rare especially after our weatherboard town hall burnt down. In their own way, these little shows gave me a glimpse of show business and, as Mum was usually involved in some way, I had the opportunity to meet the people in the show afterwards. Mum knew I was really taken in by it all.

When I was nine or ten I became a huge *Goon Show* fan and Spike Milligan's craziness never really leaves me, even today. I also loved every second of Victor Borge, the classical pianist from Denmark who was world famous for his irreverent approach to the classics. What a comedian! His best routine was playing a piece that sounded really weird and then he realised the music was upside down. Classic stuff! My hero, Harry Belafonte, also had a wonderful sense of humour.

I've always enjoyed making humour part of my performance. Make 'em laugh and make 'em cry and make 'em feel good about themselves, I always say. Over the 40-odd years of my career I've tried to add some clowning around. During my pub days in Sydney I delighted in taking off Chad Morgan, becoming Merv Currawong, stock and station agent, using cutout teeth made from a soft plastic ice-cream container. I also wore a turned-up hat with a kilt pin through it to hold the rim up, just like Chad wore. The funny nose helped to disguise me rather than suggesting that it was a Chad nose.

If anyone can write a funny song, it's Chad Morgan. I was first really aware of Chad Morgan in 1965, just after we moved to Croppa Creek. Jim Hanson, Dad's right-hand man, gave me Chad's album *The Sheik of Scrubby Creek*. Well, I immediately loved it, not only for the comedy, but also for the unashamed honesty of it. Chad is Chad; take him or leave him. I'm sure if Chad had been taken seriously he would have written many straight great songs as well. I guess his buckteeth made it hard. But apparently the girls loved him, buckteeth and all. Chad's songs immediately rang

true for me because I'd been brought up in a little country
town where everyone knew everyone else. Chad showed me
that you *can* make a career out of music in Australia without
sounding like an American or changing your accent at all.
If you know Chad, he really does sound like that. I guess after
'Old Man Emu' (which I wrote five years after I first heard
Chad's album) I faced the challenge of using my own accent
with a serious song for a change, such as 'Cootamundra
Wattle'.

Everyone has a story about Chad, especially from his
drinking days. I worked with him in the eighties in Lismore
at a country music festival. He had his own caravan, as usual,
backstage. I have a photo of him standing in the doorway
of the caravan, Chad wearing his trademark country and
western white shirt and string tie, but he has straight teeth.
He's saying to me, 'Y'see John, no one recognises me when
I haven't got my buckteeth in.' I laughed. That was funny
because Chad has a very distinctive voice and is recognisable
with or without his buckteeth! I hope I'm not telling a
secret, but after he lost his original trademark teeth in a road
accident he had two sets of false teeth made, one straight and
one protruding. On one Tamworth Festival Awards night
I joined Chad and sang 'The Sheik of Scrubby Creek' with
him; both of us with false buckteeth.

I've always got on well with Chad as he knows I respect his
extraordinary talent. It's not easy to write good funny songs,
and he's written heaps. On top of that, though, as I found
out in the seventies, no one wanted to listen to Aussie songs
with a natural accent unless it was humorous. Our inferiority
complex was rife back then. I wrote a song for Chad called

'Stoned This Afternoon'. Another one we recorded together is 'A Country Balladeer' which is on my *Chandelier of Stars* album. We recorded that in a hidden studio on the Gold Coast in Queensland. Funny thing, Chad was quite tense until we put a cameraman in the studio with him. That gave him an audience. So the video was also the take for the recording that ended up on the accompanying DVD. He was and still is, to this day, a live performer above all else. He was still doing three little shows a day in Tamworth in January 2013. What a troubadour!

In my own concerts, the humour has to be incidental, otherwise it could take over and my good songs might not be taken seriously. That's why I love to go straight to a sentimental song after a funny one. It keeps the audience awake. It's all about variety and the rule never changes as far as I'm concerned.

♫

People often imagine that Slim Dusty and I were good mates. But the truth is, Slim saw me as competition. I kind of understand why he was like that. The old showground days were dog-eat-dog, with all the country music tents in a row vying for the same walk-in customers. Slim was regarded as the King of Country Music and no one was going to take that from him as far as he and his wife, Joy McKean, were concerned. I've never had trouble with that. In fact, when *Mallee Boy* was outselling Slim's albums by about four times, I happily agreed with him being top billing at any concert where we shared the stage.

I'll never forget the night the Country Music Association of Australia put on a Country Music spectacular at the State Theatre in Sydney in the eighties. I agreed to finish the first half. Slim ended the show. My crew went about setting up our well-organised merchandise table in a good spot in the foyer. Carole Stannard, who was in charge of my shop, told me that Joy and her sister burst their way into the foyer and pushed our table aside as if it was Slim's right and privilege to be there. It underlines the competitive nature of the old showground performers. Carole was stunned.

Mary Kay and I invited Slim and Joy to dinner at our home in Epping in the 1980s but that didn't make me any closer to him. He was actually quite shy. Slim showed me by example that you could make a living singing real Aussie stories, but I have to thank Buddy Williams and Stan Coster as well. The latter wrote 77 songs for Slim, including 'By a Fire of Gidgee Coal' and 'Three Rivers Hotel'.

I continued to pay respect to Slim's status and agreed to record one of the few songs he wrote, 'I Must Have Good Terbaccy When I Smoke', for his tribute album, *Not So Dusty*. I'd already recorded this live on a very early album of my own, *The Smell of Gumleaves*. There were times over the years when I felt Slim did appreciate what I was doing. He came up to me at one of Lawsy's Mongrel Dinners and told me that he really liked my version of his 'Good Terbaccy' song. That was the closest he came to giving me encouragement. Maybe he thought I didn't need it! Do I give up-and-coming artists encouragement? If he or she is on the right track in progressing our own country music culture, you betcha!

Initially I thought Slim would welcome my success as there were, and still are, many American clones out there. When a small group of us decided to form the Country Music Association of Australia we approached Slim to be chairman as it was important to have his name attached to it. However, I was the one who was prepared to speak out publicly about our objections to the direction the awards were taking over the years. Slim never said a word publicly but he was quite riled privately. He would turn in his grave if he knew how American it has now become, in spite of my protests while in the role as president.

♫

I have always given Rolf credit for inspiring me to write 'Old Man Emu' and he subsequently recorded cover versions of 'Old Man Emu' and 'Raining on the Rock'. Then not long after that he asked me join him on stage in Melbourne and Newcastle and play jaw harp during 'Old Man Emu'. I learned a lot from him as a performer. Rolf also illustrated a children's picture book of 'Old Man Emu'. What a shame that such an influential Aussie has fallen from grace; it's hard to believe. It came as a big shock to me.

When I first took my show, band and all, to England, we invited Rolf to jump up on stage with me to sing 'Old Man Emu'. That was fun, even if we did need a shepherd's hook to get him off (just joking).

Rolf had disappointed me some time before that, at the victorious Rugby World Cup celebration in Wales. By the time the Wallabies had reached the final that year, I had become

their good luck charm. I'd sung 'Waltzing Matilda' and the
national anthem at many of their winning games, including
their Bledisloe Cup win in 1998. I'd also recorded 'Number
on My Back' which the team sang in the dressing shed. The
Wallabies were winning all the games when I had a phone
call from Rolf asking what I thought of him joining me in
singing 'Waltzing Matilda' and the anthem at Cardiff. Well,
I was gobsmacked! After all the bonding I'd done with the
Wallabies, here was Rolf trying to jump onto my bandwagon.
I knew straight away that no one would notice that I was
singing the song if Rolf was with me. He was so popular in
England. So I swallowed my pride and said, 'I don't mind
you singing "Waltzing Matilda" with me, but I think I have
earned the gig to sing the Australian national anthem by
myself.' Rolf seemed to take that in his stride. However, come
rehearsal time at the Millennium Stadium at Cardiff Arms
Park and there was his plum-in-the mouth English manager
saying to Phil and me, 'How dare you deny Mr Harris the
chance to sing the Australian anthem!' as though it was his
privilege and our duty to allow him to steal my thunder.
I was disappointed that the Australian Rugby Union couldn't
have had more influence but I guess the International Rugby
Union and the Welsh organisers had the last say.

Rolf and I rehearsed 'Waltzing Matilda' at Cardiff and
when we came to the line 'down came a jumbuck', Rolf let
out the corny bleating sound of a sheep. I said, 'Whoah, Rolf,
Aussies have a lot more respect for our song these days.' He
thanked me for the advice. Maybe in hindsight I should have
let him do it! But then I couldn't be that selfish and, besides,
'Waltzing Matilda' is our greatest Australian song and always

will be, as far as I'm concerned. It's the song that reveres the battler and puts down the squatter. I couldn't allow it to be ruined by Rolf.

I might sound a bit vindictive about this but the Cardiff Arms episode is one of the most disappointing episodes in my career. It really hurt. I could imagine the crowd thinking *Who was the bloke who sang with Rolf Harris?* If they noticed me at all. As far as I know, Rolf Harris wasn't even a rugby follower, let alone a supporter of the Wallabies. And when people ask me now what it was like singing with Rolf Harris at the World Cup, I have to bite my tongue. It's hard to explain. I would have thought that from my association with Rolf over the years he'd have understood what it meant to me. He was very selfish that day.

I must admit I felt a lot better when they played 'Number on My Back' as the victorious World Cup champion Wallabies did their lap of honour around the stadium. But when I went down to the Wallabies' dressing shed after that victory, I couldn't get past the security until one of the team coaches spotted me and told them to let me in. So who should I find in the shed already? Rolf! Soon after that I led the team in singing 'Number on My Back' and I'll never forget one of the Wallabies saying, 'What the fuck is Rolf doing down here?' It was then I realised Rolf Harris and Molly Meldrum had something in common. They were very opportunistic.

In the long run, that was a mere hiccup in a great relationship with the Wallabies. I'm very proud of the letter I have from John Eales, captain of the Wallabies during that time, thanking me for my support of him personally and the Wallabies as a team.

♫

I'm sure it was my success in singing 'Waltzing Matilda' at the rugby that made the Olympic committee think it would be ideal for me to perform it at the opening ceremony of the Sydney Olympic Games in September 2000. Funny, though, they put me on five minutes before 7 p.m., just prior to it being televised worldwide. It was seen by the Aussie audience only. The amazing thing about this was that any artist who sang before 7 p.m. was treated like a second-class performer in comparison with those who performed after 7 p.m. We were noticeably the last to be collected at the end to be driven home. Perhaps Phil Matthews, as my manager, wasn't as forceful as he should have been sometimes. I think if I was a prima donna I would have been treated with more respect, but I'm afraid an ex-farmer finds that bullshit hard to carry out. In the long run I have to be true to myself.

At the rehearsal the night before the opening ceremony, in front of a full house of those who'd missed out on tickets for the real ceremony, I was confident, the crowd joined in singing with me, and I 'killed them' as the saying goes. The big night, however, was a nightmare for me. Everything was the same as for the rehearsal, except my in-ear plugs were turned up much louder. So as I was waiting to go on, I had to turn them down on the pack hooked to my belt. Next thing, Ric Birch, the producer, said, 'You're on.' On I went and started playing my guitar but my sound was off; so I had to stop, turn it up and start again. All the way through the song I felt like crap because I had fumbled. I don't think anyone noticed, and I probably put more into the singing to compensate, but I felt absolutely shithouse afterwards. I felt jinxed.

Often things go wrong at big events when there is just one song to sing. For instance, twice I sang when Paul Keating (the prime minister at the time) was in the audience at special events and both times it was a disaster. The first one was at Parliament House, a tribute to our firefighters. I sang 'True Blue' and my lead wasn't pushed in hard enough into the guitar. This meant the acoustic instrument sounded like a distorted heavy metal guitar and was quite inappropriate. The second time was at an Olympics promotional concert. Everything was set up perfectly at the sound check. But then these bloody dancers were on before me and stomped all over my direct-input box. This meant the guitar didn't play at all through the system. There is nothing worse than sitting on stage like a stuffed monkey waiting for technicians to sort things out. The artist is always the one who looks bad on those occasions. My only performance of the TV music show, *Rockwiz* was also buggered up by a stage crewman who insisted he tune my guitar. Fine, but he handed it to me as I walked on stage, with the capo on the wrong fret so I was in the wrong key. I had to stop briefly and start again.

All these things may not seem a big deal, but the nerves are bad enough on these occasions and technical stuff-ups can throw your concentration out the window. On *Rockwiz* I skipped a whole verse, which threw the band out for several bars. I blew my best chance to expose one of my favourite songs, 'Prairie Hotel Parachilna', to a national audience. Even my performance of 'Raining on the Rock' at the ARIAs in the year I was inducted into the Hall of Fame was messed up. The technician, once again, didn't have my guitar plugged in. I sat there with my guitarist Col Watson, watching him run around the stage, half suggesting that it was my guitar. I let him know over the microphone that it was his fault and not mine. The audience was amused at my coolness, but once again I was dying inside, thinking, *Why does this always happen to me?*

But all we can do is throw a flower on the water
Look for the sun through the rain
Lay a little frangipani gentle on the water
Remember how we loved you

Chapter 32

LAY A LITTLE FRANGIPANI
GENTLE ON THE WATER

Eighty-eight Australians were killed in an Islamist attack on the tourist district of Kuta in Bali on 12 October 2002. The nightclub bombing killed 202 people and a further 240 were injured. Australians were deeply affected. This was terrorism so close to home.

I was deeply honoured when Prime Minister John Howard invited me to sing 'Waltzing Matilda' at the first Bali Memorial Service. Being a great rugby union follower, he was well aware of my performances of the song at the World Cup in 1998 and I'd met him on a number of other occasions, including at Sir Donald Bradman's memorial service. I must admit I wasn't sure if it was the right song for the occasion. But there I was, off to Bali in the Prime Minister's private plane with Phil Matthews. John and Jeanette Howard had their private room. Behind them sat the Leader of the Opposition, Simon Crean, and his wife, Carole, the prime ministerial doctor, the staff, Phil and me. Behind us in the next section were various Air Force personnel. I didn't see much of them until I attempted to take a photo of the television screen that showed how the aircraft deliberately flew around one side of Uluru so the Prime Minister could see it. I thought that was amusing as the picture showed an exaggerated flight path. That's when I was abruptly interrupted. It was entirely inappropriate, for security reasons, for anyone to take photos of the interior of the Prime Minister's plane. It was all a bit embarrassing but it gave the officer a chance to show me who was boss on the plane. I was humbled, but surprised. Simon Crean thought it was a bit over the top. I didn't really mind; it gave me something to talk about later on.

It was a bit cheeky I suppose, but I asked the Prime Minster's chief of staff whether I could spend a moment with Mr and Mrs Howard just to say thank you for the invitation to join them on such a journey. John Howard offered me a scotch and I spent about twenty minutes in their cabin. One of the things he asked me was, 'How's Slim?' I was a bit lost for words with that question. It implied I knew Slim well, which I didn't. I was certainly encouraged by his success in singing all-Australian material and I absolutely respected his standing in the industry. So I said, 'Well, to be quite honest, I don't know how Slim is. He was never very encouraging towards me.' The Prime Minister's immediate response was, 'And how's Lee Kernaghan?' I'm sure that he was subtly suggesting that perhaps I didn't encourage Lee, either. I guess politicians know about competition more than anyone else!

On our first night in Bali, Phil and I shared a dinner table with Simon and Carole Crean. I found them to be very amiable people. Carole Crean struck me as not being at all interested in politics and probably kept Simon firmly rooted in the real world. When I got to know Simon better I thought he was too down to earth to become a prime minister. It's a very tough game.

The following morning we were taken to do a sound check at Garuda Wisnu Kencana Cultural Park, a limestone quarry used as an outdoor amphitheatre, where the Balinese had left huge pillars of limestone like the ruins of an ancient building. High above and behind the stage was an enormous stone phoenix, the Garuda – dinosaur sized. As the crowd of mourners gathered, they laid candles and frangipani on the manmade pond in the foreground. I can't help feeling other's grief at funerals, so I kept out of sight and focused on my job ahead. I don't recall much of the service. I was still unsure that 'Waltzing Matilda' would be appropriate but it was the Prime Minister's choice so that was that.

You couldn't help but feel the overwhelming grief of people fighting to control their emotions during the ceremony. The time finally came for me to sing at the conclusion of the ceremony and that's when their tears flowed like a river. There are not many songs that evoke the essence of our country quite as much as 'Waltzing Matilda'. When we hear the words 'coolibah', 'billabong', 'billy boiled', and 'jumbuck' it spells out so sweetly how unique our country is. On this occasion, it brought the spirit of Australia into that Asian scene as though it had come to take the souls of the Australian victims back home. That's how it felt to the families that day and they were most grateful to me. In turn, I was grateful to John Howard for having such foresight. Before we left the quarry I sang a few more songs to help lift their spirits during the tea and refreshments that were served after the service.

After the ceremony we were quickly whisked away in the official cars. Every street corner had two or three Indonesian policemen stopping the traffic to let us through. At great speed, the cars headed for Kuta Beach. It felt like I was in a movie scene. Once the Prime Minister arrived at the beach another ceremony started; this time it was Balinese style. Canoes filled with pink bougainvillea flowers were paddled out to sea and the flowers were scattered on the water. Aussie surfers also carried the flowers on their surfboards. It couldn't have been more appropriate; the beach was the reason so many Aussies came to Bali in the first place and, of course, to experience the gracious Balinese hospitality. I could feel the healing process had begun. It was inspirational.

After this ceremony the official party was invited to walk past the wreaths, flowers and photos of the victims at the bombsite at the Sari Club. It was here that I read four lines next to a photo and felt that nothing better could be said:

> To hear your voice,
> to see you smile,
> to sit and talk to you a while,
> that would be our greatest wish today.

I thought to myself, *That's the beginning of a song*. With all the things in my mind on that sad day I could feel that this was just the start. Hence 'Flower on the Water' was written. It was first released on the *Chandelier of Stars* album but is also on *In Symphony*, the album I recorded with the Sydney Symphony Orchestra at the Sydney Opera House. The song has struck a chord not only with the families of the victims from the Bali bombings but it is often used at funerals generally. Hardly a week goes by without an email about that song or 'True Blue' being used at a friend's or family member's funeral. I am deeply touched and honoured that my songs can help people in times of sorrow.

Ten years after the bombings, in October 2012, Prime Minister Julia Gillard invited me to sing 'Flower on the Water' at the tenth anniversary memorial service, again in that same limestone quarry in Bali. Once again, the ability to write a song gave me the opportunity to share in the emotions of Australian families and left me with precious memories. I am indeed blessed.

Over the years I have met John Howard many times, as I did again in Bali in October 2012, and we always have a jovial chat. The first time I met him was at The Lodge in 1988, when he was the Leader of the Opposition and Bob Hawke was the incumbent prime minister. Bob and Hazel Hawke had invited a good number of people to celebrate New Year's Eve. The guests were all lined up in the garden to shake Bob's hand and when it came to my turn, Hazel had to tell Bob who I was. She said, 'You know, Bob, "True Blue".' 'Oh, yeah,' he said and didn't even look me in the eye. This was after I had sung 'True Blue' on three separate occasions in the same week, with Bob and Hazel in the front row, to launch the Buy Australia campaign in Sydney, Melbourne and Adelaide. However, when I was introduced to John Howard it was with a firm handshake and a real eye-to-eye contact. Aussies don't forget these things, eh? But don't get the idea that I vote Liberal or Labor or Green. I decide who gets my vote at each election.

Oh see the goanna up the gum tree
He's gonna get a feed today free
When the campers leave the lake
Bits of chook and choccy cake
It's Christmas time for him as well
See his big long belly swell

Oh it's December in Australia

(from 'Christmas Photo' © 1990 Emusic Pty Ltd)

Chapter 33

OH IT'S DECEMBER
IN AUSTRALIA

Christmas in the Mallee for me was just a wonderful family get-together with a cold chook and soft drinks. I can still hear the sounds of joy that rang out under the swamp box and river gums. I wonder if those huge mock orange trees are still there? Funny, the things you remember. I've not seen that kind of tree since. Our mob weren't drinkers in that generation but as kids, we didn't know what that meant. So I suspect there might have been a few beers hidden in car boots so Grandma and Grandpa didn't see. The goanna verse in the song 'Christmas Photo' is a recollection of those Mallee days in summer. My mother always had to get a family photo of these occasions. Such photos weren't really appreciated until years later.

Later on, many of our Christmas family gatherings were in Goondiwindi where Mary Kay's parents lived. They had a huge backyard and a clay tennis court. The big yard was ideal for a game of cricket with all the kids, the nieces and nephews, of which there were many. So being the camera enthusiast in the family, I took my mum's role in capturing that Christmas photo.

When I came up with the idea for the 'Christmas Photo' song it was a combination of the nostalgia of Christmas in the Mallee and the big gatherings at Goondiwindi. I thought all I'd have to do was get as many of the family as I could into the recording studio at Annandale in Sydney and actually take a photo. Unbeknown to them, we had microphones open so all the typical banter that went on at Christmas happened naturally. It was one of the best recording triumphs I've had. Every family nickname in the song is real. The whole family has nicknames that are used more than their real names.

I'm proud of 'Christmas Photo'. For me, the song is about celebrating a summer Christmas, as we do in Australia, instead of singing 'Jingle Bells' and songs about snow and sleighs. You might have noticed – I never tire of underlining what it is to be Australian. Aren't we lucky?

The song 'Christmas Photo' is how I came to meet Meg Doyle. As senior editor for the children's book publisher Scholastic Australia, she chose the song from my repertoire as an ideal Christmas picture book for kids in 1998. The book was retitled *Christmas in Australia*. Shamefully, I wasn't all that excited about the project at the time. I thought it was a nice little money-spinner, I suppose, but nothing compared to a hit album of songs. I was so disinterested, or blasé, I don't even remember meeting Meg when I was invited to Scholastic to see the finished product. Who knows what was going on in my mind? I suspect her immediate boss took most of my attention as he was a bit of a wanker. However, it was me, it seems, who Meg thought was the wanker.

Ken Jolly, the managing director of Scholastic, invited me on the New South Wales Variety Bash to promote the book.

Ken was not only a car enthusiast, but a great philanthropist and supporter of Variety. The company had been involved in the Bash for a number of years, taking a selected team of staff along for the ride in an old Thames school bus.

My friend and philanthropist Dick Smith started the Bash. He's an amazing ideas man. Back in 1985 he came up with this great way to extract dollars from car enthusiast mates who wouldn't normally venture onto outback bush tracks. He approached people like John Singleton, John Farnham, and others who were both well known and well off. He charged them money to come along and called it 'a drive in the bush with your mates'. They drove from Sydney to Bourke in far-west New South Wales and then to Burketown in the Gulf of Carpentaria. That first Bash raised about $250 000 and the money was donated to Variety, the Children's Charity (known as the Variety Club at the time).

That was the start of the New South Wales Variety Bash. The participants were fined for just about anything, even though they'd paid to go, and bribery became a big part of the event. Since that first one, 'the Bash', as it has become affectionately known, has attracted people from all walks of life and has raised in excess of $173 million for special-needs children in Australia. Now there is a minimum entry fee per car (currently set at $8500). Some people struggle to find this and rely on fundraising activities: from lamington drives and sausage sizzles to golf days and harbour cruises ... you name it, anything goes. These people are the real heart of what it means to be a 'Basher' nowadays. Having said that, there are generous millionaires, businessmen and philanthropists who wouldn't miss the Bash each year; philanthropists like Dick Smith. That's the great beauty of the occasion. Everybody is equal on the dusty roads as the old cars travel over horrendous potholes and rocky terrain, and through creeks and slippery mud.

Phil Matthews thought it was a great idea for me to go on the Bash. He and Scholastic came up with the idea for me to perform a concert for the children of Nyngan in central New South Wales and the surrounding district. It would be filmed for a video. This meant that I had to fly ahead of the cars to get set up for the concert in the early evening. Ken bribed Variety with a considerable amount of money to be the first car out at the start but then he and I transferred to a hire car and drove to the airport.

That night was one of the most difficult performances I have ever been a part of. Kids are fine for a few songs and I do have a number of 'family' songs, but Phil had me doing an hour-and-a half show. I was thoroughly out of my comfort zone and I think a lot of the young audience was too. The kids were stuck for that time, sitting cross-legged on the floor of the hall and the usual restlessness, fidgeting and wanting to go to the bathroom was evident to me. I've watched the video once and have since tipped several hundred of them into the council dump. What a shocker! I'll never agree to do a concert solely for kids again.

Meg Doyle had been selected to go on the Bash with Scholastic. She had to dress up as Miss Frizzle, the science teacher in the *Magic School Bus* series of books. She thought I was too full of myself to drive to Nyngan, not realising how complicated my day was. That first night in Nyngan, Meg was the only one who didn't make a fuss of me; she sat in the background, watching. While I was basically unaware of her, she was beginning to realise that maybe I wasn't just a wanker, but a wanker who'd been put through the ringers that night.

The next day I was on the Magic School Bus. My first Bash. It was amazing, bumping along the roughest dirt roads, past stations, towards Thargomindah, through the real 'sticks': the gidgee, mulga and myall country. The first day on the bus I did what typical Scorpios do and sat and observed. Who was I going to like enough to spark up a conversation with? There were only eight of us on the bus and we had to spend a fair bit of time together. It wasn't long before I reasoned that the only one I could be bothered with was that dark-haired, intelligent, quiet one: Miss Frizzle.

The bus stopped a number of times that day whenever we saw kids. I remember we stopped for three great little station kids waiting at their mailbox, watching the cars with their crazy character passengers go by. This was the kind of performance I could handle. I sang one song, 'Old Man Emu', and they couldn't believe it. By the end of the day those kids would have experienced a show they couldn't buy and ended up with caps, lollies, show bags, footballs, teddy bears and badges from the passing cars. It was like Christmas for them. What a great idea this Bash was. I was loving it!

The next day, after one of our stops, I boldly plonked myself on the bench seat where Meg had been sitting, next to the window. I took out my writing pad and started to work on a song. Miss Frizzle climbed back on board the bus and was quite taken aback.

'Your sitting in my seat,' she said.

'Well, you'll just have to sit next to me,' I replied. Which she did, much to my delight. I could tell by her persona that she was also a Scorpio. It's hard to explain, but there's an intensity in a Scorpio woman that has always been unmistakable to me: a fire, a quiet intelligence. In astrology I've read that Scorpios observe things from a distance, then go under a rock to figure it all out before making a decision. Meg's way of observing me was typical Scorpio behaviour.

'You're a Scorpio, aren't you?' I said. She was born almost exactly ten years after me in November. I could tell she was thinking, *God, there's more to this wanker than I realised.* She admitted she was a Scorpio and so our friendship started. I penned my song 'Thargomindah' on the bus while I was sitting with her; she told me that she was impressed that I could write a song as we toured through the bush. I started to break down her hard Scorpion shell. It's difficult for me not to go on about my love of the bush. I described most of the species of trees out there and what the land was used for and started to open the eyes of a girl brought up on Sydney's North Shore. By the end of that long day we were chatting like old mates.

I'm not trying to write a romantic novel here, but several days later Meg told me that I smelt nice. That's the sweetest thing a lady had ever said to me. In my career I've received many lovely compliments but that went deep.

For the rest of my time on the Bash we found ourselves in the breakfast queue together and were generally rarely apart. It felt so natural to be in each other's company. At Charleville I lent her a pair of thick socks to keep her feet warm as we sat on a bench outside the motel rooms. I would have kissed her then but there were too many people around who knew us and anyway, neither of us would allow it to go any further out of respect for our respective partners. But I knew I would never forget Meg Doyle and I was sure she felt the same way.

The night before I flew back to Sydney we went for an evening walk through the lonely, empty streets of Longreach while the rest of the Scholastic crew had a motel room party. We were like two teenagers not really knowing how to behave. We returned to the party and comments were made that we were in love. Ten years would pass before we gave in to this truth. Meg thought I had forgotten about her.

Meg never really left my mind after I left the Variety Bash in Longreach. It was as though I had known her for a long time. We felt so natural together. Back in Sydney I kept seeing women who reminded me of Meg. One day she came to my office to get a signature on a piece of artwork from the picture book for Scholastic. It was pretty obvious there was a natural connection between us that couldn't be ignored. That was a happy and sad moment for both of us. I know Phil Matthews noticed it.

After that I rang her at Scholastic a few times, discreetly. After all, she was my editor. The friendship was a bit hard on Meg because it was all on my terms. She never had my phone number, as I was afraid she might ring at the wrong time. She accepted that. Understandably, Mary Kay wasn't very happy about the phone calls and eventually demanded that I stop calling Meg. I left a message on Meg's work answering machine, after hours, saying that we were being silly keeping in contact and were never going to get more involved even though the feelings were there. I had to be cruel to Meg so

I could say to Mary Kay, without lying, that I'd stopped calling Meg. It was the only way to convince Mary Kay that I meant what I'd promised. Meg had no way of talking me out of it if she'd wanted to. There were no lingering goodbyes. I had a feeling Meg would have thrown away the socks I gave her in Charleville after that (and I was right).

A few years later Meg turned up with her partner at one of my Sydney shows and nothing had changed. I almost felt sorry for him because he could see the electricity between us as we talked again briefly. Phil Matthews had said to me earlier backstage, 'You know, Meg Doyle's out there'. Phil had seen before how she affected me.

And that's how it was until late 2005 when I was asked to sing at the Variety Children's Christmas party at Darling Harbour. I knew Meg had gone on to become more involved with Variety so I couldn't help but ask if she was around. Sure enough, I spotted her from at least 150 metres away. I hadn't forgotten her walk. Not really knowing what I was doing next, I boldly caught up with her and gave her that kiss I'd missed out on, back in Longreach. Meg was shocked but didn't back away. As she walked with me to the table where I was signing autographs she told me she thought I'd forgotten about her. 'Hardly,' I told her.

Well, that was the new beginning of sorts but Meg still didn't get my phone number. I called very infrequently in the next twelve months. One time was the day before her birthday in November. It was still only a love affair of the mind as I searched for love in Mary Kay's eyes.

I really didn't want to leave Mary Kay but I was very unhappy. Maybe she could always see me leaving her, who knows, but had she declared her love for me any time, maybe things would have been different. For years I would tell her that I loved her, and her answer was always, 'Yes, I know.'

I often went up to Springbrook on my own, as Mary Kay didn't enjoy the bush. I bought a house on the Isle of Capri at Surfers Paradise to at least get her to come to Queensland. I used to make her breakfast and go up to the farm in the hinterland most days until dinner, just like a farmer would. At the end of 2006 I started to ring Meg again, especially when I was at Springbrook.

I couldn't take the unhappiness in my marriage any longer and finally decided to ring Mary Kay and tell her when she was at Goondiwindi with her mother. There was no answer, so I sent a long letter by fax instead. In hindsight, that was a terrible way to end my marriage. A few days later we were face to face in Epping. I cried until I was out of breath. Thirty-seven years is a long time. There was such tension inside me. But it was mainly a deep sadness, as I had always believed we would be grandparents together. Mary Kay said nothing to indicate she didn't want me to go and didn't cry at all. She moved towards me to give me a hug but I rejected her, thinking, *It's all too late for affection now.*

A few weeks later, Meg was going to be in Brisbane visiting a sick friend and I invited her to my concert at the Twelfth Night Theatre. After the show that night, Steve Newton, my sound engineer, said to me, 'Do you know there's a woman in a red dress climbing into your ute?' I said, 'Who the hell do you think gave her the keys?' That is now regarded as our anniversary. We were married on the same day, 10 March, six years later in 2013 in Sydney.

We wanted a small private wedding with our closest friends and family and the setting of Mark and Caroline Jago's garden couldn't have been more perfect. Meg and I were married at their beautiful bush paradise home on a sandstone ridge, tucked away between two national parks above the Northern Beaches of Sydney.

I don't regret my thirty-seven years with Mary Kay, but I guess I wanted more out of life than what was on offer. I found myself being held back. I found myself being forced to 'act my age', to be old and over it. I felt like I still had a lifetime ahead of me. In fact, in the last seven years with Meg, more interesting things have happened to me than I could have imagined. I have proved that life can really begin in your sixties. Call me selfish, but as far as I know you get one chance only.

My relationship with Phil Matthews was definitely getting tired too. Between my marriage and my long-time manager, it felt like I was being slowed down against my will. I was being persuaded that I was past it. Meg came into my life and made me realise that I had a lot left in the tank.

At this stage my career was in limbo. Phil had retired and left me with an organisation that had collapsed. I had to fire the woman he'd hired because she was a complete disaster. Marius Els stepped in as my agent. My own staff had done all my bookings for decades up to this point. Then ... enter David Woodward, who had been hired by EMI around that same time as a freelance publicist for my 2008 album *Hillbilly Road*. David was making a name for himself in Tamworth where he was employed to work on the Country Music Festival. He seemed to appear quite often from then on, just doing whatever he could for me. I wondered whether he had another agenda in the long term, but I didn't mind if he did. David and Meg and I got on famously and we became friends. So when the time came, it was David who immediately sprang to mind as someone who might like to manage me.

David, now in his mid-thirties, was born to manage. Public relations are his forte. Anyone he contacts never forgets his personal charm whether it's face-to-face or over the phone. Born and raised in Newcastle, he has an inbuilt toughness that he disguises very well, so he is ideal for almost any task an artist needs. He has become very much a part of our family. He is also incredibly generous with his time. Nothing is too much to ask of him and his favourite expression is 'Leave it to me'. David has played a big part in bringing me out of the doldrums, with Meg by my side.

♫

When Meg and I decided to live together in 2007 the media was rather determined to make it all public. I had a corporate gig lined up about half an hour from Alice Springs, at Ooraminna on Deep Well Station, owned by Billy and Jan Hayes. Bill and Jan had agreed some years earlier to let Ted Egan build a small mock-up bush village on Ooraminna for a movie to be made of his song 'Drover's Boy'. Ooraminna was a thousand acres that had been separated off from Deep Well and developed by Billy and Jan as a tourist venture. I was first introduced to Billy and Jan in 1999 when we returned to Undoolya to do some video clips for a couple of the songs on *The Way It Is* album. Billy was Jim Hayes's brother, from the song 'Three Sons'. The movie didn't eventuate but the village remained and was ideal for corporate events, weddings and functions. I had done a corporate gig there previously as well as using it as the setting for a number of song film clips including 'A Thousand Feet' with Warren H Williams. Bill and Jan worked tirelessly at making it a highly successful tourist venue.

In light of the media attention, Phil thought the perfect solution was for Meg to escape to Ooraminna with me. Jan was so supportive and we figured we would be well out of reach of the media. But even there, a local journalist and a photographer turned up under the pretense of interviewing me for a story about my songwriting. Their real intention was to at least get a photo of Meg and me together. We were wise to them. Jan very quickly told them that their future in Alice would not be bright if they didn't clear off, which they did. Such is the respect the Hayes family commands in the area.

Over the years, Billy and Jan became great friends to us both. We often stayed in one of the little cottages there, surrounded by nature's sculptures of flint stone. There is evidence of Aboriginal occupation everywhere if you know what to look for. The broken flint was ideal for making spearheads and knives. This was where I had also taken Lawsy in December 2006. It was the end of the station bed-and-breakfast trip we went on together. When I was there with Lawsy I built a permanent stock camp utilising a huge square rock and a few steel posts. It is still there under a coolibah tree. Billy called it 'Emu's Camp'.

Billy was the most uncomplicated true bushie. He used to stir me about 'Rip Rip Woodchip', or 'Chip Chip Woodchip' as he called it. But deep down he completely understood my love of the Australian bushland. He was deeply attached to his country; as deep as the Eastern Aranda mob were. Billy had a great relationship with the traditional owners and a quiet respect for them. They still wandered over Deep Well Station. Billy didn't say much about that. Some of his white mates probably didn't understand his association with them and I respected him for it.

The last time Meg and I were out there, Jan and Billy had Ooraminna up for sale. They wanted to take life a little easier. Bush couples like Billy and Jan bond together, I believe, like no others. On a big station you have to pull together through hard times and enjoy each other's company. Partnerships out there have to be strong to survive. We had a wonderful time as usual on that visit and thoroughly enjoyed Billy's sense of humour. It had become a habit for us to spend a night around the fire at Emu's Camp with Jan and Billy, sharing a steak and a few beers and wine. Billy cooked it on the campfire that night.

Tragically, Billy, a legendary horseman and the inspiration behind Murray Hartin's poem 'Turbulence', died a few days after that. He was out on his quad bike, mustering cattle with his son, Billy Junior. He was in his element tearing around the scrub on the modern-day horse. Sadly, quads don't have eyes like a horse does and Billy didn't see the deep washaway in the grass. The quad dived into the gully and threw Billy into the air. He came down and broke his neck. He died instantly. Jan's soulmate was gone. We were devastated for Jan. It still brings tears to my eyes to think about it. Billy was absolutely true blue and his death was a loss to this country.

Meg and I returned to Alice Springs for Billy's funeral. The Alice Springs Convention Centre was filled to overflowing. Both white and Indigenous people from all over the country came to pay their respects to Billy, and his great family. At the conclusion of the public service, Jan asked us to attend the burial with the family. The small procession led by Billy's horse was heart wrenching. I offered a poem. It was based on the idea that Billy was always happiest out on the station chasing cattle. He died doing what he loved. We will always treasure both Billy and Jan's friendship.

One of the best things I have learnt through Meg is to treasure friendship. Meg is the kind of person who rarely loses contact with a friend. She has so many. In my previous life there didn't seem to be time for many friends outside of family. Weekends, when mates generally get together, have always been my work time. But Meg has taught me the joy of having good mates. I now keep in touch with more of them, new and old, like never before. I guess I am a bit like my dad; he was never one to socialise. It was always up to Mum. The invention of text messages on phones has to be the best thing for keeping in touch. I like to send a photo as well. We should never take for granted how wonderful man is at coming up with new ideas to bring the world closer together. And it's so good to be in love again. Meg is not just my wife, she is a partner in life.

Three Sons

I'm into cattle, my father was too
From great great grandfather all the way through
And we scarcely have wasted an hour of daylight
Stickin' to Herefords and it's been all right
Prepared for the lean times and save for a drought
But you can't always plan how the future turns out
Life's gettin' harder to make what we need
With low cattle prices and more mouths to feed

Oh, six generations where camels run free
I hope I am never too blind to see
How fortunate, how proud can an old fella be
Three sons in their swags 'round the stock camp with me

Sent the boys off to school to see Adelaide
How other folks live, get a job learn a trade
Couldn't keep them away 'cause their hearts are still here
My butcher, my welder, my diesel engineer

And I come in for dinner, the sun hits the range
In a matter of seconds the colours all change
From gold down to violet the soul has been burned
And I understand fully why they have returned

Cause I'm into cattle, my father was too
From great great grandfather all the way through
And we've never been guilty of wasting daylight
We work hard, we play hard and we sleep well at night

You don't wanna be a Basher
'Cause you might fall in love
With the freedom you will feel in the desert
With the friendship you will find
As the dusty roads unwind
Yeah, beware you might fall in love

You don't wanna be a Basher
It'll hook you line and sinker
You'll be grinning like a kid on a swing
You'll be keen as mustard
Even when you're busted
On the CB radio you'll sing

I'm a Basher I'm a Basher
A dirt and gravel thrasher
Driving through the bush for the children
What a way to go-o, she'll be righteoh-oh
All around the country we love

Chapter 34

AS THE DUSTY ROADS UNWIND

In 2008, Meg was to do her tenth Variety Bash. After that first one in 1998, she bought her own car, a 1962 Valiant, and took an all-female crew for the next eight years from 2000 onwards. It was a huge achievement and I told her I'd come with her on her tenth Bash, to celebrate her achievement and because the Bash had played a large part in us eventually coming together. I ended up being completely hooked on it and we continue to do them together now.

The experiences Meg and I have had together and the people we've met through the Bash are priceless memories. On the way back from the 2012 Variety Bash, which went from Balmain to Bamaga (the top of Cape York Peninsula, the most northern point of Australia), we stopped overnight in Coen. Coen is a small town, with a population of around 250, on the main road to Cape York and about 550 kilometres north-west of Cairns. After the Bash finished in Bamaga, we all had to find our way back home either by driving all the way or loading our car on a truck at Cairns. Accommodation in Coen was completely booked out by Bashers, as it was a reasonable distance from the 'Tip' for the first day southbound. We had trouble with the car air-conditioner and found an old character in Coen to fix what he thought was wrong with it. It then lasted most of the way back to Cairns.

That night in Coen, word had got around that I might sing a few songs at the local pub. It was called the Exchange Hotel but someone had climbed onto the roof, meddled with the sign, renaming it the Sexchange Hotel. This was highly amusing to tourists and I'm sure the sign will remain in its altered state. Ad-lib performances of this kind are typically the hardest gigs to do because there is absolutely no preparation. I eventually plucked up the courage and Meg and I snuck into the beer garden, with guitar in hand. There were a couple of seats kept for us at a table with JPY (John Paul Young), another regular Basher. The pub was packed. There was nowhere else to spend the evening in town. There was no backing out now. So I grabbed a bar stool and placed myself in a prominent position. With no sound system it would have been impossible if I hadn't told them quite strongly that they would have to shut up or they wouldn't hear me. Otherwise I'd go. Fortunately they all went quiet and I went straight into 'Mallee Boy'. It worked surprisingly well without a microphone. I then thought 'Crocodile Roll' would go down well, considering the number of local Indigenous drinkers who were there. It was going brilliantly when the idiot overweight publican decided to steal my thunder by appearing in drag. This was obviously his regular party trick. Naturally this instantly cruelled my performance of 'Crocodile Roll' and pissed me right off. It doesn't matter how small the show is, no entertainer can stand someone jumping on the bandwagon when you've done the hard work of capturing the audience's attention. The dickhead soon realised that I wasn't amused and disappeared back behind the bar.

I managed to get the crowd's attention again by getting JPY to join me and sing his hit 'Love Is in the Air'. JPY produced a chord chart and I accompanied him on my guitar. Nothing like a bit of improvisation! A few more songs, then I said I wanted to sing a couple of songs for the black fellas there. I heard some of the city Bashers take a huge deep breath, thinking that I was being politically incorrect, but I knew what I was doing. So I sang 'A Thousand Feet' and 'Raining on the Rock'. The young Indigenous fellas were so thankful they put on quite a show with their traditional dancing in return.

An old black bushman asked me to sing 'Granny's Little Gunyah'. I couldn't believe it. I was so annoyed with myself for not being able to sing it without going over it. Obviously, Billy and Dawn Jackson, who inspired the song, were well known and respected by the local mobs. So, in spite of being upstaged briefly by the ungracious publican, it was one of those very memorable Bash experiences and one that our Bash mates won't forget in a hurry.

Variety and the Bash have become an important part of our lives together. The Bash takes us to amazing destinations around Australia while supporting an immensely important cause. I've written two songs about the Bash since I've been with Meg. The first one was a bit of fun, mainly about the volunteer mobile workshop boys who get us back on the road and I didn't record it. The other, 'I'm a Basher', is on *The Big Red*.

♫

Like most well-known artists, I've been inundated over the years with requests for help or donations from charities and individuals. It's just not been possible to support every one of them so I've focused on those that I am most passionate about. When Bob Brown contacted me from Tasmania with his vision for the Bush Heritage Fund I thought it was a great idea. I'd been wishing I could buy some brigalow land just to protect it. Bush Heritage Australia, as it is now known, acquires or buys areas of Australian bush that are of significant conservation value and then manages the land to ensure it remains that way. With limited funds, the purchases must be carefully assessed for their value. Land that includes endangered species of flora and fauna is a priority. After the release of the *Warragul* album I worked out what my song 'Rip Rip Woodchip' had earned as one of the tracks. I decided to donate that money to three causes: the Koala Preservation Society Australia in Port Macquarie, the Malleefowl Preservation Group in Western Australia and to Bush Heritage. To the latter, I sent off $10 000, which was quite an encouraging sum of money in the eighties. Bob Brown was very pleased, as you can imagine. I'm proud to have been in a position to help at the beginning.

The friends of Bush Heritage began to build in numbers and now it is a fund that has become a significant player in Australian conservation. Sometimes people generously bequeath land in their will. If it is not overly special to Bush Heritage, they can put a conservation order on the bush areas and then resell it to raise money for far more important projects. Over the years, the purchases have been quite significant and will go a long way towards preserving our precious wildlife and bush. It's just one of the things Bob Brown can pat himself on the back for.

Some state governments will offer rate cuts if you register your land as heritage, but I don't trust them. Firstly, they'll often add your land to their list of areas that can't be developed as if it's their own contribution, giving them green credentials. Also they are known to completely abolish laws and promises made by previous governments, so Bush Heritage is the answer for me.

It astounds me how many Australians treat Bob Brown with suspicion and suspect him of being a communist. He has indirectly and directly been responsible for saving a lot of Australia in its pristine state. Our grandchildren will thank him for it. Bob Brown is a true hero. A braver man than I.

Give the man a uniform
Give the man a gun
He's your younger brother
He's your only son

This is Gallipoli
They coulda been ya mates
They coulda been me

Ya can't blame a bloke who likes adventure
He saw the posters on the wall
See the world through the sights of a rifle
Grab ya mates and go to war

And give the man a bayonet
Give the man a hat
Land him on the beaches
Eight thousand never came back

(from 'Diggers of the Anzac (This is Gallipoli)' © 1982 Emusic Pty Ltd)

Chapter 35

LAND HIM ON THE BEACHES, EIGHT THOUSAND NEVER CAME BACK

Anzac Day, it seems, has become a more significant day for many Australians than Australia Day. Why? Maybe because it defines our character as a nation. Australia Day, when the English claimed this country as their own, has lost some of its power because many of us are now more aware of what that day means to the Aborigines. Nevertheless, Australia Day always offers me an opportunity to sing about what Australia means to me, and that's great. Every one of my shows is like Australia Day, really.

Anzac Day is such an emotional experience. It's hard not to get teary as the sun comes up and while the bugle plays 'The Last Post'. It's about much more than just remembering Gallipoli. It's about remembering the sacrifice of so many young Australian men who sailed off, full of brave spirit, to endure the hell of war. It's a day when a cloud of quiet reverence swamps large crowds who come together to remember. We should not forget the contribution of the women as well.

The hundredth anniversary of Gallipoli is in 2015. I've agreed to do five shows on a cruise that follows the route of our Diggers, leaving from Fremantle in Western Australia and ending in Suvla Bay at Gallipoli for Anzac Day. I guess while I'm still at the top of my performance ability these invitations will keep coming. At the moment it seems my shows keep getting better. I hope I'll keep learning until I can't play or sing anymore.

'True Blue' has become a song that soldiers really relate to. 'Hey true blue, don't say you've gone' seems to be the line that says it all on such occasions as Anzac Day. When I wrote it, I was referring to the fair dinkum, honest, hard-working character of the Aussie. But people have taken the line more literally to mean 'don't say you've died'. I don't mind either way. I'm very proud that it has strong meaning for so many people.

I've sung at the Dawn Service at Currumbin Beach in Queensland a number of times over the years. It's held at Elephant Rock, a prominent landform jutting out into the ocean, just north of the New South Wales–Queensland border. Surfboats line the shore as a reminder of the troops landing at Gallipoli, and then they play a role in taking veterans' ashes out to sea. There is quite an eerie atmosphere as the sun comes up over the ocean. It's astounding how the crowd has built up over the years to about 10 000 people now. Channel Seven's *Sunrise* television show broadcasts the service nationally to about half a million viewers and it would be one of the most moving Dawn Services in Australia.

The Dawn Service at Anzac Hill in Alice Springs is another special one. However, it is the Dawn Service at Bomana War Cemetery just outside of Port Moresby in Papua New Guinea that I will remember the most. In 2012 I was invited to sing at the Kokoda seventieth anniversary dinner in the State Dining Room of Parliament House in Port Moresby. I was also asked to sing at the conclusion of the Dawn Service at Bomana War Cemetery just outside Port Moresby. Matt Andreatta, my sound man, and Col Watson, my guitarist, were flown in for the night as well. The dining room was adorned with the most magnificent local orchids. It was quite a night with guests of honour the Prime Minister of Papua New Guinea Mr Peter O'Neill, and his wife, and the Australian High Commissioner Ian Kemish and his wife, Roxanne Martens. Many of the guests that night were local Papuans and the song that got the best reaction that night was 'Crocodile Roll'. Especially the pig verse!

There are more Australian soldiers buried at Bomana than at any other war cemetery in the world; some 3823 servicemen, including about 700 unnamed soldiers. The year 2012 marked the seventieth anniversary of the Kokoda campaign, where Australian soldiers battled extraordinary conditions on the most rugged mountainous terrain to finally defeat the Japanese some 40 kilometres from Port Moresby. There were four veterans from the 39th Battalion present on the day, so it was a proud moment for me to sing for them and to chat with them afterwards. As the notes from the bugle were being played, the mist gradually lifted from the graves' white head stones. The atmosphere was hauntingly beautiful. The family of Private Frank Archibald, an Aboriginal solider who was buried at Bomana, had come to sing his spirit home and I was honoured when they asked me to sing at his graveside for them. I sang 'A Thousand Feet' which felt very appropriate.

I have never felt the urge to walk the Kokoda Trail as many Aussies of all ages do, in increasing numbers. I don't have a good back so I'm sure I would become a burden. But I was fortunate to see the incredible challenge the young soldiers faced while carrying packs and rifles when Meg and I were driven to Owers Corner, which marks the end of the trail, some 50 kilometres from Port Moresby. On the way to Owers Corner, Jim Stillman, one of the 39th Battalion veterans, recognised one of the simple buildings by the roadside, so we stopped and got out. The local family was only too pleased to let me take photos of Jim sitting in front of their basic home. The family was probably related to the fuzzy wuzzy angels, the local Papua New Guineans who helped the injured Australian soldiers during the battle with the Japanese. It's hard to imagine what the fate of the villagers might have been if the Australians had not stopped the Japanese more than seventy years ago.

Our time in Papua New Guinea turned out to be far more than we expected. Air Niugini, our hosts for the trip, were keen to make a fuss of us, thinking, I suppose, that I would spread the word about the country's potential as a tourist destination. Glenn Armstrong, Business Development Manager for Air Niugini, was given licence to provide Meg and I with what we wanted, and to their delight, the opportunity for us to spend a week getting to see some of the country seemed too good to pass up. And they proved to me that it is a wonderful place and its future is bright.

On our arrival at Jacksons Airport in Port Moresby we were quickly whisked away to a media conference and warmly welcomed by Australian High Commissioner His Excellency

Ian Kemish and the CEO of Air Niugini, Mr Wasantha Kumarasiri. I must admit I felt as though our hosts had exaggerated our importance but tried to remain calm, as though I was used to this kind of thing. What saved the day for me was that Meg was becoming quite emotional. She had spent three-and-a half years in Papua New Guinea as a young teenager. Her father had established the Port Moresby branch of the T&G Insurance Company. But more importantly he had been on the Kokoda Trail during the Second World War. As if that wasn't enough to impress, Papua New Guinea's Permanent Representative (Ambassador) to the United Nations in New York was Robert Aisi, a long-standing and close friend of Meg and her family. When he was a teenager at school in Armidale in the Northern Tablelands of New South Wales, Rob spent a great deal of his school holidays living with Meg's family in Sydney and he's like a brother to her. So I was quite relieved to pass the baton onto Meg who was emotional as she revealed her fond connections with the country. It was almost as if Meg had become the Queen and I was the hanger-on prince. That suited me fine. I knew very little about the country at that stage.

At that meeting we also met Justin Tkatchenko, a delightful person and quite a character. Justin was born in Australia but had obviously taken to the country like a bull to a paddock of lucerne. Always dressed in a floral shirt like a real estate salesman on the Gold Coast in the sixties (gold bracelet and all), Justin couldn't do enough for us. It turned out, in Papua New Guinea he was known as the Happy Gardener because of the TV show *The PNG Gardener* that he had hosted for many years. An orchid enthusiast, he also owned the PNG National Orchid Garden. Everywhere we went, he was recognised by the locals and several young local men shadowed us as 'security' and I'm sure they would have died for him. Even when we sat at a restaurant, his boys would eat with us. They were like family to him and we enjoyed having them around and hearing their stories. Of course, their presence made it obvious that it's not advisable to just wander off on your own in certain parts of Port Moresby.

Glenn and Justin took us to Rabaul and Kokopo, on East New Britain. Rabaul itself was fascinating, having been almost totally covered in ash as a result of the eruption of the volcanoes Tavurvur and Vulcan in 1994. The villas at our resort at Kokopo had breathtaking views over the water and the mighty volcanoes in the distance. One night after dinner they encouraged me to borrow a guitar and join the small local band playing at the bar. Firstly the guitar had to be restrung before I could attempt to play it, but it was still barely in tune. But when I sat with the band I realised that everything they played was in the same key. I tried to get them to understand that it would be better if I played 'Raining on the Rock' on my own. That went completely over their heads. So I tried to sing it in their key to their rhythm. It was a disaster from my point of view, but the other guests seemed to still enjoy it. Not my best performance but a funny one nevertheless.

We also visited an underground hospital that the Japanese had dug into the side of a hill. We had to crouch over to get through the tunnels, and the mustiness and eeriness of the place was absolutely remarkable stuff. It was obvious the Japanese meant business and were determined to work their way south to get to Australia. But it was Admiral

Yamamoto's bunker that convinced me just how close we came to being in the hands of the Japanese. The bunker is normally locked, but we gained access to thanks to Glenn and Justin's local connection. The bunker revealed a rough map of the northern coast of Australia drawn on the low ceiling. What an experience that was for us.

It's trips like the one to Papua New Guinea that make me really appreciate how my career has taken me to extraordinary places and given me the opportunity to meet with some wonderful people, many of whom become lasting friends. We left Papua New Guinea with a sense of hope for the country and a lasting impression of friendliness and generous hospitality. Meg and I plan to return to Papua New Guinea to visit more remote places. Justin told us he was intending to stand for a place in the upcoming government elections. And guess what? He is now the Minister for Sports and National Events.

On the few Anzac Days that I haven't played a role by singing 'Waltzing Matilda' or 'True Blue', I like to go to the Dawn Service in Martin Place in Sydney and then down to The Rocks for a two-up pub crawl where there are probably at least twenty games being played in that area alone. Our early Diggers played two-up and with that in mind, it's played in good spirit. It's the only day in Australia that the gambling game can be played legally on the street. Some spill over onto the footpath outside the pubs, so you have to be early to get anywhere near the game these days. I nearly always bet on tails because I'm definitely fonder of the kangaroo than I am the Queen.

Some people see Anzac Day as a celebration of war, but it's far from it, I reckon. To me it is more a reminder of the futility of war. And there is everything right in celebrating

the bravery and courage of our Diggers. It is important for
future Australian soldiers to have in their hearts the legend of
the brave Diggers. We never know when that bravery will be
called on again.

♪

I've had many letters and emails from soldiers, mainly
from blokes, and in more recent years from those serving in
Iraq and Afghanistan in particular. They often tell me how
comforting my music is to them, so far from home and their
family and friends. It's made me feel quite proud that my
music has meant so much to them. I always reply to their
emails. Often their stories touch me quite deeply. I long to
hear that they've returned safely, but as we all know only too
well, they sometimes don't. I've been told that 'True Blue' is
often sung at soldiers' funerals.

In late 2007 I was asked if I would sing at Matthew
Locke's funeral in Perth. Matthew was our first Australian
soldier to be killed in Afghanistan. If it's possible for me to do
so I won't turn down such a request. That day of Matthew's
funeral I met the most awe-inspiring soldiers of the SAS who
welcomed me warmly at the social club after the service. Over
a few beers, I listened to many brave stories and came away
feeling very proud of these men. They are the first to face up
to any enemies of our freedom and I find it very reassuring to
know they are there. Whether you think it's the right thing
for Australia to be in Afghanistan or not, as Australians we
should support them. It's a job that very few of us are able and
willing to take on. There's a dynamic energy that comes from

them that is quite confronting. I'm glad they're on our side.

During the early half of 2013 I had an email from the fiancée of a soldier in Afghanistan telling me the young couple's story. Another came from the solider himself who told me the same story. And a third one came from a wonderful lady who makes quilts for our Aussie soldiers serving overseas, Jan-Maree Ball. Coincidentally she asked me if I would sign the quilt that had been made for this same soldier and she mentioned that he was a huge fan. I knew it was the same soldier even before I read his name. Separately, both he and his fiancée had told me how he had proposed on a houseboat on the Hawkesbury River to my song 'Hawkesbury River Lovin'.

This couple told me that they will be spending their honeymoon as passengers on the 2015 Gallipoli Cruise that Meg and I will also be on, and they hoped they'll be able to have a beer or two with us. That's definitely one beer I'll be having on the ship! It will be an honour.

When I returned the signed quilt (and another for a different soldier) to Jan-Maree I included for both these courageous men my True Blue flag as a token of appreciation for what they're doing over there. I now have a terrific photo of my flag being flown above the vehicles at a compound in Karin Towt in Afghanistan. I'm proud of that because the kangaroo has traditionally been an icon used by our armed forces going back to the First World War and, of course, it sits comfortably on our air force planes. It adds to my belief that we should use the kangaroo as a truly national symbol. It's on our coat of arms standing on Parliament House and yet people still can't imagine it on our flag. What's the difference?

There you are, an Aussie in a ten-gallon hat
With your pointie-toed Cuban shoes and Yankee things like that,
And soundin' more like Haggard than a boy from Ballarat
I'm sorry but I don't understand

(from 'Go to Nashville' © 1985 Emusic Pty Ltd)

Chapter 36

I'M SORRY BUT I
DON'T UNDERSTAND

I've spent years trying to encourage young artists to be themselves, to be original rather than thinking they have to sound like Americans. It still bothers me that our country music is put in the same bag as American country music.

I first heard Sara Storer sing at a Country Music Association of Australia function in Sydney. The self-penned song she sang was called 'Man Trap'. It was quite a simple song about how she was going to build a man trap to catch a husband. She told me afterwards that she would also like to dig a hole and keep her man in it. Her sense of humour is unusual but altogether charming. She finally trapped her man, Dave, but fortunately she didn't need a hole to keep him in. It blew me away to soon discover that Sara was a Mallee girl, originally from Robinvale district, and a wheat farmer's daughter. No wonder there was an immediate connection. She was born just up the railway line from Quambatook.

Sara's sweet, pure, Aussie voice caused tears to run down my cheeks and into my beard. At last, here was a girl who understood that you don't have to put on an American twang to make it in country music. Here was someone who could carry the flame for those of us who truly believe in real Australian country music. Not long after I heard her, Jeff Chandler, an artist manager, asked me who I thought had potential. He was looking for someone he could to take on and manage. I had no hesitation in recommending Sara and he signed her up. At the next Golden Guitar Awards in 2004, Sara took home seven Golden Guitars for her first album *Chasing Buffalo*. This was a record for the most awards won in any one year in the 32-year history of the awards. But even after such an outstanding achievement, the Country Music Association of Australia received an email from some old biddy saying that Sara shouldn't have won any awards. In other words, the lady still had a complex about our accent.

Sara is living proof that a girl can sing with an Aussie bush accent and sound as pure as Joan Baez. Add to that she has the astounding gift of being able to coin a phrase with a sense of honesty, love and humour that endears her to everyone. The only thing that is holding her back from being a legend in her lifetime (in Australia) is her lack of the ego and drive that one needs to be a star. But that, of course, is a big part of her appeal. What's more, she is a natural mother and three strapping young boys are going to pull her heartstrings and keep her from pursuing a full-blown career at the moment. My bet is that her love of singing and writing will keep her in the business for a long time and her legend will grow at her own charming pace. I believe Aussies will continue to discover her and the fans will grow as they realise we have an absolute treasure in our midst, someone who we all should be really proud of. My love for her as a person and a singer-songwriter goes back to that very first time I saw her sing.

I was lucky to record a duet with Sara on her song 'Raining on the Plains', bringing me an unexpected Golden Guitar in 2004. We recorded another duet, 'Pozie', on her latest album *Lovegrass*, winning Vocal Collaboration of the Year at the 42nd Tamworth Country Music Festival in 2014. In fact, Sara scooped the pool at the awards, taking out the coveted Album of the Year award and being named Female Artist of the Year.

I don't make a habit of taking other artists on the road with me although I get many requests from people to be my support act. If I took a support act then it would leave even less time for me to be on stage and I'd disappoint the loyal fans who have paid good money to see me. I know how often my fans will say to me at the end of a concert, 'But you didn't sing such-and-such a song'. The truth is, having written around 500 songs, I can't possibly sing them all. There are some I can never leave out and that list is becoming longer. However, not long after Jeff Chandler signed up to manage Sara I suggested she come on the road with me, just for one tour. I wanted to encourage her to believe in herself and not rely on too many musicians. I could see straight away that people were trying to influence her to be like so many others. In other words, Sara didn't need to be drowned out by a band. As long as she improved her guitar playing she'd be able to entertain without all the bells and whistles. I told her it was a long road to hoe but it would stand her in good stead if she concentrated on being the Sara she's always been. I've seen so many young artists fall by the wayside because

they haven't been original and stuck to their brand. There are
a lot of forces out there to push you in different directions,
especially from record companies who rarely understand
how the artists feel. More often than not it's from people who
have never made it themselves or who are entrenched in the
American way.

The other exception I made, and only once as well, was
for my eldest daughter, Ami. We could see from an early age
that she was born to perform and sent her off to the Johnny
Young Talent School once a week. I arrived early one day to
collect her and her sister, Georgie, only to hear them singing
something like 'We are American Kids'. I was extremely
pissed off and told them I was taking the girls out of the
music school if they didn't change the word to 'Australian'.
Georgie learned guitar there but Mary Kay always said she
only took up guitar to please me. From the Johnny Young
School, Ami went to McDonald College at Strathfield, a
college that concentrated on the performing arts. It gave her
confidence and grounding. For her final exam she asked me to
accompany her on guitar while she sang 'Hawkesbury River
Lovin''. I must have been more nervous than she was because
I messed up the introduction, which amused the adjudicators,
but she sang on to get full marks for her voice.

I could see that Ami needed to entertain and write.
Mary Kay, however, encouraged her to study voice at the
Conservatorium of Music and she won a scholarship to
study opera in Germany. She was employed for a while by
Opera Australia. But she was always a writer and is making a
name for herself at folk festivals in Australia, singing mainly
her own songs and accompanying herself on keyboard. I've

always been there for her for advice, but she has needed to stand on her own two feet and not be regarded as 'John Williamson's daughter'. Her original songs are more modern folk. I'm proud of Ami's achievements. It's hard to imagine that her beautiful daughter, Lara, won't be in the music business; it will be interesting to watch as she grows up. Her father, Clemens Leske, is a renowned classical pianist. Her paternal grandparents are world renowned as well, Clemens senior for the piano and Beryl Kimber for the violin. And on Ami's side, of course, she has me and my musical parents. So look out, Lara Leske – she sounds famous already to me!

It's not often that I record other people's songs either. I made an exception with a few songs penned by a Melbourne songwriter, Bob Brown. He wrote 'Home Among the Gum Trees' in a hotel room in France. He also wrote 'Santa Bring Me a Dinosaur' and 'Big Bad Bushranger' which I recorded for my *Family Album No 2*. Bullamakanka was a thriving bush band in the eighties and they had recorded 'Home Among the Gum Trees'; along with The Bushwackers band they kept the Australian folk music scene going. Bullamakanka's haunts were north coast New South Wales and south-east Queensland. It is their version of the song that I recorded. The 'k-kangaroo' stutter in the song was their idea. They also used to sing 'a bong or two', which I cut out when I left the pub scene. Most people think I wrote the song and I rarely sing it anymore as I have too many of my own songs to fill the shows. But 'Home Among the Gum Trees', I have to admit, is one of the best singalong songs to celebrate loving our homeland. I often worked with Bullamakanka around the traps and thought they were ideal to back my song 'Goodbye

Blinky Bill', written to raise money for the New South Wales
Koala Preservation Society.

Sadly, not long after we released 'Goodbye Blinky Bill',
Rex Radonich, the banjo player, was killed in a road accident
just north of Sydney. The whole band was in the van when
a utility swung from the other side of the road and collided
with them. They all said that Rex swerved left to take the
full brunt of the collision. On the back of the single cover of
'Goodbye Blinky Bill' there is a dedication to Rex Radonich,
a really great bloke. I had a lot of time for the man the band
called, somewhat ironically, 'Blinky Bill'.

♫

I have rarely agreed to work as a support to an overseas
artist. However, in the eighties I did perform for the first half
of Johnny Cash's show in Tasmania. I'm a fan of Johnny and
had sung a couple of his hits on stage before I started writing
more material to fit an all-Australian show. There were two
concerts, one in Launceston and one in Hobart. Johnny had
his wife, June Carter, and his son with him, plus a band. His
son played a stint on the drums and was no Johnny Cash
or June Carter. I remember singing my song 'Just a Dog' in
that show in Hobart and it made quite an impression. One of
Johnny's band members was keen to listen to my songs, but
you have to be careful with Americans in the music business
that they're not out to rip you off. Unfortunately I didn't
have a song that was suitable for Johnny anyway, which was
a shame. I knew he had been a big supporter of Bob Dylan
when Dylan started out, so I reckon he would have been

generous and not claimed royalties on the recording. When I was in Nashville, I'd heard from his publisher that's what he was like.

By the time Cash came to Australia that time in 1985, I got the feeling he didn't care that much about his career anymore. There was little passion in his show. June Carter came with her deep southern accent and spoke of her husband as a 'burdened man', whatever that meant. Too many drugs? Leaving his first wife? Or that old Christian thing; come to me all those who are heavy laden? They used a screen as a backdrop and showed an old train puffing along during 'Orange Blossom Special' and other scenes to go with the songs. I didn't like that idea. I didn't think Cash needed much to present his show well. I like to leave it to the audience's imagination and have a fixed scene with big gum trees under the stars. But it took being the support for Johnny's show to make me realise what was best for me. I found his presence alone was quite awesome. When he sang a very low note and held onto it, the women, young and old, started to get out of control. Now that's real macho!

I stood next to Johnny outside the tour bus and only came up to his chest. However, under his big black coat he wore platform boots, while I was in sandshoes. I felt like I was standing with Darth Vader. He was a big man and when he sat on the armrest of the seat to chat with his band in the bus, the arm of the seat caved in. He coolly stood up and strolled back to sit with June.

In August 2012 I performed a double bill at the State Theatre in Sydney with Kenny Rogers. I performed the first half of the concert. This time I wasn't so much a support artist but a replacement for Glen Campbell. Glen Campbell's memory was failing and he was too ill to make it to Australia, so Australian artists took his place at quite short notice. The audience was there as much for Kenny Rogers as they were for Glen. I was quite pleased to get the chance to sing to Kenny's audience, knowing I couldn't go too badly if they liked country music. But more than that, I figured that I could gain some fans who potentially had never really known my songs. I believe nowadays that I can win over any Aussies who come to my show, because my songs are about them. And yes, it was a success. I had Col Watson on guitar and Dave Ellis on bull fiddle and we had a ball. I've performed in the State Theatre a couple of times before and it's a beautiful theatre to play in.

Unlike Joan Baez, who I had the privilege of meeting backstage after her concert at the Sydney Opera House in 2013, Kenny was very generous with his time. He didn't mind me introducing some friends to him and having photos taken with him. He obviously did this regularly backstage after his concerts. As it turned out, a little while later Kenny was on stage after me at the Gympie Muster. Without any prompting, Kenny asked after me and invited me to come and say g'day in his dressing room. He's a great bloke. I liked him. His performance skills were worth watching and he had a great rapport with his audience but he's definitely showing his age. So I don't imagine we'll see him in Australia much more, if at all.

I was reminded recently of another backstage meeting when I saw a television program about Michael Hutchence. I can understand why Kylie Minogue caught his eye. I met Kylie in the mid 1980s when I was awarded Best Australian

Country Record at the ARIAs. INXS had also won an award that night and I had a photo taken with them and Kylie. At the end of the night, when all the award winners stood in line for a photo, I made sure I was next to Kylie. I knew where the cameras would be pointed. A few years later, I sang 'Raining on the Rock' with Warren H Williams at the ARIAs in the State Theatre in Sydney. Kylie was there again. I walked up to her to remind her that we'd met before (any excuse would do). But once I stood face to face with her my jaw dropped and all I could say was, 'Er ... blah, blah, blubber blubber.' I was speechless. Kyie gave the cutest smile and chuckled. I'm sure she was quite used to men being gobsmacked by her.

♫

In 2010, my fortieth year in the business, Marius Els took on the role of my promoter. He and another promoter, Danny Domroe, convinced me that I should do something special to mark this milestone in my career. They suggested doing a series of concerts in the capital cities with symphony orchestras. The idea was a bit daunting for me but they convinced me to do it. Guy Noble, the main conductor with the Sydney Symphony Orchestra, was responsible for the orchestral arrangements, although he spread the job around with some fellow musical arranger friends. Col and I met Guy a few times during this process to ensure I was happy with the feel of the arrangements. Brass instruments don't suit my music, in my opinion, and Guy respected my input.

We started with the Sydney Symphony Orchestra at the Sydney Opera House. That first concert was on the night of

29 October 2010. The only rehearsal I had with the orchestra was that same afternoon. On the night, I mistakenly dropped the second verse in 'Look Out, Cunnamulla'. I kept finishing before the orchestra did. So we tried again, twice. I was dying inside because I couldn't figure out what was going wrong. Just to calm my nerves, Guy stepped off his conductor's podium and came to me with the music and started pointing to the notes. I pretended to understand what he was pointing out, but all the while I'm thinking, *What the fuck am I doing wrong?* The audience thought the whole thing was hilarious and really laughed. The third time I concentrated hard and realised my mistake. At last we finished together. The audience went off, applauding and whistling madly. All this happened in the second half, thank goodness. By then the initial adrenaline had passed and I coped with it and carried on. Had it happened in the first half I reckon the whole night would have been a disaster. My nerves would have been shot.

The night with the Queensland Symphony Orchestra started disastrously. I use in-ear monitoring (plugs in the ears like headphones). Unfortunately the plug for the left ear turned off. I performed the whole of the first half deaf in one ear. They got it right for the second half and I got a standing ovation, which proves to me an audience can be forgiving as long as you battle on with confidence. I probably performed the second half with even more enthusiasm than normal to make up for the first half. Afterwards people said they didn't realise I was struggling, which shows that acting comes into it. I was beside myself during the interval.

By the time we played with Orchestra Victoria in Melbourne, I was feeling much more confident and the musicians started to feel like a big backing band. It surprised me that many of the players in these prestigious orchestras told me how much they'd enjoyed playing with me, and that they were brought up on my music. They were certainly not the music snobs you might imagine. These were very special concerts and I'll certainly never forget them.

With my fortieth year in the business came many interviews and media articles, as well as the orchestra concerts, another album plus a tribute album, a special presentation by Governor-General Her Excellency Ms Quentin Bryce AC and to top it off, being inducted into the ARIA Hall of Fame. I don't like reading about myself, any more than I like writing about myself, but other people showed me references to me being 'an icon', a 'living legend' and so on. How do I feel about that? Well, I guess, one thing that I am proud of is, that in my late sixties, I'm still writing strong songs. I think the fact that I've never wavered from my belief in writing about us, as Aussies, has contributed; about how this ancient land is our most precious heritage, about how this island continent makes us a unique mob. Australians are still coming to understand how powerful the spirit of this place is. The emails, letters and comments after my shows prove to me that my message is ringing clear to many people. If that makes me a legend then I'm proud of it because it's not really about my fame; it's about the effect my lyrics have on people.

An icon? Well, that should be reserved for the likes of Donald Bradman. 'True Blue' has possibly become an iconic song but that's different. As soon as I hear or read the word 'icon' I think of a metallic monument or the angel on a Rolls Royce bonnet or the bulldog on a Mac truck. I would like my True Blue flag to become iconic – to represent all that is fair dinkum in Australia and my kind of patriotism. Who wants to look in the mirror and see an icon? That's weird. Maybe it's time to change how I look. I don't think people understand what it's like to be seen as a product, like a tube of Colgate toothpaste. Most rock 'n' roll album covers have great artwork on the cover. I have to have the same old dial: my own face. They say it's a selling point. It's such a relief for me to go to our mountain hideaway and be bushy again. To be able to wear the grottiest clothes, to not do my hair, not trim my beard and stay grubby all day and wear a hillbilly hat. In fact, I'd love to have an album cover with a tube of toothpaste playing a guitar but there's no Aussie brand of toothpaste that I know of. Or I'd love to have an album cover with me wearing my grubby gear. But I'm not sure my recording label, Warner, would approve.

Veteran? It can herald the end of a career. I think I'd rather earn the title when I've stopped performing. I'd rather be someone who is still being discovered by people who haven't heard me before rather than being pushed aside as a veteran or a legend. There's always the dream of writing a new song that blows all the others away. That challenge keeps me in there. At the end of it all you either *are* a legend or you're not. It's not something to aim for because Aussies don't tolerate big egos. 'A legend in his own lunchtime' is not something I want to be.

Despite the fact that people think I've made it to the top of the pile I've never really felt that I have. Andrew Denton's program *Enough Rope* didn't think I was worthy of an interview. They apparently told EMI, my record company at the time, that you have to be 'asked' to go on *Enough Rope*. Not different enough maybe? The irony is that, as a performer, it *is* different to be unashamedly Aussie. However, after forty years in the business and with five million album sales I was finally inducted into the ARIA Hall of Fame. I was sixty-six when this honour was bestowed on me. I finally felt that the industry did respect what I have achieved and I'm very proud of this award.

And you ask is he happy ... and you ask is he happy . . ?
He's got wrinkles from smiling, he feels lucky and free
And he knows what it means to live here in the sunshine
He's got wrinkles ...

He walks with Amelia down to the store
With a little cane basket for the bread and the daily Sun
Still hand in hand like babes in the meadows
And young faces turn
Love is so beautiful, it can be so deep
And a man is a king when he has his own princess
Bob wears no crown, no long flowing robe
But there in his mind he still rides on his black stallion

Chapter 37

AND YOU ASK IS HE HAPPY

For well over forty years, radio presenters and journalists have asked me the same questions. As they retire, I have to answer the same questions again with the new breed. *How did you start in music? What is your method of writing a song? Lyrics or music first?* God, I'm tired of it. And on it goes. My industry requires you to focus on yourself, your image, your next hit song, the next hit album, a new song for the show, where to tour next, how to keep the crew together. Maybe they think I don't have much else to talk about. It can be all-consuming if you let it. It's crap for a marriage, too, because you can never relax about it. And I'm an obsessive bloke. When I'm onto a new song I won't let it go until I reckon it's right. *Darling did you hear a word I've said?* It's something I've heard for forty years. I think I'm more conscious of it now and try to be more aware of what's going on around me.

So what would I rather talk about? How about God? Whoah! *That's a big one*, I can hear you thinking. Well, God has played a part in my upbringing even if I don't 'believe' nowadays. In my little childhood town of Quamby it was virtually compulsory to be a Christian: a Presbo, a methylated spiritualist, or a Mick. Sundays, come rain, hail or shine, my folks went to the Presbyterian church in the morning, after I had attended Sunday school. My main memories of Sunday school are singing, being given shiny books for good behavior once a year, and dear old Mr Fox who told us the most boring stories of the travels of Jesus. My cousins Doug and Gerald, and our mate Neil Ritchie and I carved many things into the table as the old man carried on through the Middle East. He had a map. God knows why we were presented with prizes at the end of the year. I learnt nothing, except perhaps about being good to others.

Dad was an elder of the church every year. As a successful wheat farmer he felt he owed something to God for the great seasons. As far as I'm concerned, Dad owed his success to bloody hard work and long hours on the tractor.

I thought I had finished with church by the time I was fourteen, when Mum and Dad sent me to Scotch College for four years. But I was wrong. Sundays were more boring than ever at boarding school. Morning service was at the Hawthorn Presbyterian Church and then there was another service in the evening at the school's chapel. The Scotch College chapel is a beautiful building. The interior certainly is 'godly': wonderful tall, stained-glass windows and pale, bleached timber surrounded us as the school chaplain sat three metres above us. It was all designed to make us boys feel small, I'm sure. The only way to enjoy the chapel was to join the choir. We sat way above the congregation.

The minister at the Hawthorn Church was an absolute fool. I always thought of him as a religious robot. I couldn't imagine that anyone could hold a normal conversation with him. He was a dinosaur who spat on his congregation. Of course that made it easy for the irreverent boys, when they were supposedly giving, to steal money from the collection plate by sticking chewing gum on their fingers. It wasn't the money that was important; it was just the dare (like stealing a teaspoon from Coles at Glenferrie). I remember spending time in that congregation teaching myself to double clutch in readiness for going for my car driver's licence. I was going for it in Quamby in Dad's kombi van at the end of my fourth year at Scotch.

I went through a strange period when I was about seventeen and began to go overboard about Christ. I reckon now it was a kind of self-hypnosis that had overcome us all. My study mate was a real god squadder, and another boarding house mate introduced me to a minister outside the college who liked to have intimate talks about things. That bothered me a bit. I spoke to him once and realised that the subject of sex came up very quickly. I think that snapped me out of my religious coma. However, I *did* become a Sunday school teacher for a little while when I left school. I read the biblical stories to the kids but realised I didn't really believe what I was reading. And I could see that same glazed look in their eyes as I had in mine as a kid.

The following year when we moved to Tralee at Croppa Creek, the stock route cut the property in two. There were about 300 acres on the north-east side and 3400 acres on the other. On the stock route is the little Anglican church. Mum and Dad were a real bonus to the local church community. Mum planted geraniums outside the church and could bash out a tune on the organ if the local organist (also a farmer) couldn't make it. Mum and Dad's singing was like something the locals had never heard before in the church. In fact, one lady told me that she came to the church just to hear Mum and Dad sing. Can you believe that Prince Charles, as a guest of his polo teacher, Sinclair Hill, turned up there one Sunday morning? You can imagine how full the tiny church was that day.

I used to go to church in those days just to catch up with the locals, especially old Dick Woods. He owned Takinbri on the other side of the creek. He would stand with his hand in the pockets of his houndstooth tweed jacket and waffle on: 'I say, I say, I say. A young fella landed his plane on our place yesterday and showed me a photo of the property from the air. I say, I say, I had to buy it, of course. He's making a fortune, I say, I say.' I had to laugh at this because it would take talent to get money out of old tightarse Takenbri Dick.

So church in the sixties was a social gathering for me. The conversations with the local farmers were the only reason I went, if I did at all. But over the years I've become really annoyed how people thank God for miracles. Pissed off, you could say! But I do believe in a natural force. It's called evolution. Like when a honeyeater sticks its beak into the flower of a grevillea to suck the nectar. At the same time, the grevillea dabs pollen onto the bird's head. The honeyeater goes to another bush and cross-pollinates it. There is a genius behind the wonders of nature, but it doesn't have a beard and long hair. It's not something you can pray to for help or guidance.

The greatest survival instinct, in my mind, is love. It's as natural as a baby on the mother's breast. It's the first thing we learn. Religion has successfully latched onto 'love' and called it 'God'. Love itself is god as far as I'm concerned and the only thing that will save mankind. Love, and you get it back. Hate, and you'll get it in return in spades. It's just logic.

All my ramblings here remind me of an incident in my struggling years in the early eighties, performing solo in some fairly wild pubs. The Blacktown Inn was, at that time, a bikies' pub. I set up my two speakers and stomp-box stage on a regular night there for a couple of months. By then I had learned that behind the eyes of every person there is a connection if you appeal to his or her inner self. Bikies' outfits and tattoos present a hard outer shell but are merely a shield to hide their softness. Like any tough guy, a bikie has love of his mum behind those eyes. I'll never forget one short-in-stature bikie who came up to me one night and said, 'Hey John, don't tell the guys I said so, but they would love to hear your song "Wrinkles".' It was a moment that convinced me that I was right about the connection between us all.

Hey True Blue
Don't say you've gone
Say you've knocked off for a smoko
And you'll be back later on
Hey True Blue, Hey True Blue
Give it to me straight
Face to face
Are you really disappearing
Just another dying race
Hey True Blue

(from 'True Blue' © 2003 Emusic Pty Ltd)

Chapter 38

GIVE IT TO ME STRAIGHT,
FACE TO FACE

You don't mess about when you've got blood in your piss.

Alarm bells rang the morning of my performance with Orchestra Victoria on Friday 20 May 2011. I noticed the colour of my urine didn't look right. I'd been uncomfortable in that area for a while but the specialist I'd been referred to hadn't come up with anything much at all. I rang his surgery first thing Monday morning. Before long I was in St Vincent's Hospital in Sydney for a cystoscopy. On 1 June I received the diagnosis: bladder cancer.

It was a shock but I wasn't scared. I'm a bit of a fatalist. I didn't feel like it was terminal. But I was certainly worried about what they had to do to fix it, especially if the cancer was bad enough for my bladder to come out. The surgeon had described the alternatives which included making a new bladder out of a piece of my bowel but that also meant the prostate would have to be removed. He explained that losing the prostate doesn't improve your libido (to put it mildly).

I think the surgeon's preferred option was to remove my bladder, to make sure we got rid of it all. I didn't like the idea of a bag though, so I was keen to try the other treatment option: a method of flooding the bladder with the BCG vaccine, which is what they use to treat tuberculosis. This sounded like the best of a bad deal. They flood your bladder with this poisonous solution through the 'old fella' once a week for six weeks.

The first lot of BCG treatments ended on 6 August. It didn't work. The cancer was still there. I decided to give it another go. The second lot finished on 20 December. Then they had to wait a while for things to settle down again before doing the exploratory stuff with the camera under a general anaesthetic. The treatment didn't stop any of my scheduled performances. It just meant Meg and I had to miss the Variety Bash that year.

My bladder got the all clear in the middle of January 2012. That's nearly three years ago now and after regular cystoscopies every six months, it's still clear. Now I've got a little bit of cancer in the prostate, but no panic. Hopefully it will stay 'little' until the end of 2015 and then I'll probably get the prostate cut out. Bugger it! It's not worth the worry.

Another health hiccup arrived in January 2014. I thought I was having problems with indigestion. The short version is that I had a stent put in a main artery to the heart because the artery was 95 per cent blocked. Bloody hell! But again, it was business as usual with the shows, although there have been some tricky moments as a result of this.

At the Byron Bay Blues Festival in March 2014, there was a bloody incident on stage, literally. We'd got there a minute before the show was due to start – it was supposed to be a 20-minute drive but the traffic was dreadful. My heart was pounding; I wasn't nervous, just worried we weren't going to get there on time. A few songs in, halfway through 'Mallee Boy', my nose started bleeding profusely. It was going down the back of my throat. The audience couldn't see it so I kept going, but midway through 'Galleries of Pink Galahs' I had to stop playing guitar to put my finger on my nostril to stop the flood. The band lost it as soon as I stopped playing. I lead everything, and they didn't know what was going on, so I had no choice but to stop and explain to everyone that I had a blood nose, and that I was on blood thinners because I'd had a stent put in. They were all right behind me and tissues suddenly appeared from everywhere. So I stuffed some up one nostril and carried on for about four songs. All seemed to be okay so I pulled the tissues out, and a huge long trail of blood came out with it! It just wouldn't stop so I had to plug it up again.

Anyway, I got through it, still did an hour show and absolutely killed it! The whole audience was right behind me, urging me on: 'You can do it!' It's proof that the show *will* go on.

The moral of the story is that I got onto the cancer pretty quickly, it didn't really slow me down and now I'm good as gold. I'm not yet seventy so it looks like it's going to be a bumpy ride to get to 93, my dad's final age.

I've taken you away from all y'friends
Y'family is all around the world
I led you up the Hillbilly Road
To horseflies and lizards

Chapter 39

I LED YOU UP
THE HILLBILLY ROAD

I'm often asked, why Springbrook?

In the Mallee, while we never worked on Sunday, Mum and Dad only ever took two weeks' holiday a year. Mum was never keen to go to the same place, but every Christmas, after harvest, it was time to head to the beach. I have vague memories of a trip to Sydney and Brisbane and it rained the whole time. That was not good for camping. One year we went to Mildura simply because it had an Olympic swimming pool, one of the first in the bush. We swam with delight in that pool every day. That year I discovered flippers. Wow! I could swim twice as fast and go a lot further before I ran out of breath. One day the New Zealand Prime Minister Robert Muldoon was there inspecting the pool and I gave him a demo of my speedy swimming. Even today I prefer to swim with small flippers. My feet are skinny and as useless as two sticks. I reckon there should be flippers under the aeroplane seats as well as a life jacket.

By the time I was a teenager, Mum had discovered Surfers Paradise ... the Gold Coast. Wow! This was really something different: two-storey motels with swimming pools! We were all so happy there that they invested in a couple of units on the Boulevard. The building was called The Sands. Eventually it was knocked down and rebuilt and called Zenith. Poor Mum and Dad never made much out of the units. The managers were crooks.

Many years later, in 1976, Mary Kay and I stayed in their unit at Zenith. I was keen to see some rainforest up in the mountains and Mum said, 'You need to take a drive to Springbrook.' So off we went up the winding road, not knowing what we would see. I just loved the road and the subtropical scenery. But more than that, it was also the little patches of old dairy country where the forest trees were much more visible in a paddock and were able to show off their beauty. While I have a reputation for being a greenie, I also respect how hard the previous generations worked, scratching out a living from the bush. So the patches of kikuyu grass with the magnificent rainforest specimens are a heritage worth preserving. That is different to clearing for closer settlement and I will fight against it. What's left should be left as it is.

So after walking under the waterfall at Purling Brook Falls and checking out the view from the Best of All Lookout and the many wonders high up where the rainforest becomes temperate, I noticed a 'For Sale' sign as we coasted back down the hill: ten acres for $20 000. Walking through the bush on the block led to the discovery of an unbelievable view of the Numinbah Valley. I remember thinking that the old dairy country I could see below had a lot of ornamental foreign trees on it. Not having seen rainforest specimens in the open before, I assumed that they were from the northern hemisphere. After all, Aussies planted many trees that were not native to our country while we were still unaware of the beauty of our own trees.

It was important to me, when I purchased the block, to know what was there. Now I can look at it from above, where the cottage is, and point out where things are. My bit of rainforest was selectively logged in the past but all the original species are still there. I have a red cedar tree that would be hundreds of years old. It was left because it was not tall and straight. It probably covers half an acre. What a heritage to leave future generations! I do have my eye on a crow's ash tree that was felled maybe forty years ago. They took a three-metre log and left the rest. It has so much natural oil in it that it's still as solid as the day it was cut. The timber is rare now. It's been highly prized as ideal for dance floors because of its high oil content. We cut the end off and my mate Mick made a huge chopping block out of it. If you count the rings, it adds up to being about 400 years old. The young crow's ash trees on the paddock are very ornamental; their pale green leaves contrast beautifully with the dark green hoop pines. All this diversity on just 170 acres will give you some idea why I object to clear-felling old growth forests. It's unimaginable to think of my small forest being turned into a tree farm with two or three species of trees when there are thousands of different living things relying on it being left as it is. A bird, bat or lizard has claimed every hollow branch. It's a city with no empty accommodation. Now our neighbour runs about 50 head of cattle on the grass. The lantana on the edge stops them venturing into the forest. Lantana, an introduced species, isn't that bad in this situation; it dies away in the forest shade and protects the soil when the forest is cleared.

When Meg and I got together, there was really nowhere to go except the cottage at Springbrook. At that stage it didn't have power. I used a generator. The kitchen was very basic. The few chipboard cupboards were beginning to swell. The gas fridge was inadequate and on it went. Hardly, I guess, what Meg expected. Mary Kay had never shared my dream of one day living there so back then it didn't seem to be worth developing the cottage when it was really just a man's shack.

So here we were, completely in love but both out of very comfortable suburban homes. It was romantic, sure, but I think Meg was wondering what the hell she had fallen into. I also had a rented apartment in the centre of Sydney but it was in a state of needing refurbishing too. In fact, every time we had dinner with friends, I felt as if I had let Meg down terribly as all our mates had beautiful kitchens. But it was just a matter of time. Meg now has two kitchens that are state of the art, you might say. Not extravagant, but beautifully designed by Meg to suit her great love of cooking. Me? I'm a short order cook. I can do any kind of breakfast or pasta, but I rarely cook anything else because Meg finds cooking relaxing and usually hunts me out of the kitchen. For the cottage at Springbrook, I'm glad she chose deep cherry-red drawers and cupboards with touches of timber here and there. They add colour to the place and are a perfect foil for the wooden rafters and soft lichen green walls.

I'm not as hell-bent on perfection as Meg. I love to let things just happen to a degree. That way the cottage will end up with character that we didn't expect. My mate Mick, who is very clever with hardwood, turned up and suggested a great idea for the architraves using the hoop pine I've had cut and stored in 'Willoshed'. Mick built the fireplace surround back in the late eighties out of the bridge timbers of the old Neranwood bridge. Before we constructed it we had to dig the gravel from the cracks. The high shelf above it is made from a large collapsed stool from outside the Purling Brook store. I bought it by giving ten dollars to the local bushfire brigade. The fireplace will always set the tone of the cottage. But originally that space was a cupboard. I just love the way the things develop and change organically. A mistake is often a godsend.

In Australia we are surrounded by astounding resources. With that in mind, a stroll down a riverbed can be a real treasure hunt. Places such as the Pilbara in Western Australia inspire me constantly. I'm now obsessed with rocks and what I can do with them at our bush home. My permanent outdoor barbecue area at the cottage at Springbrook resembles a stock camp, but also has an old enamel fuel stove. I love to spend time around the fire, smoking forequarter lamb chops and cooking vegies in a camp oven. It keeps me in touch with the simpler life of our forefathers and I love it. I have a good collection of kerosene lamps that light up the tall trees around me and it becomes 'home' after the sunset has calmed my mind. I can fully understand how drovers and miners always prefer to spend their days that way.

I thought that by now, in my late sixties, I would spend a lot of time with my grandkids, but I'm still as creatively active and enjoying the stage as ever. Perhaps even more so.

Up at our mountain hideaway I've been preparing for twenty years for the day when I could spend time doing things with grandkids. I have a big pile of mulga, gidgee and other timber to make things for them. Now that Hawkesbury, my oldest grandchild, has reached a good age of seven, that time is getting closer, I hope. It's a young adventurer's paradise up there. I can't wait to show him my secret cubby house in the forest made of stone. Someone recently was quoted saying 'Johnno is an eight-year-old in a sixty-year-old body.' Hey, that's flattering to me. I'm pleased to hear it!

I've always been away with the pixies when my mind is on creative ideas. Meg gets a little frustrated with me when I'm not listening but at least I'm 300 per cent better than my own father. I wonder if he ever heard what I said. I have inherited that problem but I fight against it. I was a hopeless student. A dreamer. Still am. On the other hand I can concentrate for days on the lyrics of a new song. Or completely construct a building in my head, or a painting.

What about my attempts at art? Well, maybe I crave art because I'm not bound to stick to what I'm known for, like I am as a songwriter. I know on which side my bread is buttered, so I'm not about to lose my fans by expanding too far musically. But painting and sculpture – there's no limitation for me. I'll die happily exploring my limits. No one has to like it at all. That's real freedom.

I've always found it easy to design lettering, so it's understandable that I ended up designing some of my album covers. My first contribution was a painting of the Mallee tree and ute on the back of the *Mallee Boy* cover. A few years later I completely designed and painted both sides of the

Warragul album. Then I painted the cover for the 'Rip Rip Woodchip' single.

Years ago when we covered the floor of the extension at our Epping house with cork tiles there was a pile of the tiles left over. These 30-centimetre squares were the ideal surface to paint landscapes of my favourite areas in Australia. They were reproduced as greeting cards. We sold most of them as merchandise to fans, but I kept some for my own use as well. I still use them to respond to special fan emails and letters. I've never really pursued that part of my creativity so therefore I'm not much more than an illustrator at this stage. The special edition of *The Big Red* album also includes illustrated cards that relate to some of the songs. They're just rough sketches really. I'm always drawing, especially when I'm in Sydney, or waiting around somewhere, so they were put to good use with the album. I mainly draw for fun and not for my profession. It's not surprising, then, that my earliest recollection of drawing is sketching Donald Duck.

♫

The *Hillbilly Road* album is very much about the early period of my new life with Meg. 'Beach of Love' was loosely written about the fact that Meg loves swimming, a couple of kilometres a day if she can. 'Catch a Virgin' I wrote when she had to go back to Sydney while I stayed another week at Springbrook. 'Better Than a Picture' was inspired by one of the incredible views of the wilderness from the property. 'Dark Irish Eyes' is about her. And 'Hillbilly Road', Meg's favourite on the album, was written the night before her birthday when she was a little teary about being away from her family and friends.

In the long run, however, it was another song with a Springbrook connection on *Hillbilly Road* that struck the biggest chord with my audience: 'Cydi'. Our neighbours at Springbrook, Ross and Denice Gilbert, have a daughter Jennifer who I noticed was always in her dad's shadow as she was growing up. She loves cattle and the bush and is the apple of her father's eye. I'd also had an email some years before from a lady in western New South Wales, describing a woman on the land who took over the family property when her dad was killed in the Second World War. This lady had run the farm ever since. The name 'Cydi' came from my ex brother-in-law's description of his son, Jason, who was nicknamed Sidekick, which became Sidie. I realised that Cydi would be a good girls' name. I'm very proud today that quite a few baby girls have been named Cydi since the album was released. I'm sure many of the parents don't realise it's short for Sidekick. The other thing that gives me a buzz is how often a young woman will come up to me after a show and tell me that she is her dad's Cydi. It's the kind of comment that makes a songwriter very happy; it's great to know that a song has such an effect on people.

♬

Cydi

She walks like her old man, over active and thin
She laughs at all the same things, that makes her father grin
She's only 15, no brothers in her clan
And her father calls her Cydi, his right hand man

She can drive a tractor, or curse a useless dog
Shear a sheep, strain a fence or cut a nine foot log
She was meant to be a boy, it didn't go to plan
But her father loves his Cydi, his right hand man

But the boys in the town today are turning their heads
Is that really Cydi, that tomboy kid of Ed's?
She used to kick the footy, win every race we ran
Ed knew the world was changing, for his right hand man

You won't find her in the kitchen, she won't make her bed
She'd rather make a sheep grate with a welder in the shed
Or just be out there in the bush doing what she can
Just being with her father, his right hand man

And her mother takes her shopping, it's time she bought a dress
Looking in the mirror, 'Not bad' she must confess
But I'd rather have that pair of jeans and boots if I can
She's still her fathers Cydi, his right hand man

And the boys in the town today are turning their heads
Is that really Cydi, that tomboy kid of Ed's?
She used to kick the footy, win every race we ran
Ed knew the world was changing, for his right hand man

Yet her father loved his Cydi, his right hand man

There's inevitably been a little bit of Meg on the albums since *Hillbilly Road*. I consider 'Rescue Me' on *The Big Red* to be my best love song. And it's been nice to know that a song about a new romance does strike a chord with many people my age. Second marriages are very common these days. When Meg and I married in March 2013 I wrote a song for the occasion, which is on my fiftieth album, *Honest People*. I'm still writing love songs like I'm in my thirties, but I sometimes think that perhaps the song is for a younger person to sing.

I keep saying that I probably only have one more original album in me. I don't need to write any more songs because it's already hard to fit all the songs I like doing into the show. But despite that, when a good idea comes I have to work on it. It actually keeps me playing guitar at home and my voice in good shape. It's still fun creating songs from nothing. But bugger it; that means having to try it out on my audience. If they like it, then I almost feel obliged to record it. And if it's recorded, then it has to be promoted and that means touring. It's a train I've been on since 1970, but it *is* going slower nowadays.

People often ask me if I get tired of the travelling. The answer is, I get tired of airports. As for performing, I currently have on stage with me the 2013 Musician of the Year at Tamworth, Col Watson, on guitar. Dave Ellis on bull fiddle is highly respected in jazz and classical fields. He played bass on the *Mallee Boy* album and two other albums. What a pleasure this trio is. The best combo ever. I'm bringing back earlier songs now that never sounded so good. My stomp-box is still my drummer.

Of course, touring always places demands on those left at home. For this reason I've never been on the road much more than three weeks at a time. It's a lot easier for *me* now because Meg is willing and happy to be my personal assistant as well as carrying on her own small business in children's literature. She loves travelling around this country as much as I do and does at least 50 per cent of the driving when we're on the road. At the end of every show I come out after half a beer and she is right beside me while I sign autographs and CDs. She keeps me in touch with special fans who have emailed their story or their wish to meet me personally. Sometimes there are families who literally plan their trip to Australia from overseas to coincide with a show and Meg points them out. I enjoy this part of my work. It keeps me in touch with which songs my fans like. I even get ideas from their comments. It's also nice to see my audience face to face. The little kids are a delight; I never forget how much it meant to me when I was a kid when a performer said hello to me at the charity shows in Quamby. I don't mind admitting that I'm aware that a handshake and 'how y' going' with a fan is never forgotten. Each handshake or photo is like a brick in my foundation of loyal fans. After 44 years I'm standing on quite a high wall. I can't understand entertainers who don't like signing autographs. It's tiring, admittedly, but at the same time the love out there is invigorating. We are not above our audiences.

♫

As the producer of my own albums I have always felt more comfortable in a down-to-earth setting where we could sit around, jam and rehearse the songs in the casual setting of a backyard. *Hillbilly Road*, *The Way it Is*, *Gunyah* and

Chandelier of Stars were all recorded at Epping in suburban Sydney. Steve Newton, my engineer at the time, rented the house from me and converted the garage into a studio called Enrec, after his late brother, Eric Newton. *Pipe Dream* was also recorded in his garage before that. Steve also felt more at home in his own environment. I lived in Epping as well during this time so it really was like having my own studio.

The final product on an album is my decision in terms of the musical elements coming together. That is, the balance of the instruments, the performance and how far out the voice sits and so on. However, I've always listened to and asked for other opinions. So over these albums, Steve and Phil Matthews, my manager at the time put in their two bobs' worth. There would even be arguments, but the buck always had to stop with me. After all, I was the one who was paying and I'm the one who has to live with the result for the rest of my life. So I can't blame anyone but myself for recordings that don't gel. And no matter how hard you try, you never achieve that magic on every track. There are just so many factors. I sometimes think that a hit is a fluke, but generally for my market it's when the lyrics hit the spot for a lot of people.

At one stage, Steve and Phil reckoned it was time I handed over the production to someone else. I fought against them quite vigorously. Rightly or wrongly, much of the fun as a creative writer is also to create the recording. As soon as I write a new song I begin to hear some of the production, like where the bass comes in, what kind of guitar, harmonies and so on. Also, I believe in letting good session players have an input, that's why they get the job – they're also creative. A couple of times I've let another producer have a go and

I hated the result. It wasn't my sound. It's a bit like allowing an architect free rein to design your home: you can end up with something you can't live in. Having said that though I co-produced my fiftieth album, *Honest People,* with someone who approaches music the way I do: Matt Fell. In other words, he is not too fixed with ideas before I record, and allows a song to develop using different sounds. It can be so much fun and it's the unexpected that so often makes the difference.

♫

In December 2013 I resigned as president of the Country Music Association of Australia (CMAA). It caused a great deal of unexpected controversy. I was the only founding member of the CMAA who was still on the board. It was formed in 1992. I'm very worried that the Aussie culture of our music will be watered down by people who don't care about anything but their own agendas. They judge our music using an American yardstick. You may think that what I've said is because of my own agenda. Maybe so, but it's also for my country, not just for me. I've been criticised for not staying on to effect change but I've done all I can, mainly by example. Unfortunately that wasn't enough. I was only one vote.

I have 25 Golden Guitars. I don't need any more. I have always encouraged new artists who aren't worried about sounding like our American counterparts. Surely we can, and are, developing music about our country that is unique. Imagine if Willie Nelson or Johnny Cash tried to sound like us. They would be laughed out of the business. It's all about believing in yourself and our unique character. I just can't

say 'I'm fair dinkum' with an American accent; it would
sound ridiculous. I think some of us are well on the way to
developing a music that isn't in the same bag as the United
States. It's music of, and for, our country, which is different
to 'country music' in the musical genre sense. Perhaps we will
come up with another name for it one day.

In the not too distant future I predict that the pseudo
American accents at the Tamworth Festival will be frowned
upon. People will think, did we really sing like that in the
old days? As I've often said publicly, the likes of Slim Dusty,
Buddy Williams and Stan Coster kept open the gate that
Banjo Paterson and Henry Lawson unlocked. I've given that
gate a nudge and I hope artists like Sara Storer will push it
further. Unfortunately I see many Australian country music
artists who pay homage to Australia while being entrenched
in the American country music culture. I am not knocking
artists like Keith Urban who have beaten the Americans at
their own game, but I can't call it Australian country music.

At the Tamworth Festival in January 2013 I was reminded
of the good people in our music industry. I was terribly sick.
My greatest fear with touring is the singer's enemy – the
common cold or flu. For years I've prided myself on never
cancelling a show because of a bad throat. On the morning
of my regular evening concert in the Tamworth Town Hall,
I'd already appeared on the *Sunrise* TV show and couldn't
sing live as planned. I didn't know if I'd be any better by that
night. Before I fell into a deep sleep on the floor, David, my
manager, said 'Leave it to me'. His favourite expression! By
the time sound check came around he and Meg had contacted
artists who were in town to see if they were willing to sing

one of my songs in my show. Mike McClellan, Troy Cassar-Daley, John Stephan, The Sunny Cowgirls, Shane Nicholson, Harmony James, Anne Kirkpatrick, Tania Kernaghan, Chelsea Basham and my daughter Ami. Wow! We could never afford all that talent if we had to pay them. A lot of the time we didn't know what key the artists were going to sing my songs in, but Dave Ellis on bass, Col Watson on guitar and me on acoustic and stomp-box managed all the different keys. Those boys can do anything and just adapted. It was the first time I've felt like a real musician. I didn't know I had it in me. I managed to croak through a song in between the others and the audience absolutely loved it. And it was fun to sing rough-voiced harmonies to my songs and be able to concentrate on my guitar. We donated part of the takings that night to Variety the Children's Charity.

I was blown away that all these beautiful artists knew my songs and were delighted to perform them with me. What a generous bunch of people. It will go down as a very memorable Tamworth. Despite the negativity over my CMAA resignation I believe these people are my mates in the industry and I'd help them out in the same way.

It all depends how much you really want it
Be sure that you choose it carefully
The joy after all is in the journey
Of being what you really wanna be

Chapter 40

BEING WHAT YOU
REALLY WANNA BE

I have to admit saying to someone in the early eighties that I wanted to become a famous Australian. I think he thought I was a wanker when I said it. I was trying to say that it wasn't important to me to be a world star. I just wanted to be appreciated by my own people for singing our own songs and making a difference. If the songs communicated to the world, great, but I haven't tried to achieve that. I must admit though, when I hear a mob of Aussies singing Don McLean's 'American Pie' I feel as if I haven't achieved the ultimate as a writer. But I haven't given up just yet. It's the human condition to always want more. I tell myself often to be content to be alive and healthy and in Australia.

I had an idea that the theme of birds would hold my autobiography together. I've loved our native creatures since I was a kid. I can't explain the magic I felt as a boy when I spotted a new bird. I can probably tell you exactly where I saw a certain bird for the first time. The Quambatook council dam was where I first saw the red-legged avocet with his strange upward bent beak; the grey fantail behind the Quambatook cafe in the lane; the sacred kingfisher in the Church of England front yard. They all have their little territories. The pretty little goldfinch used to nest in our fruit trees but I ignored it because it was English. The black-faced shrike had a mud nest in the gum tree where we used to swim in the Avoca River. I'm sure the tree and the old swinging rope will still be there. The nankeen night herons would stay in the gum plantation opposite our first house until dark. For my egg collection we plaited the combungi grass on the bank of the river and could walk out to the middle where the musk duck nested. That was our biggest prize – an egg larger than a domestic duck's. Its shell was a pale green and as hard and thick as porcelain. On the way through the reeds we found the reed warblers nests made out of the combungi seeds on top of the stalks. If I heard a reed-warbler today it would take me immediately to the Avoca River.

Isn't it amazing how you can tell an Australian location by the birdcalls? The whipbird is the sound of our rainforest. As you head north there is a dove that is definitely the sound of the Tropical North. The sound of spring where I used to live in Epping is the wattlebird that reminds me of an old-fashioned hedge clipper. The currawongs in Sydney sing differently to the ones at Springbrook in Queensland. The corellas sound like the outback. Mobs of galahs take me back to the farming country. Bloody sulphur-crested cockies are everywhere. I hunt them away from our cottage at Springbrook. They love to wake you up very early, just like they did at Croppa Creek. The blue-winged kookaburra up Cape York Peninsula sounds like he's practising to be like the common jackass. Up there you can hear the carpenter bird at night. It sounds like someone nailing down an iron roof on a shed. It's certainly quite annoying when you're trying to sleep.

I could go on forever how I remember throughout my adult life where I first saw a native bird that heralded from the pages of my bird books and my Gould League days. I was disappointed to discover that the Gould League seems to exist mainly in Victoria these days. I wish it was promoted in schools nationally. I'd love to see a competition for birdcall mimicking, especially for kids. I'm sure there must be thousands of mimics out there who could help me. I'm not bad on the kookaburra and white cocky calls but I bet there are fantastic mimics out there who would blow me away. A few years ago I was performing in the Ipswich Civic Centre theatre when I heard a butcherbird. It wasn't an individual call but the really difficult call common to butcherbirds. It was someone in the audience.

I have listened to those birds and the way we talk to describe things. We have our own melody if you just listen. There is no such thing as noteless speech. There is music in the way we speak, just as the Irish have a lilting in their speech. We are much drier.

The 44 years since I wrote 'Old Man Emu' have been quite a journey. Or a hell of a career, as my recent album was titled. One of my greatest achievements is that my songs have stood clear from my influences. While others have inspired me, from both here and overseas, I believe I've created a country style that is uniquely Australian. I've allowed people and the bush to speak to me. I've never said I'll retire from showbiz because I don't trust that I can. Fate seems to have led me in the right direction so far, so I don't worry too much. After losing my brother Robin and my own brush with cancer, I'm thankful for every day.

♪

I guess in the long run I'll be remembered for a few songs; certainly for 'True Blue'. I hope it will become part of our nation's heritage. At the moment, the Wallabies and the Australian cricket team use it as a victory song. 'Flower on the Water' has become a song for funerals for many people. 'Cootamundra Wattle' and 'Cydi' I hope will last as songs of love of family. I'm glad 'Raining on the Rock' seems to be the one to describe the heart of Australia. 'Old Man Emu' will always amuse kids. Of course, I can't predict what songs will last when I'm gone, but a handful would be nice.

My achievements outside of music? Well, the cottage I've created on a cliff in south-east Queensland will bring joy to Aussies forever. It may burn down one day in a bushfire but there is no doubt with such a view, people will persevere and rebuild it again and again. When I decided to build there, many people thought I was mad. Now our friends are gobsmacked and love being there with us.

I think, in the end, my greatest joy has been in creating things. Hopefully I will drop dead in the middle of messing about with rocks or timber or building a chook yard. A creative life is a gift. I get up early every day in the mountains so I don't miss a moment of daylight. If I stay healthy, my dream of manmade paths through the rainforest will be achieved. I really do want to share my privilege of being a caretaker of an amazing piece of Australia. Speaking of health, my small dose of prostate cancer creates concerns but I refuse to let it bother me. I already have too many reasons to be thankful for living this long.

I wonder what I did to deserve this life. I regard myself very lucky to have been brought up in a bush town, a farmer's son. I'm very lucky to have had a musical family and a mother who introduced me to wildflowers. But above all, I'm lucky to be able to string words together about how I feel. All these things are gifts. When you receive a gift, you should be thankful. You shouldn't feel that you are better than others; quite the opposite. Sure I am proud of what I have achieved. That's what makes life worthwhile. I have indeed had a fortunate life. I've lost half my hearing already but while I still have my hands and eyesight, I have a life. If I end up bedridden in the finish I'll be happy if I've at least got a pocketknife and some gidgee wood to whittle.

The Joy is in the Journey

Everyone has their disappointments
Days when nothing seems to go your way
It all comes down upon you in the evening
But tomorrow morning brings another day

You'll never make a mark just being lucky
You have to earn your place in the sun
By crossing every bridge that comes before you
And darlin' it's the same for everyone

It all depends how much you really want it
Be sure that you choose it carefully
The joy after all is in the journey
Of being what you really wanna be

So don't let a setback change your dreams
Dig your heels in take it on the chin
It's only there to make your armour stronger
The game of life is always there to win

You'll never make a mark just being lucky
You have to earn your place in the sun
By crossing every bridge that comes before you
And darlin' it's the same for everyone

DISCOGRAPHY

To follow is a complete list of John's repertoire over more than four decades, from the first record, *John Williamson*, in 1970 to his fiftieth album, *Honest People*, in 2014.

A number of these titles are no longer available in their original form or format. Information on all John's current releases can be found at johnwilliamson.com.au

JOHN WILLIAMSON | *Fable, 1970*

Old Man Emu; Melbourne Green – Melbourne Blue; The Pitt Street Farmer; The Morning After; Susan-Gaye; Autumn of Our Love; Little Babies; Under the Bridge; Beautiful Sydney; Should I Tell Her; W-W-Wallaby; The Unexplored Shadows; Through an Eagle's Eye.

COMIC STRIP COWBOY | *Mercury/PolyGram, 1976*

Comic Strip Cowboy; Engine Driver; Six Boys in Blue; Boyhood Story; Big Country Round; Freedom Frog; Vegetable Soup; Highway to the Grave; J.C. Bulginpockets; Goin' Round the Bend; Four Points and Forty Bucks; Dingo Dog.

ROAD TO TOWN | *Mercury/PolyGram, 1978*

Water Water Everywhere; Heaven's Right Here; Lonesome Playground; Leave the Lights On; Gotta Get Back; I Still Cry; Springbrook; Only a Dog; Send Down the Rain; Road to Town; Murrumbidgee Madness; Waratah Rock 'n' Roll Ball.

COUNTRY GREATS – JOHN WILLIAMSON | *Mercury/ PolyGram, 1978*

Old Man Emu; The Pitt Street Farmer; Vegetable Soup; It's a Grab It While It's Goin' Kinda Life; Lonesome Playground; W-W-Wallaby; Come Ride a Country Road; Comic Strip Cowboy; Engine Driver; Tearjerkers; Madame Tooshay; Melbourne Blue – Melbourne Green.

TRUE BLUE | *Festival, 1982*

Old Man Emu; Big Country Round; Boyhood Story; Under the Bridge; Heaven's Right Here; The Breaker; Murrumbidgee Madness; True Blue; A Granda Plan for Landa; Only a Dog; Springbrook; Send Down The Rain; Hawkesbury River Lovin'; Diggers of the Anzac (This Is Gallipoli).

FAIR DINKUM J.W. | *Festival, 1982*

Country Football; Kill the Night; (Why Don't We) Separate and Be Lovers?; Botany Bay; Wrinkles' Road Train; Ryebuck Shearer; (You've Gotta Be) Fair Dinkum; Just a Dog; Silver-haired Showman; With My Swag upon My Shoulder; Love of a True Blue Girl; Your Body Feels Like Heaven to Me; Brisbane Ladies.

SINGING IN THE SUBURBS – LIVE | *Festival, 1983*

It's Good to Be Me; Lillee and McEnroe; The Vasectomy Song; The Sheik of Scrubby Creek; Waratah Rock 'n' Roll Ball; Bound for South Australia; And the Band Played Waltzing Matilda; Singing at a Party; Chain Around My Ankle; I Can't Feel Those Chains Any Longer; Botany Bay; Stuffed If I Know; Home Among the Gum Trees; Waltzing Matilda.

THE SMELL OF GUMLEAVES – LIVE | *Gumleaf/Festival, 1984*

Dad's Flowers; The Bush Barber; Good Tobacco When I Smoke; The Trees Have Now Gone; The Last of the Pioneers; Queen in the Sport of Kings; I've Always Been a Drover; I'm Fair Dinkum; Drunken Duncan; Stoned This Afternoon; Billabong; Only 19; We Will Stop the War; I'll Be Gone.

ROAD THRU THE HEART | *Gumleaf/EMI, 1985*

The Dusty Road We Know; Old Lou; Go to Nashville; The Shed; You and My Guitar; The Least That I Can Do (Song for Ethiopia); I Had a Dream; Someday an Eagle; See You Next Year, Mate; Alice Springs; Coober Pedy; Stan Coster (Poem); Short of a Quid; Goodbye Again.

HUMBLE BEGINNINGS | *Gumleaf/Festival, 1985*

Old Man Emu; Melbourne Blue – Melbourne Green; The Pitt Street Farmer; Little Babies; Gum Tree; W-W-Wallaby; Misery Farm; Freedom Frog; Comic Strip Cowboy; Engine Driver; Vegetable Soup; Highway to the Grave; J.C. Bulginpockets; Goin' Round the Bend; Dingo Dog; A Dog with No Hair (Pub with No Beer); Six Boys in Blue; Four Points and Forty Bucks; It's a Grab It While It's Goin' Kinda Life; Come Ride a Country Road, Tearjerkers; The Buddies Song (Have a Go); Water Water Everywhere; Lonesome Playground; Leave the Lights On; Gotta Get Back; I Still Cry; Road to Town.

ALL THE BEST | *Gumleaf/Festival, 1986*

You and My Guitar; Goodbye Blinky Bill; Just a Dog; Wrinkles; Diggers of the Anzac; Old Man Emu; The Shed; Hawkesbury River Lovin'; The Breaker; I'm Fair Dinkum; The Bush Barber; Dad's Flowers; Billabong; Chain Around My Ankle; I Can't Feel Those Chains Any Longer; The Vasectomy Song; Stuffed If I Know; Home Among the Gum Trees.

MALLEE BOY | *Gumleaf/Festival, 1986*

Mallee Boy; Galleries of Pink Galahs; Back at the Isa; Raining on the Rock; Three Rivers Hotel; Cracker Night; True Blue; Humpin' M'Bluey; The Budgie Song; I'm in the Mood; Cootamundra Wattle; Paint Me a Wheelbarrow; Diamantina Drover; Show Me a Better Way.

BOOMERANG CAFÉ | *Gumleaf/Festival, 1988*

It's a Way of Life; Old Man Verandah; Sail the Nullarbor; Westown; Welcome All to Broome; Crocodile Roll; The March for Australia (A New Beginning); The Boomerang Café; The Truckie's Wife; My Dad Snores; You're a Miner; The Only One; One More for the Road.

WARRAGUL | *Gumleaf/Festival, 1989*

Dingo; Why They Call Him Sundown; Station Cook; Drover's Boy; Ancient Mountains; Charters Towers; Boogie with M'Baby; Special Girl; 40 Years Ago; Amazing Day; Longreach Is Praying; Bill the Cat; Big Bad Bushranger; Rip Rip Woodchip; Shelter.

J.W.'S FAMILY ALBUM | *Gumleaf/Festival, 1990*

Christmas Photo; Camel Train to Yamba; Teach Me to Drive, Dad; Just a Dog; The Flight of the Blowfly; Goodbye Blinky Bill;Crocodile Roll; On My Ukelele; Big Bad Banksia Man; Old Man Emu; Koala Koala; My Dad Snores; Old Sow; When We Were Kids; A Proud Man (Alan Border); Home Among the Gum Trees.

WARATAH STREET | *Gumleaf/Festival, 1991*

Songs for My Guitar; Tubbo Station; Winter Green; Waratah
Street; A Bushman Can't Survive; Wobbly Boot Hotel
(Boggabilla Pub); Goodiwindi Pork; Will Our Grandchildren
Sing; A Flag of Our Own; The Big Depression; Ami, Take Your
Chances!; Georgie; Beachcomber From Wollongong; Millions
of Women; Papa Whisky November.

AUSTRALIA CALLING: ALL THE BEST VOL 2 | *Gumleaf/
EMI, 1992*

This Is Australia Calling; I'll Be Gone; Rip Rip Woodchip;
Mallee Boy; Cracker Night; Boomerang Café; Budgie Song;
Boogie with M'Baby; I'm in the Mood; Waratah Street;
A Bushman Can't Survive; Drover's Boy; Papa Whisky
November; Crocodile Roll; Cootamundra Wattle; Shelter;
Bill the Cat; Beachcomber From Wollongong; Galleries of
Pink Galahs; Raining On the Rock; A Flag of Our Own;
True Blue.

LOVE IS A GOOD WOMAN | *Gumleaf/EMI, 1993*

Good Woman; Misty Blue; Millions of Women; The Truckie's
Wife; Leave the Lights On; Kill the Night; (Why Don't We)
Separate and Be Lovers; The Only One; (You've Gotta Be)
Fair Dinkum; Love of a True Blue Girl; The Dusty Road We
Know; Heavens Right Here; Goodbye Again; Your Body Feels
Like Heaven to Me; I Still Cry; Special Girl; Tubbo Station;
Winter Green.

MULGA TO MANGOEs | *Gumleaf/EMI, 1994*

Aussie Balladeer; The Farming Game; Seven Year Itch; River Crying Out; The Buckled Bicycle; All Steamy; Sydney 2000; Last Night a Love Song; Tropical Fever; Fool to Love You; Little Piss Piddle; Tony M'Mate; Christmas Waltz; At Lightning Ridge; Pickin' on the Murray; My Oath to Australia.

Includes Bonus CD: **LET'S LAUGH WITH JOHNNO – LIVE:**
Vasectomy Song; Lillie and McEnroe; Sheik of Scrubby Creek; Waratah Rock 'n' Roll Ball; I Wish Mate, I Wish; Full Moon Girl; Dog with No Hair; My Dad Snores; Teach Me to Drive, Dad; The Bowls (Bush Poem); I Still Call the Commercial Home; Drunken Duncan; Big Bum On the Toilet Seat; Boogie with M'Baby; Bill the Cat; Crocodile Roll.

TRUE BLUE – THE VERY BEST OF JOHN WILLIAMSON (25TH ANNIVERSARY) | *Gumleaf/EMI, 1995*
This is a compilation including **ALL THE BEST VOL. I & VOL. 2**

You and My Guitar; Goodbye Blinky Bill; Just A Dog; Wrinkles; Diggers of the Anzac; Old Man Emu; The Shed; Hawkesbury River Lovin'; The Breaker; I'm Fair Dinkum; The Bush Barber; Dad's Flowers; Billabong; Chain Around My Ankle; I Can't Feel Those Chains Any Longer; The Vasectomy Song; Stuffed If I Know; Home Among the Gum Trees; Waltzing Matilda; No One Loves Brisbane Like Jesus; This Is Australia Calling; I'll Be Gone; Rip Rip Woodchip; Mallee Boy; Cracker Night; Boomerang Café; The Budgie Song; Boogie with M'Baby; I'm in the Mood; Waratah Street; A Bushman Can't Survive; Drover's Boy; Papa Whisky November; Crocodile Roll; Cootamundra Wattle; Shelter; Bill the Cat; Beachcomber From Wollongong; Galleries of Pink Galahs; Raining on the Rock; A Flag of Our Own; True Blue.

FAMILY ALBUM NO. 2 | *Gumleaf/EMI, 1996*

Kitchy Kitchy Koo; The Timbercutter (Who Couldn't Complain); You Come Back to Tassie; Santa Bring Me a Dinosaur; Walkin' on the Beach; Little Piss Piddle; The Golden Kangaroo; On Our Selection; My Heart Will Find You; Special Girl; My Oath to Australia; Big Bad Bushranger; Country Football; Little Brick; Bananas.

BOUND FOR BOTANY BAY | *Gumleaf/EMI, 1996*
[*Formerly titled* FAIR DINKUM J.W. | *1982*]

Country Football; Kill the Night; (Why Don't We) Separate and Be Lovers?; Botany Bay; Wrinkles' Road Train; Ryebuck Shearer; (You've Gotta Be) Fair Dinkum; Just a Dog; Silver-haired Showman; With My Swag Upon My Shoulder; Love of a True Blue Girl; Your Body Feels Like Heaven to Me; Brisbane Ladies.

OLD MAN EMU | *Gumleaf/EMI, 1997*
[*Formerly titled* TRUE BLUE | 1982]

Old Man Emu; Big Country Round; Boyhood Story; Under the Bridge; Heaven's Right Here; The Breaker; Murrumbidgee Madness; True Blue; A Granda Plan for Landa; Only A Dog; Springbrook; Send Down the Rain; Hawkesbury River Lovin; Diggers of the Anzac (This Is Gallipoli).

HOME AMONG THE GUMTREES – LIVE | *Gumleaf/EMI, 1997*
[*Formerly titled* THE SMELL OF GUMLEAVES – LIVE | 1984]

Dad's Flowers; The Bush Barber; Good Tobacco When I Smoke; The Trees Have Now Gone; The Last of the Pioneers; Queen in the Sport of Kings; I've Always Been a Drover; I'm Fair Dinkum; Drunken Duncan; Stoned This Afternoon; Billabong; Only 19; We Will Stop the War; I'll Be Gone.

COUNTRY CLASSICS – JOHN WILLIAMSON | *Reader's Digest, 1997*

DISC 1: Old Man Emu; Comic Strip Cowboy; Big Country Round; It's a Grab It While It's Goin' Kinda Life; Boyhood Story; Leave the Lights On; Springbrook; Only a Dog; Murrumbidgee Madness; Hawkesbury River Lovin'; Diggers of the Anzac; The Breaker; Just a Dog; Wrinkles; The Vasectomy Song; And the Band Played Waltzing Matilda; Chain Around My Ankle; I Can't Feel These Chains Any Longer; Home Among the Gum Trees; Waltzing Matilda

DISC 2: Queen in the Sport of Kings; I Was Only 19; Dad's Flowers; The Shed; Go to Nashville; You and My Guitar; Have You Ever Been Short of a Quid; Mallee Boy; Galleries of Pink Galahs; Raining on the Rock; True Blue; Cracker Night; Three Rivers Hotel; The Budgie Song; Cootamundra Wattle; Diamantina Drover; I'm in the Mood; Goodbye Blinky Bill; Crocodile Roll; Sail the Nullarbor; Boomerang Café.

DISC 3: It's a Way of Life; The Truckies Wife; Welcome to Broome; My Dad Snores Boogie with M'Baby; Bill the Cat; Drovers Boy: Shelter; Rip Rip Woodchip; Big Bad Bushranger; Waratah St; Papa Whiskey November; A Bushman Can't Survive, A Flag of Our Own; This Is Australia Calling; I'll Be Gone; Tropical Fever; Sydney 2000; My Oath to Australia.

PIPE DREAM | *Gumleaf/EMI, 1997/1998*

On the Improve; Wedding Ring; The Blues Sometimes; Coolabah Blue; Pipe Dream; Vegie Bill; Prettiest Girl in the Kimberley; The Girl I Met; Missin' The Kisses; Power Over Me; Woman on the Land; Bush Telegraph; Rosewood Hill; Old Pancho; Sir Don.

Includes Bonus CD **BEHIND THE DREAM:** Behind the Dream; Old Farts in Caravan Parks; All Good News; Raining on the Rock;

JOHN WILLIAMSON FOR AUSSIE KIDS – LIVE | *Gumleaf/EMI, 1998*

The Budgie Song; On My Ukelele; Old Sow; Cracker Night; Big Bad Bushranger; My Dad Snores; Crocodile Roll; Little Piss Piddle; Big Bad Banksia Man; Goodbye Blinky Bill; Rip Rip Woodchip; The Golden Kangaroo; Santa Bring Me a Dinosaur; Christmas Photo; Old Man Emu; Home Among the Gum Trees; Waltzing Matilda; True Blue.

BOOGIE WITH M'BABY – LIVE | *Gumleaf/EMI, 1998*

Vasectomy Song; Lillee and McEnroe; Sheik of Scrubby Creek; Waratah Rock 'n' Roll Ball; I Wish Mate, I Wish; Full Moon Girl; Dog with No Hair; My Dad Snores; Teach Me to Drive, Dad; The Bowls (Bush Poem); I Still Call the Commercial Home; Drunken Duncan; Big Bum on the Toilet Seat; Boogie with M'Baby; Bill the Cat; Crocodile Roll; Old Farts in Caravan Parks.

THE WAY IT IS | *Gumleaf/EMI, 1999*

Campfire on the Road; A Thousand Feet; Three Sons; Queensland Bungalow; Wonthaggi; Mountain Hideaway; Singing in the Rain; Would I Be the One; We're Still Here; Happy Birthday My Old Friend; Railwayman; Great Ocean Road; Purple Roses; Do I Love You?; Thargomindah (The Way It Is); The Land of the Truly Free.

JOHN WILLIAMSON'S AUSTRALIA | *Reader's Digest, 1999*

This Is Australia Calling; Sail the Nullarbor; Raining on the Rock (with Warren H. Williams); Shelter; Cootamundra Wattle; The Boomerang Café; And the Band Played Waltzing Matilda; I Was Only 19; I Can't Feel These Chains Any Longer; True Blue; Sir Don; Goodbye Blinky Bill; Rip Rip Woodchip; Waltzing Matilda.

WALTZING MATILDA – LIVE | *Gumleaf/EMI, 2000*
[*Formerly titled* SINGING IN THE SUBURBS – LIVE | *1983*]

It's Good to Be Me; Lillee and McEnroe; The Vasectomy Song; The Sheik of Scrubby Creek; Waratah Rock 'n' Roll Ball; Bound for South Australia; And the Band Played Waltzing Matilda; Singing at a Party; Chain Around My Ankle; I Can't Feel Those Chains Any Longer; Botany Bay; Stuffed If I Know; Home Among the Gum Trees; Waltzing Matilda.

ANTHEMS – A CELEBRATION OF AUSTRALIA |
Gumleaf/EMI, 2000

True Blue; Home Among the Gum Trees; Rip Rip Woodchip;
This Ancient Land: Corroboree 2000; Galleries of Pink
Galahs; Diggers of the Anzac; Sydney 2000; Advance
Australia Fair; River Crying Out; This Is Australia Calling;
The Land of the Truly Free; My Oath to Australia; Diamantina
Drover; Raining on the Rock; A Flag of Our Own; Sir Don;
The Baggy Green; A Number on My Back; Waltzing Matilda
2000; Shelter.

GUNYAH | *Gumleaf/EMI, 2002*

Sing You the Outback; Frangipani Bay; Cape York Peninsula;
Granny's Little Gunyah; Butter Outa Grass; A Mighty Big
River; Around Jindabyne; The Devil's Boots; Salisbury Street;
You Are My Foundation; Buried in Her Bedclothes; The Kiwi
and the Emu; Telephone in My Pocket; Big Brother, Little
Brother.

LAUGH ALONG WITH JOHN WILLIAMSON | *Gumleaf, 2002*

Old Man Emu; Crocodile Roll; The Budgie Song; Bill the Cat;
Little Piss Piddle; Cracker Night; Christmas Photo; The Shed;
Murrumbidgee Madness; On Our Selection; Bush Telegraph;
Dad's Flowers; Vasectomy Song; Bush Town; Old Farts In
Caravan Parks.

THE GLORY OF AUSTRALIA | *Gumleaf, 2002*

True Blue; Aussie Balladeer; Cootamundra Wattle; Short of
a Quid; A Bushman Can't Survive; On the Improve; Woman
on the Land; Wrinkles; Three Rivers Hotel; Galleries of Pink
Galahs; Raining on the Rock; Shelter; My Oath to Australia,
Sydney 2000; Waltzing Matilda

WANDERING AUSTRALIA | *Gumleaf, 2002*

Mallee Boy; Tubbo Station; At Lightening Ridge; Hawkesbury
River Lovin; You Come Back to Tassie; Coober Pedy; Sail
the Nullarbor; Welcome to Broome; Amazing Day; Station
Cook; Ancient Mountains; Alice Springs; Back at the Isa;
Springbrook; Papa Whiskey November.

OLD FARTS IN CARAVAN PARKS – LIVE | *Gumleaf/EMI,*
2003 [*Formerly titled* BOOGIE WITH M'BABY – LIVE | *1998*]

Vasectomy Song; Lillee and McEnroe; Sheik of Scrubby
Creek; Waratah Rock 'n' Roll Ball; I Wish Mate, I Wish;
Full Moon Girl; Dog with No Hair; My Dad Snores; Teach
Me to Drive, Dad; The Bowls (Bush Poem); I Still Call the
Commercial Home; Drunken Duncan; Big Bum on the Toilet
Seat; Boogie with M'Baby; Bill the Cat; Crocodile Roll; Old
Farts in Caravan Parks.

TRUE BLUE TWO │ *Gumleaf/EMI, 2003*

True Blue – 21st Anniversary; You Are Very Welcome; Keep
Australia Beautiful; Sing You the Outback; A Thousand
Feet; Campfire on the Road; Three Sons; Raining on the
Plains; On the Improve; Amazing Day; Back at the Isa; Vegie
Bill; Prettiest Girl in the Kimberley; At Lightning Ridge;
Coolabah Blue; Camel Train to Yamba; Old Farts in Caravan
Parks; Buried in Her Bedclothes; Wonthaggi; Tropical Fever;
Mountain Hideaway; Raining on the Rock; Forty Years Ago;
Dusty Road We Know; Truckie's Wife; Purple Roses; Woman
on the Land; Salisbury Street; It's a Way of Life; My Dad
Snores; Kitchy Kitchy Koo; Big Brother, Little Brother; Big
Bad Bushranger; A Mighty Big River; This Ancient Land; You
Come Back to Tassie; Sail the Nullarbor; The Baggy Green;
Sir Don; Kiwi and the Emu; A Number on My Back; Waltzing
Matilda (Rugby Version)

MATES ON THE ROAD – LIVE │ *Gumleaf/EMI, 2003*

Mallee Boy; Dear Little Quambatook; Chook Routine; It Goes
Without Saying; Cracker Night; Forty Years Ago; Salisbury
Street; Hawkesbury River Lovin'; The Flight of the Blowfly;
Boomerang Café; Buried in Her Bedclothes; You and My
Guitar; Galleries of Pink Galahs; Cootamundra Wattle; Old
Man Emu; Teach Me to Drive, Dad; Cape York Peninsula;
Crocodile Roll; Wrinkles; Diamantina Drover; Amazing Day;
Three Sons; Keeper of the Stones; A Thousand Feet; What
a Place; Raining on the Rock; Chain Around My Ankle; I Cant
Feel Those Chains Any Longer; Diggers of the Anzac; Waltzing
Matilda; A Number on My Back; True Blue; A Bushman Can't
Survive; Glory to Australia; Mates on the Road.

FROM BULLDUST TO BITUMEN | *Gumleaf, 2004*

Humpin' M'Bluey; Springbrook; Mountain Hideaway; No
One Loves Brisbane Like Jesus; Queensland Bungalow;
Charters Towers; Papa Whiskey November; Granny's Little
Gunyah; Frangipani Bay; Cape York; Peninsula; Crocodile
Roll; Old Farts in Caravan Parks; Three Rivers Hotel; Sing You
the Outback; Back at the Isa; Diamantina Drover; Waltzing
Matilda; Longreach Is Praying; Thargomindah; Show Me a
Better Way

CHANDELIER OF STARS | *Gumleaf/EMI, 2005*

Little Girl from the Dryland; Chandelier of Stars; Bells in
a Bushman's Ear; Cowboys and Indians; Skinny Dingoes;
The Camel Boy; Keeper of the Stones; Desert Child;
Renner Springs; A Country Balladeer; Firestorm; Flower
on the Water.

WE LOVE THIS COUNTRY | *Gumleaf/EMI, 2005*

We Love This Country; Campfire on the Road; On the
Improve; Wobbly Boot Hotel; Cape York Peninsula; Vegie Bill;
Welcome All to Broome; Singing in the Rain; Alice Springs;
You Come Back to Tassie; Bush Telegraph; Pickin' on the
Murray; Around Jindabyne; Beachcomber from Wollongong;
Old Farts in Caravan Parks.

JOHN WILLIAMSON – COUNTRY CLASSICS 2 | *Reader's Digest, 2006*

DISC 1: We Love This Country; Beachcomber from Wollongong; Tubbo Station; A Mighty Big River; Wonthaggi; You Come Back to Tassie; Pickin' on the Murray; Coober Pedy; Alice Springs; Campfire on the Road; Westown; Vegie Bill; Prettiest Girl in the Kimberley; Cape York Peninsula; Frangipani Bay; Back at the Isa; Charters Towers; At Lightening Ridge; Coolabah Blue; On the Improve.

DISC 2: Old Farts in Caravan Parks; Lillee and McEnroe; Sheik of Scrubby Creek; Waratah Rock 'n' Roll Ball; I Wish Mate, I Wish; Full Moon Girl; Dog with No Hair; The Flight of the Blowfly; Teach Me to Drive, Dad; The Bowls; I Still Call the Commercial Home; Drunken Duncan; Big Bum on the Toilet Seat, Little Piss Piddle; Christmas Photo; Bush Town; No One Loves Brisbane Like Jesus; Dear Little Quambatook; Chook Routine; I'm Fair Dinkum.

DISC 3: A Thousand Feet; This Ancient Land; Raining on the Plains; When We Were Kids; Wrinkles; Wobbly Boot Hotel; A Country Balladeer; True Blue; A Proud Man; The Baggy Green; Sir Don; Sing You The Outback; Woman on the Land; River Crying Out; The Land of the Truly Free; Keep Australia Beautiful; Raining on the Rock; Firestorm; A Number on My Back; Waltzing Matilda.

THE PLATINUM COLLECTION | *Gumleaf/EMI, 2006*

DISC 1: Old Man Emu; The Breaker; True Blue; Hawkesbury River Lovin; Diggers of the Anzacs; Wrinkles; And the Band Played Waltzing Matilda; Good Tobacci When I Smoke; Queen in the Sport of Kings; I'll Be Gone; The Shed; You and My Guitar; Goodbye Blinky Bill; Just a Dog; Billabong; I Can't Feel Those Chains Any Longer; The Vasectomy Song; Home Among the Gum Trees; Mallee Boy; Galleries of Pink Galahs.

DISC 2: Raining on the Rock; Cracker Night; Cootamundra Wattle; The Budgie Song, Diamantina Drover; Sail the Nullarbor; Boomarang Café; Boogie with M'Baby; Bill the Cat; Rip Rip Woodchip; Shelter; Big Bad Bushranger; Waratah Street; A Bushman Can't Survive; A Flag of Our Own; Papa Whiskey November; This Is Australia Calling; Tropical Fever; Vegie Bill; Prettiest Girl in the Kimberley; Sir Don.

DISC 3: Campfire On the Road; A Thousand Feet; Three Sons; Purple Roses; This Ancient Land; Corroboree 2000; The Land of the Truly Free; The Baggy Green; A Number on My Back; Waltzing Matilda 2000; Sing You the Outback; Cape York Peninsula; Salisbury Street; Buried in Her Bedclothes; Raining on the Plains; Old Farts in Caravan Parks; Glory to Australia (Live); Mates on the Road; Chandelier of Stars; Desert Child; Flower on the Water; We Love This Country.

WILDLIFE WARRIORS – IT'S TIME | *Gumleaf/EMI, 2006*

Wildlife Warriors; It's Time; Rip Rip Woodchip; Dingo;
Humpin' M'Bluey; It's a Way of Life; Send Down the Rain;
Goodbye Blinky Bill; Koala Koala; A Thousand Feet; Ancient
Mountains; River Crying Out; Rosewood Hill; Home Among
the Gum Trees – Steve Irwin Memorial; True Blue – Steve
Irwin Memorial; The Trees Have Now Gone.

HILLBILLY ROAD | *Strinesong/EMI, 2008*

Flowers on the Concrete; Drink a Little Love; Dark Irish
Eyes; Hillbilly Road; Catch a Virgin; Cydi; Pmarra Knatcha
(My Home in the Bush); Australia Is Another Word for Free;
Better Than a Picture; Rivers, Wood 'n' Wire; Beach of Love;
Tomorrow's Worries. Bonus Track: The Joy Is in the Journey
(from the Australian Folk Musical Quambatook)

**ABSOLUTE GREATEST: JOHN WILLIAMSON, 40 YEARS
TRUE BLUE** | *Strinesong/EMI, 2010*

CD 1: Absolute Greatest: Mallee Boy; Raining on the Rock
(live) (with Warren H. Williams); Galleries of Pink Galahs;
Hillbilly Road; Flower on the Water; Rip Rip Woodchip;
A Bushman Can't Survive; Wrinkles; Wintergreen; Australia Is
Another Word for Free (with Warren H. Williams and Amos
Morris); Salisbury Street; Cootamundra Wattle; Hawkesbury
River Lovin'; You and My Guitar; Three Sons; Cydi; Chandelier
of Stars; Boogie with M'Baby (live); Diggers of the Anzac
(This Is Gallipoli); Old Man Emu; True Blue; Island of Oceans
(with Shannon Noll).

CD 2: Absolute Tribute: Flower on the Water (Wendy Matthews); Salisbury Street (The Waifs); Galleries of Pink Galahs (Shannon Noll); Cootamundra Wattle (Kasey Chambers); Chandelier of Stars (James Reyne); Paint Me a Wheelbarrow (Sara Storer and Greg Storer); Tubbo Station (Songbirds); You and My Guitar (Ash Grunwald); Truckie's Wife (Ami Williamson); Raining on the Rock (Troy Cassar-Daley); Wintergreen (Ordinary Fear of God); Hillbilly Road (Adam Harvey); Old Man Emu (Tommy Emmanuel).

JOHN WILLIAMSON: IN SYMPHONY | *Strinesong/EMI, 2011*

Overture/Island of Oceans; Wintergreen; Cootamundra Wattle; Hawkesbury River Lovin': Salisbury Street; Flower on the Water; Boogie with M'Baby; Tubbo Station; You and My Guitar; A Bushman Can't Survive; Galleries of Pink Galahs; Cape York Peninsula; Look Out Cunnamulla; Prettiest Girl in the Kimberley; Chandelier of Stars; Raining on the Rock; Waltzing Matilda; True Blue; Old Man Emu. (Recorded with the Sydney Symphony Orchestra, Guy Noble, Conductor)

THE BIG RED | *Strinesong/Warner, 2012*

Kissing on a City Corner; The Big Red; Marree Girl; Prairie Hotel Parachilna; Rescue Me; Hang My Hat In Queensland; Look Out Cunnamulla; Mates Around the Fire; The Weight of a Man; I'm a Basher; Movie Star; The Men of League.

A HELL OF A CAREER | *Strinesong/Warner, 2013*

CD 1: Old Man Emu; True Blue – 21st Anniversary Version; Hawkesbury River Lovin'; Diggers of the Anzac (This Is Gallipoli); Wrinkles; Queen in the Sport of Kings (Live); I Can't Feel Those Chains Any Longer (Live); Mallee Boy; The Budgie Song; Galleries of Pink Galahs; Raining on the Rock (Live with Warren H Williams); Cootamundra Wattle; Sail the Nullarbor; Westown; Boomerang Café; Amazing Day; Boogie with M'Baby (Live) ; Ancient Mountains; Bill the Cat; Dingo; Goodbye Blinky Bill.

CD 2: Island of Oceans; Rip Rip Woodchip; A Flag of Our Own; A Bushman Can't Survive (Live Orchestra Version); Wintergreen; Papa Whisky November; Prettiest Girl in the Kimberley (Live Orchestra Version) ; Sir Don; Three Sons; A Thousand Feet (with Warren H Williams) ; The Baggy Green; Sing You the Outback; Salisbury Street; Glory to Australia (Live) ; Chandelier of Stars; Flower on the Water; The Joy Is in the Journey; Hillbilly Road; Cydi; The Big Red; Hang My Hat in Queensland (Live Orchestra Version) ; Prairie Hotel Parachilna (Live)

HONEST PEOPLE | *Strinesong/Warner, 2013*

Heatwave; Keep Walking; Song for Luke and Mel; What You Wish For; Will She Marry Me; Call Me Blue; Interval (Instrumental); It's All About Love; Grandpa's Cricket; Kings and Queens; Girt by Sea; Honest People; Clouds over Tamworth.

NOTES

The photos that appear on the endpapers were taken in my shed, where I keep a lot of the Australiana and memorabilia that I collect.

Why the Waratah Street sign? I just like the name of the street, so I wrote a song and then used it as the name of the album. I have an actual enamel street sign as well as the sign that was made when I sang the song on *The Ray Martin Show*.

There are a lot of old ginger beer bottles in the shed. They take me back to the time when even reasonably small towns like Swan Hill in Victoria had their own soft drink factories. Those ginger beer bottles are pretty special – they're a reminder that we used to produce our own things in Australia. They're worth a bit, but I've stopped collecting them because I do have a lot of them.

Holdens were big in Quambatook in the early fifties. There were a lot of Holdens in our little town, and I remember someone had a kangaroo on the bonnet. I'd forgotten you could buy them, just for the Holden, and then I spotted one in an antique shop in Port Fairy when I was there for the folk festival. So I paid a bit for it. It's now on my 1951 ute.

The slouch hat with the emu feather? Obviously 'Old Man Emu' was my first hit so I'm quite fond of emus. I've been called 'Emu' and I have an EMU333 number plate. I've always been intrigued by the feathers they used in the Light Horse infantry. I discovered it was started in the Darling Downs region; they always wore an emu badge and they actually collected the emu feathers off the barbed wire fences while riding around the farms. They stuck the feathers in their hats. So it was the Light Horse Regiment from Toowoomba that started it, then the whole Light Horse infantry adopted it.

'Whitlam for Werriwah' is a collectable election poster; I paid about $90 for it a long time ago now, and I stuck the quote on it. Makes it more interesting, I think. I've always been into the real entertainers, so I've got a Jimmy Durante and a Groucho Marx figure. To me, there's more to music than just the music so I look up to those guys as much as songwriters. If I could find a statuette of Harry Belafonte or Victor Borge I'd have them in the shed too. There's Happy, one of the Seven Dwarfs – he is a great entertainer. So are Popeye and Olive Oil, and the *Bugs Bunny Show* characters – all the things I loved as a kid. I've collected a few cows too – the shed is on an old dairy farm. Larson comic strips got me into cows. He was so good at making weird characters out of cows and I've cottoned onto it. I especially like the black and white ones.

I've got a few books in the shed: information on Australian subjects, books about Australian legends. Some of them have been given to me and I've bought a few. And there's the Bushman radio – it doesn't work but its valves are all there, and it serves as another reminder of the fact that we used to manufacture in Australia.

ACKNOWLEDGEMENTS

I am blessed that my wife, Meg, an experienced editor, pushed me all the way. I know no one who can stick to a task like her. Thank you, Babe.

My publisher, Andrea McNamara, has encouraged me with her delightful charm. The Penguin team has left me with no doubt that I am with the right people.

THE · AUSTRALIAN
WORKER
SOLD HERE